Camping
Idaho

Help Us Keep This Guide Up to Date

Every effort has been made by the author and editors to make this guide as accurate and useful as possible. However, many things can change after a guide is published—trails are rerouted, regulations change, techniques evolve, facilities come under new management, etc.

We would love to hear from you concerning your experiences with this guide and how you feel it could be improved and kept up to date. While we may not be able to respond to all comments and suggestions, we'll take them to heart and we'll also make certain to share them with the author. Please send your comments and suggestions to the following address:

The Globe Pequot Press
Reader Response/Editorial Department
P.O. Box 480
Guilford, CT 06437

Or you may e-mail us at:

editorial@GlobePequot.com

Thanks for your input, and happy travels!

A **FALCON** GUIDE®

Camping
Idaho

Randy Stapilus

FALCON GUIDE®

GUILFORD, CONNECTICUT
HELENA, MONTANA
AN IMPRINT OF THE GLOBE PEQUOT PRESS

FALCONGUIDE ®

All photos by Randy Stapilus unless otherwise noted.
Maps created by Trailhead Graphics © Morris Book Publishing, LLC

ISSN: 1548-2642
ISBN-13: 978-0-7627-2454-3
ISBN-10: 0-7627-2454-4

Manufactured in the United States of America
First Edition/Second Printing

To buy books in quantity for corporate use or incentives, call **(800) 962–0973, ext. 4551,** or e-mail **premiums@GlobePequot.com.**

Contents

NORTHERN IDAHO

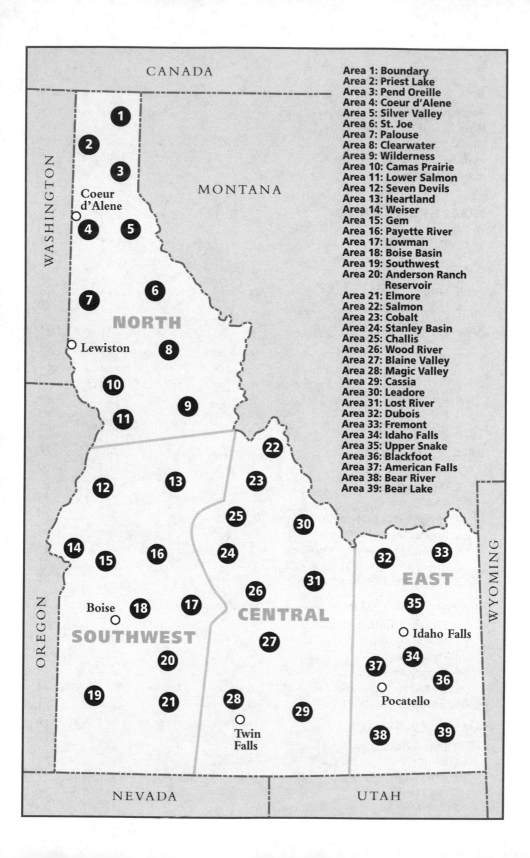

CANADA

WASHINGTON

MONTANA

Coeur
d'Alene

NORTH

Lewiston

OREGON

Boise

SOUTHWEST

NEVADA

CENTRAL

Twin
Falls

EAST

WYOMING

Idaho Falls

Pocatello

UTAH

Area 1: Boundary
Area 2: Priest Lake
Area 3: Pend Oreille
Area 4: Coeur d'Alene
Area 5: Silver Valley
Area 6: St. Joe
Area 7: Palouse
Area 8: Clearwater
Area 9: Wilderness
Area 10: Camas Prairie
Area 11: Lower Salmon
Area 12: Seven Devils
Area 13: Heartland
Area 14: Weiser
Area 15: Gem
Area 16: Payette River
Area 17: Lowman
Area 18: Boise Basin
Area 19: Southwest
Area 20: Anderson Ranch
         Reservoir
Area 21: Elmore
Area 22: Salmon
Area 23: Cobalt
Area 24: Stanley Basin
Area 25: Challis
Area 26: Wood River
Area 27: Blaine Valley
Area 28: Magic Valley
Area 29: Cassia
Area 30: Leadore
Area 31: Lost River
Area 32: Dubois
Area 33: Fremont
Area 34: Idaho Falls
Area 35: Upper Snake
Area 36: Blackfoot
Area 37: American Falls
Area 38: Bear River
Area 39: Bear Lake

SOUTHWEST IDAHO

EASTERN IDAHO

Acknowledgments

People in Idaho love to criticize the federal agencies so visible around the state: the (U.S. Department of Agriculture) Forest Service, the Bureau of Land Management, and others. At the risk of outraging a number of Idahoans, however, this must be said: The personnel of the Forest Service, Bureau of Land Management, and other agencies—federal, state, and local—have without exception been wonderfully helpful in providing background information for this book. However many campgrounds you visit, however many campers you talk to (and we talked to plenty of campers and others in the course of researching the campgrounds), you still can't know enough about all of those campgrounds to develop a full, comprehensive picture without help from the people who actually manage them.

These very helpful people include (among many others) Clem Pope at the Krassel Ranger Station (Payette National Forest); Dennis Thompson and Jill Hill at the Burley District (Bureau of Land Management); Rick Just at the Idaho Department of Parks and Recreation; Bill Boggs at the Idaho Falls District (Bureau of Land Management); Sherri Lesch at the Weiser Ranger Station (Payette National Forest); Maury Young at the Montpelier Ranger Station (Caribou-Targhee National Forest); Ron Goold, campground host at Warm Lake (Payette National Forest); Mary Price at the St. Maries Ranger Station (Panhandle National Forest); Eileen Ball at the Palouse Ranger Station (Clearwater National Forest); Teresa Seloske at the Slate Creek Ranger Station (Nez Perce National Forest); Jan Albertson and Becky Nedrow at the Ashton Ranger Station (Caribou-Targhee National Forest); Pam Brown at the Burley office of the Bureau of Reclamation; Kathy Williams at the Malad Ranger substation (Caribou-Targhee National Forest); Melissa Fowler at the Lost River Ranger Station (Salmon-Challis National Forest); Dan Misciagna at the Bonners Ferry Ranger Station (Panhandle National Forest); and Dion Wilson at the Island Park Ranger Station (Caribou-Targhee National Forest).

Besides all these land managers, I got a great deal of help from land users, including Steve Pline, Marianne Konvalinka, and Bruce Perry.

Many thanks to the terrific editorial staff at the Globe Pequot Press, especially Scott Adams, Cary Hull, and Charlene Patterson. And of course to Linda Watkins, who helped with every stage of this book and read the final edition.

Map Legend

Interstate Highway	〔90〕
U.S. Highway	〔95〕
State Highway	〔33〕
County Road	CR36
Forest Road	FR448
City	Boise ◉
Town	○ Challis
Campground	Λ
River or Creek	
Reservoir or Lake	
State Line	IDAHO
National Park or Recreation Area	
National Forest	
Wilderness Area	
Indian Reservation	

How to Use This Guide

Campgrounds are listed in this book by their relation to an easily located city, which should make planning your trip easier. Specific information on campgrounds includes the following:

Location: Distance and direction from the reference city, along with special features such as lakes or streams.

Sites: Indicates how many camping sites are available, and in some cases breaks them down by type of site (tent camping as opposed to RV spaces, where that is applicable).

Facilities: Available services, as of the time of our check on each campground, are noted here. These include availability of drinking water, toilets, fire rings, and so on.

Fee per night: Indicates the fees as this book went to press, but because fees are subject to change, we advise that you check ahead. These listings should, however, give you an idea of which campgrounds are more or less expensive.

> $ = Less than $10
>
> $$ = $10 to $15
>
> $$$ = $16 to $20
>
> $$$$ = More than $20

Elevation: Idaho's campgrounds range in elevation from about 700 feet above sea level to more than 10,000 feet above.

Road conditions: Many of Idaho's campgrounds are accessible by good roads, but some are extremely remote and on challenging roads.

Management: This section tells you which agency—federal, state, or local—is responsible for this campground and provides contact information. In many cases, private concessionaires operate campgrounds for the public agencies.

Reservations: Indicates whether reservations can be made for a specific campground (some are first come, first served), and if so, how to make them.

Activities: What can you do once you get there? This list gives you an idea of your options at each campground.

Season: Here we indicate when each campground is open, but this can change from year to year, since many campgrounds are opened as snow clears away (and closed as it arrives). However, camping is tolerated in some campgrounds that technically are closed, though no services are provided there by the managing agency.

Finding the campground: These are the recommended directions from a nearby city or town, preferred over other possible routes.

The campground: A general description of the campground.

The quick reference charts with each area give information about the campground services available, along with opening and closing dates. Following is the key to abbreviations used in these charts:

Sites: U = Undeveloped

RV length: maximum footage given

Toilets: F = Flush, V = Vault

Fee: $, $$, $$, $$$$ (explained above)

Recreation: B = Boating, F = Fishing, H = Hiking, S = Swimming

About Idaho

Idaho is not often called a border state, but in many ways it is: a place in between the Rocky Mountains of the West and the Pacific Northwest, between the Great Basin deserts and the great interior forests. All of the states can legitimately claim great variety in their landscapes and attractions, but Idaho can stake a claim stronger than most.

Many visitors to Idaho probably have little idea how much variety there is; the interstates in southern Idaho and on one short strip of the Panhandle provide little clue. To get to Idaho's highest places, you have to get far from the interstates; the state's greatest peak, Mount Borah, is near the center of the state, a couple of hours from any of the state's large population centers. Much the same is true of Idaho's lowest spots, such as Hells Canyon, said by some (depending on how you measure) to be the deepest gorge in North America.

Most of Idaho is mountainous, like Nevada or western Montana. There is a massive valley, the Snake River plain, crossing southern Idaho nearly from Wyoming in the east all the way to Oregon, and smaller plains elsewhere. But much of Idaho is too mountainous to make civilization an easy proposition.

Idaho is one of the most lightly populated states. The largest urban area is around Boise; its population is rapidly approaching the half-million mark. Somewhat less than half as many people live in the Pocatello–Idaho Falls area in the east, and a third large population center is based around Coeur d'Alene in the north. Almost three-fourths of all the people of Idaho live in these areas, and they are the locus of almost all of the population growth in the 1990s—Idaho was one of the half dozen fastest-growing states in the nation in that decade. Traditionally, the "resource industries"—timber, mining, and agriculture—provided the economic base for the state. Today agriculture is still a lead industry, but high-tech and service industries (including tourism) are at least as important.

The intrepid souls who do explore Idaho find an endless array of vistas, landforms, and environments. Huge portions of it are off-limits to encroaching civilization. About two-thirds of Idaho is publicly owned, and while some of that land is used for timber harvesting or other "multiple use" purposes, most of it is in a natural state. Idaho also has several of the largest wilderness areas in the nation—roadless areas where people can come but not stay or even leave behind a trace of their presence.

Interstates (84, 86, 15) connect the main population centers in the Snake River valley in the south, and a short strip of Interstate 90 runs across the Panhandle in the north. But Idaho's highway system remains a work in progress. Many miles of paved highways in Idaho did not exist half a century ago, and new highway miles were paved even in the 1990s. Just one paved road—U.S. Highway 95—links north and south in Idaho; most of it is two-lane, and long stretches are narrow and twisting. Governors have called it "the goat trail." Other highways range from twisted and full of switchbacks in mountain areas to long and straight in the valleys. Generally they are passable by all recreational vehicles.

Off-highway travel, much of which is also off-pavement, is another matter. Some backcountry roads are relatively flat and straight, allowing for long runs of 50 miles per hour or even more. But those are unusual; most are more challenging, and most backcountry travel should be estimated at 20 miles per hour or even less. Many forest roads were developed for logging trucks and are only as finely graded as are needed for those heavy-duty vehicles. Large recreational vehicles often can and do make their way onto mountainous dirt roads, but the quality varies widely. A carefully driven four-wheel-drive vehicle can traverse nearly all maintained backcountry roads, but even in this case, note the qualifiers (*carefully* driven and *nearly* all).

Get a good, detailed map for the area you're planning to visit. The Forest Service has good maps available for its forest areas. If you don't know what kind of road you're setting out on, ask someone at the agency that manages the backcountry land and the road (most often, in Idaho, the Forest Service and the Bureau of Land Management, or the county).

Time of year matters. Snow survives in the highest elevations well into summer, and even in June and July high-elevation dirt and gravel roads can turn into mud pits. In some places snow can start again as early as mid-September. Sudden blizzards in the fall have trapped many a backcountry traveler. Be prepared when you travel. Make sure you have water, food, first-aid supplies, and extra clothing and blankets to manage through cold weather. That applies even in summer in the higher reaches.

In the great center of the state, dominated by mountain ranges and wilderness areas, you will find few roads of any kind. Some areas are losing roads: The U.S. Forest Service has said it will close some roads in forest lands, another reason to supplement your review of maps with a check-in at agency offices.

Northern Idaho

Northern Idaho, especially the Panhandle, tends to see more rain and snow, and it has more large bodies of water. The state's two largest lakes, Coeur d'Alene and Pend Oreille, are located in the far north. Though a central Washington desert area lies between much of northern Idaho and the Pacific Ocean, a great deal of northern Idaho does resemble the Pacific Northwest region: forested, lush, well watered.

Campgrounds near the two large lakes often are in high demand, partly because they are located near the large population centers of Coeur d'Alene and Post Falls in Idaho and—just a half hour away—the Spokane, Washington, metro center. Those seeking a more remote getaway, however, can find it in many places through this region. Most of northern Idaho is national forestland, and campgrounds are scattered through remote forestlands from the Canadian border (one of them is literally walking distance from the border) south to Riggins (the traditional border with southern Idaho—and the place where the time zone switches from Pacific in the north to Mountain in the south).

Southwest Idaho

About half of Idaho's population resides in the southwestern part of the state, nearly all of those within about 50 miles of Boise. That puts a crowding pressure on campgrounds especially close to Boise, and on summer weekends most public campgrounds within 100 miles of Boise fill up well before sundown on Friday. That's especially true because few camping opportunities exist on the desert plains around Boise itself (in what is called the Treasure Valley); most of the camping is found in the mountains above.

Travel a little farther, and spend more time off paved road and more on gravel, and many more possibilities open. The vast Owyhee Mountains south of Boise and the Snake River are a tremendous resource for truly primitive camping; few formal campsites exist here, but "dispersal camping" is popular all over this huge (and little-known) region. North of Boise and on up to the popular Cascade Lake and Payette Lake areas near McCall, campgrounds are all over, some directly on highways and others buried deep in the backcountry.

Central Idaho

Southern Idaho generally is more arid than the north. There are sand dunes in southwestern and far-eastern Idaho (and camping is allowed next to them), and large regions of the south are dry enough to qualify for desert status. That statement comes with a big qualifier, though, because the mountains of Idaho often store substantial water in their snowpacks, and because Idaho has a massive river system centering on the Snake River. The Snake—running from eastern Idaho (where it enters the state from Wyoming) through the south to form part of the borders with Oregon and Washington, and leaving Idaho at Lewiston—has a huge system of tributaries. About 87 percent of Idaho is watered by the Snake River system. (Many Idahoans familiar with its backcountry speak not of which county they are in, but of which river basin: "That was in the Payette Basin," or "Up in the Lochsa.") Those waters have transformed much of Idaho, and nowhere is that more true than in south-central Idaho. The central part of the Snake River plain in the southern part of the state is commonly called "the Magic Valley" because of how irrigation has magically transformed a desert once uninviting to any settlers into a well-populated green garden.

This central region is some of the most rugged in the state. The Sawtooth Mountains in the very middle of Idaho—near Stanley—are stunning for their jagged peaks, and for the spectacular mountain lakes (Redfish is the most popular) at their feet. South of there lie enormous lava fields, a region called Craters of the Moon, and the opportunity (for those who pick their sites carefully and plan ahead) for mind-bend desert camping. Farther south still, south of those irrigated fields and south of the Snake River plain, are more mountains, a region remote and little known outside the state, with scenery ranging from the City of Rocks to a mountain campground situated higher than 10,000 feet—and a view spreading out a hundred miles to the north, all the way (on a clear day) to the Sawtooth Mountains.

Eastern Idaho

On a national level, eastern Idaho has been overshadowed by neighboring Yellowstone and Grand Teton National Parks. But "the Idaho side" just west of those parks has just as many outdoor activities to offer.

It has lakes as scenic as those in northern Idaho—Henry's Lake, Bear Lake, the Blackfoot Reservoir, Palisades Reservoir among others—which are renowned locally (and among savvy fishermen) but remain little known nationally. It has some of Idaho's most popular rivers, such as the Salmon to the north and the Henry's Fork (of the Snake River) to the east (both of which are lined with some of the best campground locations in Idaho). Some of these areas are so popular locally that campgrounds fill up fast on weekends, but many of the more remote places (especially away from the Island Park and Palisades Reservoir area) are often lightly used, even in summer.

Idaho's Campgrounds

Idaho is a popular state for camping, and it draws many thousands of recreation-minded visitors every year. It has hundreds of campgrounds, and they run the full spectrum, from extremely primitive to the most up-to-date and crisply modern (even among some of the public campgrounds). This book covers public campgrounds run by government agencies. In Idaho that covers most of the landscape, because about two-thirds of Idaho is publicly owned.

Many campgrounds fall into easily defined categories, but some occupy gray areas. In some cases more than one government agency is involved, and in others government and private entities both have a role. In recent years actual on-ground management of many federal campgrounds (and the overwhelming majority of public campgrounds in Idaho are federal) has been contracted to someone else, sometimes a local government but more often a private contractor, who might hire a campground host, or take reservations, or physically manage the campground location directly, or all of these things. This guide covers "public" campgrounds rather than private ones; the rule of thumb usually adhered to is: Who owns and controls the land where the campground is located? If the land underlying the campground is publicly owned, generally it is listed here.

Another gray area: When is a public camping area sufficiently "primitive" or undeveloped that it ceases to be a "campground"? In Idaho campers are allowed to drop anchor on vast stretches of Bureau of Land Management (BLM) and Forest Service lands and many other public lands as well. This practice, called dispersed camping, is actually encouraged in some places (especially some of the more popular national forests), to the point that some limited facilities such as fire rings are located in these places. Even so, the Forest Service doesn't consider these to be "campgrounds." The Bureau of Land Management has placed picnic tables and toilet facilities at a number of remote spots where people have periodically camped, and you'll get varying answers as to whether some of these are actually "campgrounds." This guide has parsed through these case by case and generally has included those sites that have been well enough developed to fit most people's idea of a campground. Still, for variety (and for those determined to rough it), some very primitive locations have been included here, and some are primitive enough to include not even any designated camping spaces, just a loosely defined region in which people camp.

The Idaho Recreation and Park Association, which consists of campground managers of many kinds, describes itself as "a non-profit, professional organization founded in 1959 and is made up of individuals from municipal, county, state, and federal park and recreation agencies, private corporations, hospitals and institutions, colleges, commercial enterprises, commissions, and advisory boards. IRPA also serves as a voice for parks and recreation in local, regional, state, and national legislation." The association can be contacted through its Web site at www.idoc.state.id.us/IRPA/IRPA.html.

Most federal and state camping areas in Idaho have a fourteen-day limit: After that, you have to pack up and move (usually at least about 30 miles

5

away). There are variations, however. Some national forest lands have a sixteen-day limit, and the rules are also looser on some other agency lands.

A system of fees applies to use of many federal lands, and annual passes and senior citizen passes are available in some cases. Check ahead to find out which options work best for you.

One other general comment: The seasons of use are often more flexible than the dates noted in this guide suggest. Campgrounds often open and close, as a matter of practice, with the seasons; many mountain campgrounds open when the snow melts away and close when the snow falls anew. In the case of many (though not all) public campgrounds, the opening and closing dates noted here represent the dates when maintenance by the agency starts and stops. Camping outside these periods, while often cold and without services, is usually allowed (for the hardy). If you have questions along these lines, check with the local camp administrative organization noted in the guide.

National Park System

Oddly, considering the amount and high quality of public land in Idaho, there are no national parks in Idaho (unless you count the small strip of Yellowstone National Park on Idaho's eastern border). The National Park Service does, however, administer a number of lands in the state. It operates two campground areas in Idaho, the City of Rocks National Reserve and the Craters of the Moon National Reserve. (There have been efforts to redesignate Craters as a national park.) These ordinarily are more developed campgrounds than the national forest campgrounds. Craters has a relatively modern campground, while the City of Rocks is somewhat more primitive.

National Forests

The Forest Service controls the majority of Idaho's public campgrounds. Its forests and grasslands take up 21.8 million acres of land in Idaho, about a third of the whole state, more than any other organization. These lands are incredibly variable. Some are true forests and others desert flats; some are mountainous, while other areas are more like plains. Some are essentially dry desert in character; others are wet with lakes and streams.

The Forest Service manages the lands for "multiple use," which can include timber production and other commercial uses as well as recreation.

Though its campgrounds are not all alike, most have similar facilities and amenities. Most are shaded, feature fire rings and picnic tables, and supply drinking water and vault toilets. Most do not have utility hookups. They are varied in size, from only a few spaces to scores of spaces. Fees range from free, in a few cases, to nearly $20 a night on the high end. Many, but not all, have group spaces.

Conditions and uses of Forest Service campgrounds also vary widely. In some places all-terrain vehicles are essentially banned; in others special trails have been sct up for them. In some places camping is strictly restricted to designated campgrounds; in others campers are encouraged to disperse to non-designated locations as well as designated campgrounds. In some places the Forest Service operates campgrounds directly through oversight by rangers and seasonal employees; other areas use "concessionaires," privately hired campground managers who live on-site.

Many, but not most, national forest campground sites in Idaho can be reserved through a national reservation system available by a toll-free phone number or online. The online service provides information about specific sites so that you can reserve (if it's available) the site closest to the lake, or the rest-room, or the woods.

Some rules and conditions vary from forest to forest, and others are relatively standard. The maximum stay in national forests (with some exceptions, such as campgrounds hosts) almost always is fourteen days. In almost all cases, where a fee is charged for camping at all, the Forest Service charges an extra fee for second vehicles. While some national forest campgrounds do have trash deposit facilities, you're best off assuming a "pack it in–pack it out" policy—that is, expect to haul away your garbage, not leave it behind.

Bureau of Land Management

The Bureau of Land Management (BLM) oversees about four dozen camp-grounds (as defined in this guide) in Idaho. The bureau manages public lands that were in a sense "left behind"—neither reserved as park or forest land nor given or sold to private owners. Many BLM lands in Idaho are desert and plains lands, but there are many beautiful locations among them, and they include many large and small bodies of water.

BLM campsites usually are less developed than those in national forest lands; ordinarily include toilet facilities, fire rings, and sometimes drinking water; and tend to be very remote, although there are some striking exceptions to the rule. On the other hand, fees tend to be small (and many locations are free), competition for spaces is relatively light, and restrictions on use are usually far less than in most other public lands.

Bureau of Reclamation

An agency little known in eastern states, the Bureau of Reclamation is highly important throughout the West and remains important in Idaho today. BuRec is the nation's premier dam builder, and in Idaho that has resulted in irriga-tion of vast areas, with the arrival of civilization as a result. The bureau still directly controls many of those "project" areas, which include many of the state's reservoirs. Recreation sites, sometimes but not always including camp-ing facilities, are attached to many of them.

The Bureau of Reclamation manages or owns the land underlying ten campgrounds in Idaho. All are located near bodies of water, and all are espe-cially popular with boaters and anglers.

State Parks

The state park system is a relatively recent development in Idaho; in 1950 Idaho had only two relatively undeveloped parks. That has changed drastically, as the state has thoroughly developed a wide range of properties all over the state since then.

The state Department of Parks and Recreation operates seventeen campgrounds, many of them large, most of them well developed with services that rival the best private campgrounds. They also tend to be more expensive than the federal lands.

Local Government

Local governments across Idaho operate scores of parks, but almost all of them are picnic and recreation sites only, with no overnight camping allowed. There are exceptions. Ada County, for example, owns a campground site adjacent to the Western Idaho Fairgrounds at Garden City, where RVers can stay (mainly in connection with events at the fairgrounds). Bingham County runs an elaborate recreation complex, which includes camping, on the shore of American Falls Reservoir. In a few communities, such as Pocatello, camping is allowed in some parks but only with permission from the governing body (the city council, in this case). In one especially complex case, the city of American Falls has a cooperative agreement with the Bureau of Reclamation to operate a recreation area (including camping), but the management of the site is assigned to a private contractor. Bonneville County operates a camping complex on the Ririe Reservoir on Bureau of Reclamation land.

Idaho Power Company

One other category of campground also straddles the line between public and private. When Idaho Power Company, the state's largest electric utility, was awarded licenses to build hydroelectric dams on the Snake River, it agreed to provide park and recreation areas near those dams. In the years since it has done just that, operating a series of parks along the Snake River from American Falls in eastern Idaho to Hells Canyon along the Oregon border. They are operated by a private company but as an outgrowth of government regulation. Some of these—all of them recreation areas in the Hells Canyon region—allow camping, and others allow day use only. The Idaho Power recreation areas all are popular for boating and fishing in the reservoirs and hiking and hunting on the lands nearby. The following three campgrounds are all in Idaho. Idaho Power also operates one recreation area, Copperfield Camp, on the Oregon side of Hells Canyon, and it has sixty-two RV and ten tent camping sites.

- Woodhead Park in the Hells Canyon complex at the Brownlee Reservoir. Idaho Power's largest park area, it covers sixty-five acres and was heavily refurbished in 1995. It has 124 RV sites with electricity hookups and fifteen tent sites; all have water, picnic tables, and fire rings.

- McCormick Park in the Hells Canyon complex at the Oxbow Reservoir. Its twelve acres include thirty-four RV sites with hookups for water and electricity and several tent camping locations with electric power hookups.

- Hells Canyon Park in the Hells Canyon complex at Hells Canyon Reservoir. Its grassy, partly shaded lands overlooking the reservoir include twenty-four RV sites, some with electricity and water hookups, and some space for tent campers. Picnic tables and barbecue stands are available as well.

Private Campgrounds

Idaho has lots of private campgrounds, especially in the more popular vacation spots and population centers. Almost all offer basic hookup and related services; some offer much more, and a minority are truly plush resort facilities. This book does not include private campgrounds.

Idaho Outdoors

If you plan to spend time camping in Idaho, there are a number of important things you need to know.

Overstaying Your Campground Welcome

There are limits to how long you can stay in a given camping area or region. National forests in particular have discovered some campers who stay all summer—or even longer—especially in areas near high-cost communities such as Sun Valley. Stay limits are imposed on most public campsites around the state. Most national forests in Idaho have a fourteen-day stay limit; some in eastern Idaho have a sixteen-day limit. Note the limits when you enter the campground or make your reservation.

Zero Impact Camping

If you want your camping trip to be a real success, you won't think only about having fun; you'll also think about how to leave zero impact on the environment. Here are some important reminders:

Some public campgrounds have resident Dumpsters for your garbage—or at least some of your garbage—but the safest course (unless you know otherwise) is to assume that you will pack out everything you pack in.

Don't tempt wildlife to your campsite by throwing leftovers from a meal on the ground or into the fire ring; either dispose of leftovers in a trash container or store them in a secure vehicle for later disposal.

If the campground has a utility sink for cleaning dishes, use it. Avoid washing dishes in streams or lakes.

If a fire ring is provided at your campsite, use it. Resist the urge to build really large fires; a fire that is too big can easily get out of control. Don't throw trash that won't burn—such as glass, cans, or aluminum foil—into your fire; you'll leave an unsightly mess.

Never leave a fire unattended. Make sure that any fire you set is 100 percent snuffed out before you leave. Like other western states, Idaho has been prone to massive forest fires in recent years, and many of them have been a direct result of campers who fail to turn their flames entirely to ashes.

Some campgrounds have strict rules about where to place tents and RVs to minimize the impact on the areas around the campgrounds. Be sure to adhere to these rules.

When walking to and from the bathhouse, or when hiking, stay on established paths and trails to avoid damaging sensitive areas.

When hiking, bury your human waste at least 100 feet from water sources under 6 to 8 inches of topsoil. Don't bathe with soap in a lake or stream—use prepackaged moistened towels to wipe off sweat and dirt, or bathe in the water without soap.

ATVs and Motorbikes

One of the more controversial (it easily leads to arguments) topics in the Idaho backcountry and in camping circles is the role of motorized off-road vehicles. Advocates and critics of snowmobiles (which often are used on off-road trails on public lands) and jet boats (which run on regulated sections of a number of Idaho rivers) have loudly voiced disagreements. Of most direct import to campers is the category of ATVs and motorbikes.

ATVs (all-terrain vehicles) and motorbikes are highly popular in some areas. They can be great fun, and they allow for a lot more exploration of the landscape than hiking by foot. On the other hand, they make a lot of noise and sometimes tear up the landscape.

State and federal governments in Idaho have reacted to the demand and criticism not by banning but by limiting and regulating ATV use.

The state of Idaho requires that owners of all ATVs and motorbikes used off-road register with the state Department of Parks and Recreation. The cost is $10, and the owner places a sticker provided by the department on the vehicle. (Nonresidents have up to thirty days to register.) State law also requires that a noise suppression system be placed on the vehicle.

As to where they can be used, the various landowning agencies have set up specific ATV-use areas. A number of ATV trails have been established around the state (most often by the Forest Service). Generally they require that the vehicles be turned off and pushed inside campground boundaries.

Horses

Horses may no longer be our primary means of transportation, but in western states like Idaho, they're still plenty popular when it comes to recreation. With that in mind, a number of campgrounds around the state have set up facilities for those who want to take horses (and other animals, such as llamas) into the backcountry. These sites are scattered all over the state, from the St. Joe Basin in north-central Idaho to several in central and southeastern Idaho.

Horse-friendly trails can be found all over Idaho. In general horses should be kept just outside campgrounds. (You'll often see notices to that effect.)

Bears

A great deal of Idaho backcountry is bear country. That shouldn't make you reluctant to camp in Idaho, but it should make you alert to the possibility of a bear encounter.

Everyone who spends much time in Idaho's backcountry builds up a few bear stories—some frightening, some amusing, some simply awe-inspiring. The basic lesson to be taken from them is that while bears are a wonderful and important part of the Idaho wilds, they are best encountered (if at all) at a distance, preferably a considerable distance. Don't be one of those foolish visitors who think of bears as cute and cuddly. They are neither. While most are not particularly aggressive and will simply amble away from you if given a chance, all should be treated with great caution and respect.

Don't give them any reason to move in your direction, and foremost that means keeping your food securely contained (except while actually eating or preparing food), with no stray smells drifting about. Apart from meals, keep your food some distance from your person. Remember that bears smell things much better than we do, and they can be relentless in pursuit of food. Some smart backcountry visitors string their food high up in trees in caches, well beyond a bear's reach. At the least, lock it securely inside a motor vehicle. If you think that putting your food back in the ice chest will be enough, consider this story, told by an experienced backcountry lodge manager who left home for a few weeks in early winter. When she returned to her house, the front door had been ripped away and muddy bear tracks led to the kitchen, where the front door of the refrigerator was similarly torn off, and all the food inside consumed.

Opinions differ about the best tactic in case of a bear encounter, though everyone agrees that simply turning your back and running away is a bad idea (the average bear can almost certainly outrun you). If you're planning to spend extended time in the Idaho deep backcountry, you may first want to read one of several books on dealing with bears.

Idaho has two types of bears, black and grizzly. Almost all Idaho bears are black bears; those are smaller than the grizzlies and more even-tempered. Ordinarily they will simply walk off or climb a tree upon encountering a human. Grizzlies are larger and have a hump atop their shoulders; they are more aggressive and easily provoked. Beware of them. The staff at the local ranger station should know if grizzlies have been spotted in the area, so ask before you enter.

Other Big Mammals

Moose are most common in eastern Idaho, especially in the region near Yellowstone National Park, but they can be found statewide, especially in the wilderness areas. They may look like friendly amblers, but these big creatures can be dangerous. Keep your distance.

Elk, deer, and antelope are very common (tens of thousands of them are harvested in hunts every year), and they often can be seen in and around campgrounds and other locations. Antelope are especially common in eastern Idaho; the population periodically explodes on Idaho National Engineering and Environmental Laboratory lands, where they cannot be hunted, and herds of them have been known to block highway traffic in the area.

Mountain goats and Rocky Mountain bighorn sheep are relatively rare in Idaho but not endangered: A small number of hunting tags for these animals are issued each year. They usually keep to the most remote regions and the most mountainous country; they are rarely spotted from the highway or from most campgrounds.

Mountain lions, or cougars, are not commonplace in Idaho but have been seen in many remote areas around Idaho. Unprovoked cougar attacks do occur in the wild in Idaho; a newspaper editor in Idaho Falls even has written a book about them. Bobcats and Canada lynx also are found in Idaho.

Wild canines are well represented. Coyotes can be found statewide, especially in the desert lands of southern Idaho, and several species of foxes are often seen as well, sometimes close to human settlement. Wolves are often spotted in the Sawtooth Mountain region and elsewhere.

Small Mammals

As part of its Fourth of July celebration, the small city of Council for many years has held porcupine races. Porcupines from nearby forests are collected, encouraged to race in an open field, and then released back into the woods.

They are just one example of the many smaller mammals found in Idaho's wild country (though porcupines are not tiny; they often are about the size of a midsize dog). The handiwork of beavers can be seen in many wild places. Other small mammals in Idaho include squirrels, muskrat, Idaho pygmy rabbits, raccoon, badgers, marten, mink, otters, and skunks. While rare in Idaho, wolverines are not unheard of.

Fish

Think "fish" and "Idaho," and trout and salmon spring first to mind. And rightly so, though some species and some stream locations are off-limits for fishing. The rules change from time to time along with fish population, so be sure to get a copy of fishing regulations published by the state Department of Fish and Game (and available in most sporting goods stores and other locations around the state) before sinking a line.

Trout in Idaho include the rainbow, cutthroat, brook, Dolly Varden, golden, and Kamloops varieties, and the allied steelhead, which is among the most prized of fishing catches in Idaho. About a dozen trout fish hatcheries are located around Idaho, regularly releasing many fish into streams in the state.

Salmon include the chinook, sockeye, and kokanee. Some salmon are endangered, and fishing of salmon is carefully restricted.

Other fish in Idaho streams include the perch, largemouth and smallmouth bass, whitefish, sturgeon, and bullhead catfish.

Northern Idaho

Area 1: Boundary

Where do you go to live if you want to get away from it all? This is one of the places—the farthest northern reach of Idaho, hugging the Canadian border. In fact, a fair number of the people who live here came here for just that reason. There are two border crossings here, Eastport and Porthill, but you don't get a sense of international bustle in this country.

The only population center in the area is Bonners Ferry, and it is a small city. (The most visible attraction is the Kootenai Tribal Casino on the east side of town.) Overall, this is thinly settled country, with a number of people living deep in the hills and woods.

Much of this mostly mountainous land is managed by the Kaniksu National Forest (part of the Idaho Panhandle National Forest); all of the public campgrounds here are operated by the Forest Service. A couple of them are among the prettiest camping sites in the state. Moose and white-tailed deer are often seen in this area, along with a wide variety of birds in the wetlands and small lakes that dot the region.

For more information:

Bonners Ferry Chamber of Commerce
P.O. Box 1609
Bonners Ferry, ID 83805
(208) 267–5922
www.bonners-ferry.com

Idaho Panhandle National Forests
3815 Schreiber Way
Coeur d'Alene, ID 83814
(208) 765–7223
www.fs.fed.us/ipnf/

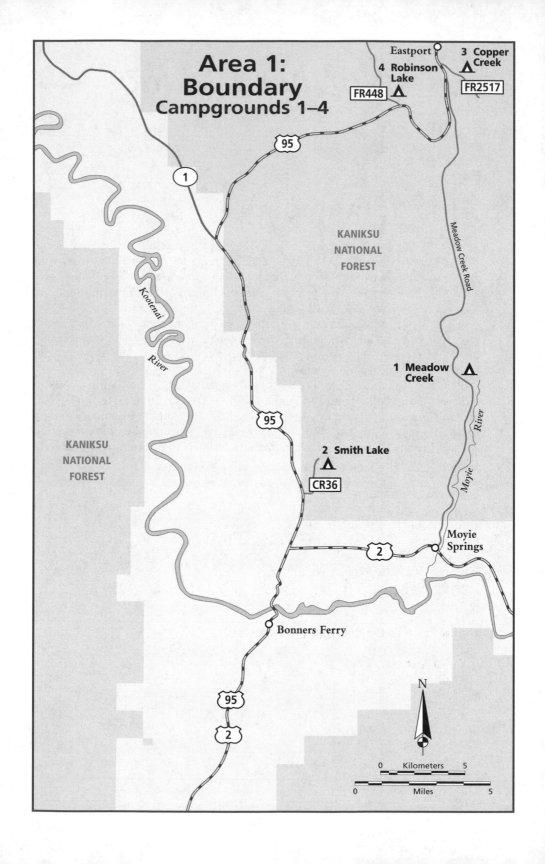

Area 1

	Town	Sites	Max. RV length	Electric	Picnic	Fire rings	Toilets	Showers	Water	Dump station	Disability access	Recreation	Can reserve	Fee ($)	Season	Stay limit (days)
1 Meadow Creek	Bonners Ferry	22	22		•	•	V		•			F		$	May–Oct.	14
2 Smith Lake	Bonners Ferry	7			•	•	V		•			BHS			May–Oct.	14
3 Copper Creek	Eastport	16	32		•	•	V		•		•	FH		$	May–Oct.	14
4 Robinson Lake	Eastport	10	32		•	•	V		•		•	BFHS		$	May–Oct.	14

1 Meadow Creek

Location: Northeast of Bonners Ferry
Sites: 22
Facilities: Drinking water, vault toilets, fire rings, river access, pets allowed
Fee per night: $
Elevation: 2,400 feet
Road conditions: Forest road is mildly rugged but passable for most motor vehicles in good weather conditions. Take it slow and easy.
Management: Forest Service, Bonners Ferry Ranger District, (208) 267–5561
Reservations: No
Activities: Fishing, picnicking
Season: May 15–October 1 (depending on weather)
Finding the campground: From Bonners Ferry drive north on U.S. Highway 95 for 3 miles, then east on U.S. Highway 2 for 2.5 miles to the city of Moyie Springs, then north (away from Moyie Springs) on Meadow Creek Road for 11 miles.
The campground: Located at the Moyie River, this is a good spot both for fishing in the Moyie and for hiking and huckleberry picking. The area is forested and mountainous, well within the Purcell Mountain Range—the campground is several hundred feet higher than Moyie Springs. The camping sites are well shaded and generously spaced.

2 Smith Lake

Location: North of Bonners Ferry
Sites: 7
Facilities: Drinking water (hand pumps), fire rings, vault toilets
Fee per night: None
Elevation: 3,000 feet
Road conditions: The off-highway portion of the drive here is not long, and the lower levels of it are good, but after the first mile or so it turns tough.

Management: Forest Service, Bonners Ferry Ranger District, (208) 267–5561
Reservations: No
Activities: Boating, swimming, hiking, picnicking
Season: May 15–October 31
Finding the campground: Drive north of Bonners Ferry on US 95 for 5 miles, then east 2 miles on Boundary County Road 36.
The campground: Check for directions before heading up here into the mountains, since the signs sometimes don't do the job. Once you arrive, you'll find a boat ramp and open picnic area; the camping area is generally forested.

3 Copper Creek

Location: South of Eastport
Sites: 16
Facilities: Drinking water, fire rings, barrier-free access (three sites), vault toilets
Fee per night: $
Elevation: 2,500 feet
Road conditions: Good highway, then decent gravel road the last mile to the campground
Management: Forest Service, Bonners Ferry Ranger District, (208) 267–5561
Reservations: No
Activities: Fishing, hiking
Season: May 15–October 1 (depending on weather)
Finding the campground: From Eastport drive on US 95 south 1 mile, then east on Forest Road 2517 for 1 mile.
The campground: Here's your chance to camp only a short hike away from the Canadian border. You're less than 2 miles from the small community of Eastport, which has limited services but a variety of supplies available. (There are duty-free shops here, too.) Close by the campground, a short walk to the east, you'll find spectacular Copper Falls, one of the most scenic waterfalls in Idaho. Three of the camping sites here are disabled-accessible.

4 Robinson Lake

Location: South of Eastport
Sites: 10
Facilities: Drinking water, fire rings, barrier-free access (three sites), vault toilets
Fee per night: $
Elevation: 2,800 feet
Road conditions: Narrow and hilly but paved, all the way into the campground
Management: Forest Service, Bonners Ferry Ranger District, (208) 267–5561
Reservations: No
Activities: Boating, fishing, hiking, picnicking, swimming

Season: May 15–October 1 (depending on weather)
Finding the campground: From Eastport drive 7 miles south on US 95, then a half mile north on Forest Road 448.
The campground: You don't exactly camp on the shores of this little lake, but the water is just over a walkable berm. Not far away, herons and ospreys nest. The campground area is nicely forested and hilly, with a couple of fast-moving streams flowing through. There's just enough space to keep campers from piling on top of one another. The spaces are spread out well.

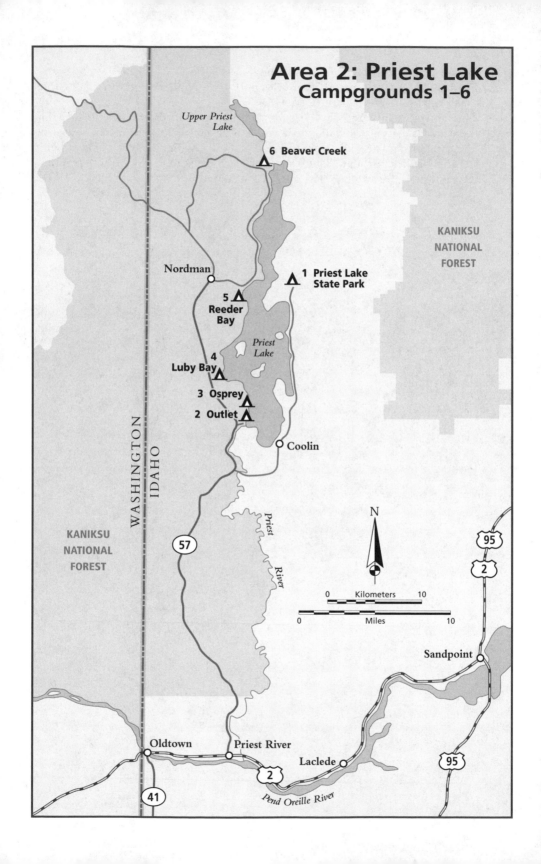

Area 2: Priest Lake

The future of Priest Lake has been a hotly fought topic for years in northern Idaho. Should its waters, its 72 miles of shoreline, and its wonderful wooded terrain be protected from further development? Or should more people be allowed to build their homes here? How should the state lands in this area be managed?

What's absolutely clear is that this is a very popular destination. This is one of the most lushly vegetated parts of Idaho, with evergreens and spruce growing thick and ferns and many other plants in the underbrush. Vacation homes line up along the western side of the lake (the state park is located on the eastern side), and the small community of Coolin at the southern base of the lake is a busy marina center.

Priest Lake's 25,000 acres are renowned for canoeing and other boating, fishing (it holds a record for a giant Mackinaw catch), and hiking. There are a number of private resorts and camping sites along with the public sites noted here. It is one of Idaho's premier destinations.

The campgrounds here are among Idaho's prettiest waterfront locations. In addition to the camping sites noted here, several not accessible by road merit mention. On Kalispell Island (on the southern part of the lake, near Luby Bay campground) the Forest Service operates twelve camping areas, each with from one to seven sites. Just south of this island is Bartoo Island, which has seven camping areas, two of them intended for group use. These are strictly pack in–pack out sites (some of these island sites require use of portable toilets). Several Forest Service campgrounds also are located on Upper Priest Lake but are accessible only by hiking trail or boat. Check with the Priest Lake Ranger District at (208) 443–2512 for more information.

While most of the area close to the lake is relatively developed, the region generally is packed with a wide range of wildlife. You'll find moose and white-tailed deer in the area, as well as coyotes—and bears. Most are black bears, but there are a few grizzlies about, so be careful to use bear etiquette in the area (see previous chapter on Idaho Outdoors).

Most of the campgrounds here, as in so much of Idaho, are National Forest campgrounds.

For more information:

Priest River Chamber of Commerce
P.O. Box 929
Priest River, ID 83856
(208) 443–3191
www.priestlake.org

Area 2

	Town	Sites	Max. RV length	Electric	Picnic	Fire rings	Toilets	Showers	Water	Dump station	Disability access	Recreation	Can reserve	Fees ($)	Season	Stay limit (days)
1 Priest Lake State Park	Priest River	151	50	•	•	•	F,V	•	•	•		BFHS		$$–$$$	Year-round	
2 Outlet	Priest River	31	22		•	•	F			•		BFHS		$	May–Sept.	14
3 Osprey	Priest River	16	20		•	•	V			•		FHS		$	June–Sept.	14
4 Luby Bay	Priest River	52	60		•	•	F		•	•	•	FHS	•	$$	May–Oct.	14
5 Reeder Bay	Priest River	24	50		•	•	F			•	•	FH		$$	May–Oct.	14
6 Beaver Creek	Priest River	40	60		•	•	F,V			•	•	FHS	•	$$	May–Sept.	14

1 Priest Lake State Park

Location: North of Priest River
Sites: 151
Facilities: Drinking water, electric and water hookups, dump station, barrier-free access, fire rings, flush and vault toilets, showers, minimart, laundry, lake access, pull-through sites, pets allowed
Fee per night: $$–$$$
Elevation: 2,400 feet
Road conditions: Paved in places, good gravel in others; quality lessens on the farthest north reaches.
Management: Idaho Department of Parks and Recreation, (208) 443–6710
Reservations: Available via Web site www.idahoparks.org
Activities: Boating, fishing, hiking, picnicking, snowmobiling, swimming, waterskiing
Season: All year, technically; as a practical matter, about May 1 through October 31 (depending on weather)
Finding the campground: From Priest River (the town) drive 25 miles north on Idaho Highway 57, and then follow the sign to Coolin; the park covers a wide tract of land east of Coolin.
The campground: Priest Lake State Park has three camping areas. Dickensheet is located about 4 miles south of Coolin, next to the Priest River (not the lake). Rafts and canoes can be launched there and taken up and down the Priest River. The Indian Creek area is 11 miles north of Coolin and is where park headquarters are located; fishing, boating, and waterskiing in the lake are popular here, as is snowmobiling in the winter. Groceries, propane, marina services and boat rentals, restaurants, and indoor lodging all are available here. Farthest north, 23 miles north of Coolin, is the Lionhead area (named after a local rock formation), a favorite both for boating and for relaxing on a fine white-sand beach. Hiking trails are accessible in all these locations.

2 Outlet

Location: North of Priest River
Sites: 31
Facilities: Drinking water, fire rings, flush toilets
Fee per night: $$
Elevation: 2,400 feet
Road conditions: Good highway and relatively smooth gravel road within the campground
Management: Forest Service, Priest Lake Ranger District, (208) 443–2512
Reservations: Call (877) 444–6777 or visit Web site www.reserveamerica.com—recommended at least four days in advance.
Activities: Boating, fishing, hiking, picnicking, swimming
Season: May 25–September 10 (depending on weather)
Finding the campground: From Priest River (the town) drive 25 miles north on ID 57, then 1 mile northeast on Forest Road 237.
The campground: Shady, well-manicured (without becoming city-park civilized), and sloping down to Priest Lake, which you can see through the trees. Site facilities (fire rings and table) are above average in quality.

3 Osprey

Location: North of Priest River
Sites: 16
Facilities: Drinking water, fire rings, vault toilets
Fee per night: $
Elevation: 2,400 feet
Road conditions: Good highway and relatively smooth gravel road within the campground
Management: Forest Service, Priest Lake Ranger District, (208) 443–2512
Reservations: No
Activities: Fishing, hiking, picnicking, swimming
Season: June 15–September 10 (depending on weather)
Finding the campground: From Priest River (the town) drive 25 miles north on ID 57. One mile north of the well-marked Outlet campground, turn east onto driveway and continue to Osprey.
The campground: Facilities here are relatively primitive compared with some of the other public campgrounds in this area, but its location on the lake is second to none. The campground area's slope down to the lake amounts to stadium seating for a lake view. This site, like most of the others around Priest Lake, does get plenty of use in the summer.

4 Luby Bay

Location: North of Priest River
Sites: 52
Facilities: Drinking water, dump station, fire rings, barrier-free access, flush toilets, amphitheater

Fee per night: $$ (and second-vehicle fee)
Elevation: 2,350 feet
Road conditions: Excellent highway north along Priest Lake, then 1 mile of gravel road leading up to the campground
Management: Forest Service, Priest Lake Ranger District, (208) 443-2512
Reservations: Call (877) 444-6777 or visit Web site www.reserveamerica.com—recommended at least four days in advance.
Activities: Fishing, hiking, picnicking, swimming
Season: May 20–October 5 (depending on weather)
Finding the campground: From Priest River (the town) drive north about 28 miles on ID 57 to Lamb Creek Village area (see campground sign), and then turn right (east) and drive 1 mile on gravel road.
The campground: Unusual for most Forest Service campgrounds, this one is located near a small community, Lamb Creek. There, campers can see (and prospectively use) a boat launch and marina and can check out a historical museum. Like most of the other Priest Lake campgrounds, this one is on a shady, sloped lakeshore. Several large parking spurs are available for maneuvering those larger vehicles. The amphitheater is sometimes used for talks on nature subjects and occasionally by scouting and other groups. The Forest Service does impose a two-day minimum stay for most weekends and a three-day stay on holiday weekends. The maximum stay is fourteen days.

5 Reeder Bay

Location: North of Priest River
Sites: 24
Facilities: Drinking water, fire rings, flush toilets, barrier-free access
Fee per night: $$
Elevation: 2,400 feet
Road conditions: Good—paved up to the campground and easy travel inside
Management: Forest Service, Priest Lake Ranger District, (208) 443-2512
Reservations: Call (877) 444-6777 or visit Web site www.reserveamerica.com—recommended at least four days in advance.
Activities: Fishing, hiking, picnicking
Season: May 25–October 5 (depending on weather)
Finding the campground: From Priest River (the town) drive 39 miles north on ID 57 to Nordman; there, turn east on Forest Road 1339, the paved road (there's just one in the area), and continue for 3 miles.
The campground: This is the "flattest" campground among the Priest Lake Forest Service campgrounds and the least tree-covered. Neither of these things are necessarily negatives, though; Reeder probably is the easiest of the group for some campers to set up their temporary quarters. The most remote of the major Priest River campgrounds, it gets a little less use than some of the others. Facilities are above average, including flush toilets (unusual for Forest Service campgrounds), and the lake view is perfectly good.

6 Beaver Creek

Location: North of Priest River
Sites: 40 group sites available
Facilities: Drinking water, flush and vault toilets, fire rings, lake access, barrier-free access, restaurant on-site
Fee per night: $$
Elevation: 2,500 feet
Road conditions: Good, with easy access for almost any vehicles, all the way to the campground
Management: Forest Service, Priest Lake Ranger District, (208) 443–2512
Reservations: Call (877) 444–6777 or visit Web site www.reserveamerica.com— recommended at least four days in advance.
Activities: Fishing, hiking, picnicking, swimming
Season: May 20–September 3 (depending on weather)
Finding the campground: From Priest River (the town) drive 39 miles north on ID 57 to Nordman, and then turn right and drive 12 miles northeast on Reeder Bay Road.
The campground: The two main loops here are in a forested area overlooking one of the northernmost reaches of Priest Lake. Make your reservations four days or more before your arrival. There are security gates at the campground entrance, and they are closed from 10:00 P.M. until early morning. A large, thirty-five-person group site is available; reservations are strongly recommended for its use. There's a good-size roped-off swimming area at shore side.

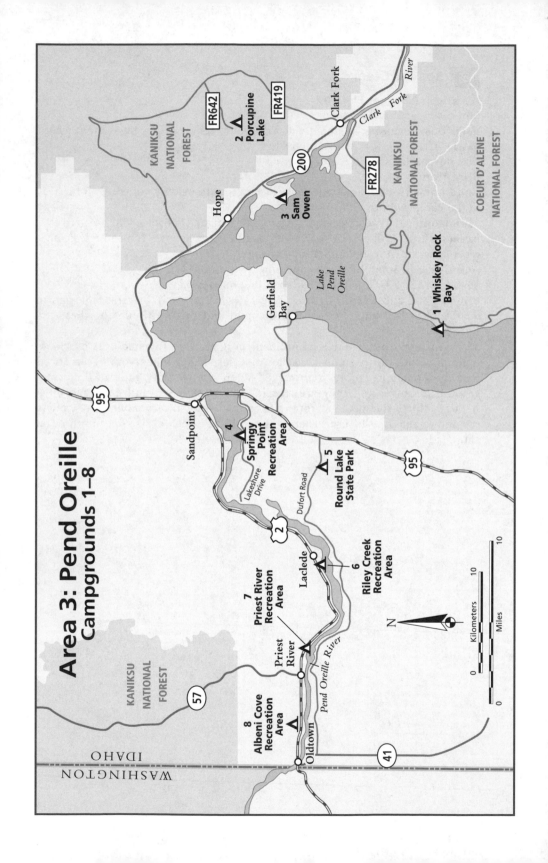

Area 3: Pend Oreille
Campgrounds 1–8

WASHINGTON

IDAHO

KANIKSU NATIONAL FOREST

KANIKSU NATIONAL FOREST

KANIKSU NATIONAL FOREST

COEUR D'ALENE NATIONAL FOREST

Clark Fork

Clark Fork River

Hope

Sandpoint

Garfield Bay

Lake Pend Oreille

2 Porcupine Lake

FR642

FR419

3 Sam Owen

FR278

1 Whiskey Rock Bay

4 Springy Point Recreation Area

Lakeshore Drive

Dufort Road

5 Round Lake State Park

6 Riley Creek Recreation Area

Laclede

Pend Oreille River

7 Priest River Recreation Area

Priest River

8 Albeni Cove Recreation Area

Oldtown

200

95

95

2

57

41

N

Kilometers
0   10

Miles
0   10

Area 3: Pend Oreille

It's a close call, but some say Lake Pend Oreille—Idaho's largest lake—is even more beautiful than the better-known Lake Coeur d'Alene to the south. Certainly more of it is easy to view, since U.S. Highway 2 and then Idaho Highway 200 run along most of its northern shoreline. Pend Oreille (pend o-ray) is thought to mean "ear pendants"—or intended to mean that—but a book called *Names on the Land* by George Stewart notes "it is not even good French." It is suspected to have been named in reference to the nearby Indians, since it was given the name some decades before the lake was mapped—hence, before anyone knew its shape.

This probably is Idaho's foremost lake for boating; you can find a number of marinas along the north shore. It is also one of Idaho's best for fishing, especially for trout. Moose are especially prevalent in this area, so keep a look out for the big creatures. Big birds nest along the lake: They include eagles, herons, and ospreys.

The lake itself is only the beginning of the attractions here, however. Sandpoint is a true jewel among Idaho's smaller cities, an arts center with many galleries in its downtown and which hosts a series of major regional arts events through the year. Don't let Sandpoint's small size fool you: This is a restaurant center, too, and the shopping possibilities are led by the downtown store of Coldwater Creek, the headquarters of the major national catalog company.

The whole area is strewn with hiking possibilities. Not least of these is the Schweitzer Mountain Ski Area just north of Sandpoint.

Don't forget the other cities along the lake: Priest River, Hope, Clark Fork. All of them are worth a visit.

For more information:

Greater Sandpoint Chamber of Commerce
P.O. Box 928
Sandpoint, ID 83864
(208) 263-2161
www.sandpoint.org/chamber

Priest River Chamber of Commerce
P.O. Box 929
Priest River, ID 83856
(208) 448-2721
www.priestlake.org

Idaho Panhandle National Forests
3815 Schreiber Way
Coeur d'Alene, ID 83814
(208) 765-7223
www.fs.fed.us/ipnf/

Area 3

	Town	Sites	Max. RV length	Electric	Picnic	Fire rings	Toilets	Showers	Water	Dump station	Disability access	Recreation	Can reserve	Fees ($)	Season	Stay limit (days)
1 Whiskey Rock Bay	Clark Fork	9	16		•	•	V		•			BS			May–Oct.	14
2 Porcupine Lake	Clark Fork	5			•	•	F		•		•	BFS			May–Oct.	14
3 Sam Owen	Hope	80	30		•	•	F		•	•	•	BFS	•	$	May–Oct.	14
4 Springy Point Recreation	Sandpoint	40	40		•	•	F	•	•	•		BFS	•	$$	May–Oct.	
5 Round Lake State Park	Sandpoint	53	35	•	•	•	F	•	•	•		BFHS	•	$$–$$$	Year-round	
6 Riley Creek Recreation	Priest River	68			•	•	F	•	•	•	•	BFS	•	$	May–Sept.	
7 Priest River Recreation	Priest River	20			•	•	F	•	•	•		BS	•	$–$$	May–Sept.	
8 Albeni Cove Recreation	Priest River	14	30		•	•	F	•	•	•		BFS	•	$$$	May–Sept.	

1 Whiskey Rock Bay

Location: Southwest of Clark Fork
Sites: 9 (3 on Lake Pend Oreille)
Facilities: Drinking water, fire rings, vault toilets, pets allowed
Fee per night: None
Elevation: 2,000 feet
Road conditions: Expect a drive of well over an hour from Clark Fork over a sometimes rugged forest route. The road is sometimes steep, and it has switchbacks. This road is accessible for RVs in the summer (not recommended in the spring); check for conditions for other vehicles.
Management: Forest Service, Sandpoint Ranger District, (208) 263–5111
Reservations: No
Activities: Boating, picnicking, swimming
Season: May 15–October 1
Finding the campground: From ID 200 in Clark Fork, drive 30 miles southwest on Forest Road 278. Those planning to tent it may prefer to boat across the lake (a distance of 10 miles) from Garfield Bay.
The campground: The southeast side of Lake Pend Oreille (along the section of the lake that jags south about 35 miles) has but one campground—and it's a beauty, partly forested, partly open-air. The view of the lake, and mountains beyond, is not sweeping but is well framed by mountains and shoreline. Boating is popular here, and so, though overland travel certainly is possible, many campers get here by boat from across Pend Oreille. Be aware that facilities and services are limited and not close at hand, so pack carefully before setting out.

2 Porcupine Lake

Location: Northwest of Clark Fork
Sites: 5
Facilities: Drinking water, barrier-free access, dump station, fire rings, flush toilets, lake access, pull-through sites, pets allowed
Fee per night: None
Elevation: 4,800 feet
Road conditions: Gravel mountain roads, with the last half-dozen miles a steep and sometimes rough climb. Give your vehicle a good looking over, and check in with the local ranger station, before tackling this trek.
Management: Forest Service, Sandpoint Ranger District, (208) 263–5111
Reservations: No
Activities: Boating, fishing, picnicking, swimming
Season: May 1–October 1
Finding the campground: From central Clark Fork, drive along Forest Road 419 (Lightning Creek Road) about 9 miles north of Clark Fork, and then drive 6 miles west on Forest Road 642 (Porcupine Creek Road).
The campground: A small campground, remote and relatively hard to get to. Still, for those who crave getting away from it all and crowd avoidance, Porcupine Lake is one of the best in the region. The lake is a small and usually cool mountain lake.

3 Sam Owen

Location: East of Hope
Sites: 80
Facilities: Drinking water, fire rings, dump station, flush toilets, barrier-free access, covered picnic shelter, lake access, pull-through sites, pets allowed
Fee per night: $
Elevation: 2,100 feet
Road conditions: Partly paved, partly gravel, well maintained and smooth—but watch out for occasional nasty potholes.
Management: Forest Service, Sandpoint Ranger District, (208) 263–5111
Reservations: Call (877) 444–6777 or visit Web site www.reserveamerica.com.
Activities: Boating, fishing, picnicking, swimming
Season: May 1–October 1
Finding the campground: From Hope drive 3 miles southeast on ID 200 and then 2 miles west on Bonner County Road 1002.
The campground: One of the larger public Panhandle campgrounds, Sam Owen is carefully organized. You'll find nice forest cover and some distance between many of the sites. The lake access is not immediately evident from most of the campground—you don't get the great lakeside view you get in some other regional sites—but it isn't far away, either.

4 Springy Point Recreation Area

Location: South of Sandpoint
Sites: 40
Facilities: Drinking water, flush toilets, showers, fire rings, dump station
Fee per night: $$
Elevation: 2,100 feet
Road conditions: Lakeshore Drive is mostly paved.
Management: U.S. Army Corps of Engineers, (208) 437-3133
Reservations: Call (877) 444-6777 or visit Web site www.reserveamerica.com.
Activities: Boating, fishing, picnicking, swimming
Season: May 13-October 9
Finding the campground: From Sandpoint drive 1.5 miles south on U.S. Highway 95, and then turn west onto Lakeshore Drive and drive about 2 miles.
The campground: An expansive, well-shaded camping site, with rolling hills and an intermittent look at Lake Pend Oreille from the south side. Sites are spread out, so campers aren't on top of one another. Amenities are above average, and firewood is available for purchase.

5 Round Lake State Park

Location: South of Sandpoint
Sites: 53
Facilities: Drinking water, dump station, fire rings, flush toilets, showers, lake access
Fee per night: $$-$$$
Elevation: 2,100
Road conditions: Good; nearly all paved
Management: Idaho Department of Parks and Recreation, (208) 263-3489
Reservations: Available via Web site www.idahoparks.org
Activities: Boating, fishing, hiking, picnicking, swimming
Season: All year, technically; as a practical matter, about May 1 through October 31 (depending on weather)
Finding the campground: From Sandpoint drive 10 miles south on US 95, over the bridge across Lake Pend Oreille, and then 2 miles west on Dufort Road to the park entrance.
The campground: Round Lake is a small, relatively shallow (about 37 feet at its deepest), circular (as its name implies) glacial lake only a few miles south of Pend Oreille, and one of Idaho's older state parks (established in 1965). It's a good place for boating and swimming, and a beach area is close to the campground. This is a well-shaded area, with ponderosa pines and Douglas firs dominating among the many tall trees. Wildlife is abundant in the area; keep a lookout for the black bears, and watch as well for raccoons, porcupines, white-tailed deer, and many others. Fishing is said to be good in the lake as well, since a variety of trout species hang out there.

6 Riley Creek Recreation Area

Location: East of Priest River
Sites: 68
Facilities: Drinking water, dump station, flush toilets, fire rings, showers, barrier-free access
Fee per night: $
Elevation: 2,100 feet
Road conditions: Paved to the campground
Management: U.S. Army Corps of Engineers, (208) 437-3133
Reservations: Call (877) 444-6777 or visit Web site www.reserveamerica.com.
Activities: Boating, fishing, picnicking, swimming
Season: May–September
Finding the campground: From the city of Priest River, drive 8 miles east on US 2 to Laclede, and then turn right (south) and drive on the Riley Creek Road 1 mile nearly to the river.
The campground: This is an attractive, shaded, well-maintained campground. A residential area also facing the Pend Oreille River is adjacent, so bear in mind that you have neighbors. This area often gets busy on summer weekends, so plan to arrive early.

7 Priest River Recreation Area

Location: East of Priest River
Sites: 20
Facilities: Drinking water, dump station, fire rings, flush toilets, lake access, showers
Fee per night: $-$$
Elevation: 2,100 feet
Road conditions: Paved into the campground
Management: U.S. Army Corps of Engineers, (208) 437-3133
Reservations: Call (877) 444-6777 or visit Web site www.reserveamerica.com.
Activities: Boating, picnicking, swimming
Season: May–September
Finding the campground: From the city of Priest River, drive 1 mile east on US 2, and then turn right (south) at the campground sign.
The campground: Shaded in places, open-air in others, this campground is nearly on the Pend Oreille River and has a nice overlook. It is especially well set up for small groups, with a small open-air theater and recreation facilities. This recreation area also is a popular picnic spot among Spokane-area residents looking for a little away time, so be aware that summer weekends may be busy.

8 Albeni Cove Recreation Area

Location: West of Priest River
Sites: 14
Facilities: Drinking water, dump station, fire rings, flush toilets, shower

Fee per night: $$$
Elevation: 2,100 feet
Road conditions: Paved to the campground
Management: U.S. Army Corps of Engineers, (208) 437-3133
Reservations: Call (877) 444-6777 or visit Web site www.reserveamerica.com.
Activities: Boating, fishing, picnicking, swimming
Season: May 13-September 10
Finding the campground: From Priest River drive 6 miles west on US 2 (2 miles east of Old Town); campground is about 1 mile south of the highway (follow the signs).
The campground: The best shaded of the Army Corps sites in this area—and all of them have nice shade trees—this one, as one camper there said, "makes you feel like you're in your own world." The campground is directly across from the Albeni Dam, which has some effect. The boat launch may, depending on time of year and the amount of water in the area, be usable or not. Call ahead if boating from here is your intent. Reservations are advised during the summer. The local Army Corps office notes that many people ask whether utility hookups are available here; the answer is: No, they are not.

Area 4: Coeur d'Alene

Probably only Sun Valley edges out Coeur d'Alene as the best-known Idaho vacation spot. The city is perched on the northern shore of the like-named lake, and both deserve their international renown. The visitor centerpiece is the Resort, a large hotel and convention center on the lake; there are associated downtown shopping centers and even a floating golf green nearby. Charter boats are available for tours around Lake Coeur d'Alene.

The Coeur d'Alene area is one of Idaho's fastest-growing, holding its own with growth in the Boise area in the 1990s. It is located only a half hour away from the metro area of Spokane, Washington, which gives visitors here access to that city's amenities. That also means that the Coeur d'Alene area is a close-by playground for the population of Spokane, which can make some parts crowded at times.

You can, however, engage in all sorts of outdoor activities here. You'll find fishing, swimming, and boating in Lake Coeur d'Alene (and in several nearby lakes, such as Fernan and Spirit) and camping and hiking in a variety of locations. One of the best nature walks in the area is adjacent to downtown Coeur d'Alene. Tubbs Hill, which juts out into the lake, is an undeveloped nature preserve, home to a vast variety of birds and a range of other animals as well.

For more information:

Coeur d'Alene Chamber of Commerce
1621 North Third Street
Coeur d'Alene, ID 83814
(208) 664–3194
www.coeurdalene.org

Idaho Panhandle National Forests
3815 Schreiber Way
Coeur d'Alene, ID 83814
(208) 765–7223
www.fs.fed.us/ipnf/

1 Farragut State Park

Location: East of Athol
Sites: 108
Facilities: Drinking water, barrier-free access, electric and water hookups, fire rings, dump station, flush and vault toilets, showers, pull-through sites, pets allowed
Fee per night: $$–$$$$
Elevation: 2,250 feet
Road conditions: Paved to the campground
Management: Idaho Department of Parks and Recreation, (208) 683–2425
Reservations: Available via Web site www.idahoparks.org

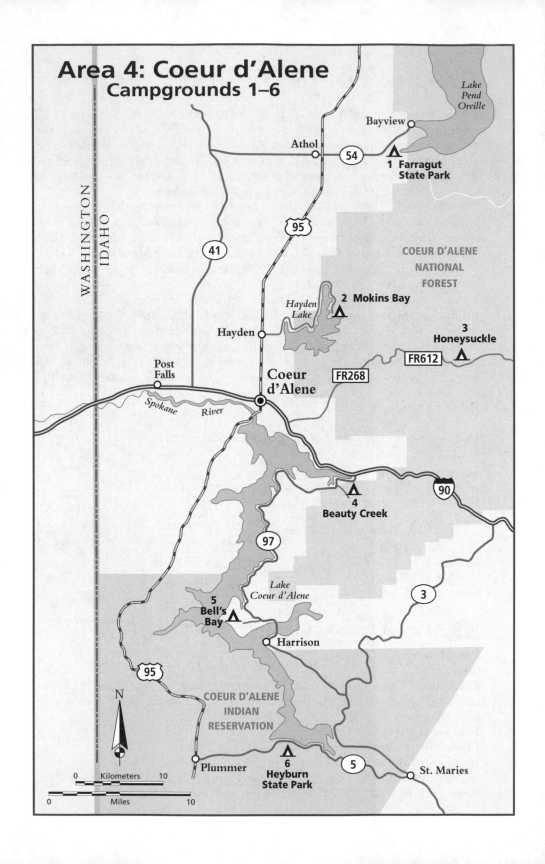

Area 4

	Town	Sites	Max. RV length	Electric	Picnic	Fire rings	Toilets	Showers	Water	Dump station	Disability access	Recreation	Can reserve	Fees ($)	Season	Stay limit (days)
1 Farragut State Park	Athol	108	31	•	•	•	F,V	•	•	•	•	BFH	•	$$–$$$$	Year-round	
2 Mokins Bay	Hayden Lake	16	22		•	•	V		•			BF		$$	May–Sept.	14
3 Honeysuckle	Coeur d'Alene	8	16		•	•	V		•		•	FH		$$	May–Sept.	
4 Beauty Creek	Coeur d'Alene	15	32		•	•	V		•		•	BFH	•	$$	May–Oct.	14
5 Bell's Bay	Harrison	26	22		•	•	V		•		•	BFS	•	$	May–Sept.	14
6 Heyburn State Park	Plummer	132	55	•	•	•	F	•	•	•		BFS	•	$$–$$$	Year-round	

Activities: Boating, fishing, hiking, picnicking
Season: All year, technically; as a practical matter, about May 1 through October 31 (depending on weather)
Finding the campground: From Hayden drive north 14 miles to Athol on U.S. Highway 95, then turn right (east) on Idaho Highway 54 and continue 7 miles to the park entrance.
The campground: Farragut is located on the southernmost reach of Lake Pend Oreille, not Lake Coeur d'Alene. It has one of the most distinctive histories of any park in Idaho. During World War II, the area was taken over as a naval training base. After that, a failed attempt was made to turn it into a college campus; only years after that was the land turned into a state park. It is now one of the more expansive and well-appointed state campgrounds.

2 Mokins Bay

Location: East of Hayden Lake
Sites: 16
Facilities: Drinking water, LP gas, fire rings, vault toilets
Fee per night: $$ (extra vehicle fee)
Elevation: 2,300 feet
Road conditions: Paved up to the campground
Management: Forest Service, Coeur d'Alene River Ranger District, (208) 769–3000
Reservations: No
Activities: Boating, fishing, picnicking
Season: May 15–September 15
Finding the campground: Drive about 1 mile north of central Hayden on US 95 and then turn east on Lancaster Road for 5 miles. Turn left (north) on Hayden Lake Road and follow it about 11 miles north of and around Hayden Lake

to its east side, to Mokins Bay. At that point turn east at the PUBLIC CAMP sign; the campground is another 200 feet beyond. The drive from Hayden is about 30 minutes.

The campground: The west and north sides of Hayden Lake are privately owned, an upscale resort area. (Bing Crosby had a home there.) The east side, and beyond, is public land and open for limited camping. The countryside is gorgeous, of course, and so is the lake. This is a popular campground, and it is first come, first served, so be sure to check for availability.

3 Honeysuckle

Location: Northeast of Coeur d'Alene
Sites: 8
Facilities: Drinking water, fire rings, barrier-free access, vault toilets
Fee per night: $$
Elevation: 2,800 feet
Road conditions: The way here from Coeur d'Alene is almost all gravel mountain road, some of it rough.
Management: Forest Service, Coeur d'Alene River Ranger District, (208) 769–3000
Reservations: No
Activities: Fishing, hiking, picnicking
Season: May 20–September 15
Finding the campground: From the east end of Sherman Avenue in downtown Coeur d'Alene, drive 11 miles northeast on Fernan Lake Road (which becomes Forest Road 268), then 11 miles east on Forest Road 612.
The campground: Northeast of Coeur d'Alene is a region relatively few people traverse; though not far from a large metro area, these mountains (Monument Mountain is southeast of the campground) are relatively lightly visited. They're good getaway spots close to a busy metro area.

4 Beauty Creek

Location: East of Coeur d'Alene
Sites: 20
Facilities: Drinking water, fire rings, barrier-free access, vault toilets
Fee per night: $$ (and extra vehicle fee)
Elevation: 2,150 feet
Road conditions: Paved on Idaho Highway 97 up to the last mile, then easy and relatively flat gravel road into the campground; an easy drive
Management: Forest Service, Coeur d'Alene River Ranger District, (208) 769–3000
Reservations: Call (877) 444–6777 or visit Web site www.reserveamerica.com.
Activities: Boating, fishing, hiking, picnicking
Season: May 1–October 1 (subject to change)
Finding the campground: From Coeur d'Alene drive 7 miles east on Interstate 90, turn off at exit 22 (Harrison–St. Maries exit), drive west 2.5 miles on

ID 97, turn left (east) at the campground sign, and continue 1 mile southeast on Forest Road 438.

The campground: Beauty Creek is about 1.5 miles away from Lake Coeur d'Alene, but a creek (sometimes dry in the summer and laden with big, climbable rocks) does run in front of the campground area. This is forested mountain country, but the mountains around are gentle. The campground itself is in an open meadow, and some of the sites are fairly close together. This would be a good site for several families camping together. Firewood is available for a small fee.

5 Bell's Bay

Location: North of Harrison
Sites: 26
Facilities: Drinking water, fire rings, barrier-free access, vault toilets
Fee per night: $
Elevation: 2,600 feet
Road conditions: Good, though not fast. ID 97 along the lake is spectacular for viewing, but it hugs the rugged coast closely, so don't expect to make freeway speeds. Of the last 3 miles off the highway to the lakeside, the first and last miles are paved, and the middle mile is washboarded gravel. The last half mile is a steep drop down to the lake; take it slowly if you're hauling a heavy load.
Management: Forest Service, Coeur d'Alene River Ranger District, (208) 769–3000
Reservations: Call (877) 444–6777 or visit Web site www.reserveamerica.com.
Activities: Boating, fishing, picnicking, swimming
Season: May 15–September 15
Finding the campground: Drive east from Coeur d'Alene 7 miles on I–90, turn south on exit 22 (Harrison–St. Maries), and drive 25 miles south on ID 97. At the campground sign, drive west 3 miles to the campground.
The campground: This is the only public campground with both a great setting and great views of Lake Coeur d'Alene. There's a boat dock onto the lake—one of a small number of public docks on this lake—and there are good RV spaces under the trees. This may be the most impressive campsite and value, overall, in the Coeur d'Alene area.

6 Heyburn State Park

Location: East of Plummer
Sites: 132
Facilities: Drinking water, electric hookups, flush toilets, showers, dump station, fire rings, playground, pull-through sites, pets allowed
Fee per night: $$–$$$
Elevation: 2,250 feet
Road conditions: Paved
Management: Idaho Department of Parks and Recreation, (208) 443–6710

Reservations: Available via Web site www.idahoparks.org

Activities: Boating, fishing, picnicking, swimming

Season: All year, technically; as a practical matter, about May 1 through October 31 (depending on weather)

Finding the campground: Plummer is 42 miles from Coeur d'Alene. From Plummer drive east on Idaho Highway 5 for about 12 miles; the park is just off the highway between Plummer and St. Maries.

The campground: This is one of the larger public campgrounds in Idaho. Heyburn is located just south of the southern end of Lake Coeur d'Alene, near the point where the St. Joe River pours into it. The park is one of the largest of Idaho's state parks, thoroughly forested, and pockmarked with marshy areas. The combination makes for an unusually strong collection of wildlife and plants (which include ponderosa pines estimated to be more than 400 years old). Hikers can check out a half dozen forest trails winding around the park. Animals include deer, moose, muskrat, black bears, raccoon, skunks, bobcats, and even mountain lions (though those are not often seen by casual visitors).

Area 5: Silver Valley

The people and the campgrounds are in different places in this region.

The people are in the Coeur d'Alene Basin, which more than a century ago became one of the premier mining districts in the United States. Billions of dollars worth of silver, and lesser amounts of other valuable metals, were mined in the valley running from the present communities of Kingston to Mullan, an area so rich it was called the Silver Valley. Since the early 1980s, however, this activity has diminished and little mining still is undertaken. Wallace and Kellogg do have mining-era historical exhibits and tours well worth a visit, and Kellogg is ground zero for the world's longest single-stage gondola, leading up to the Silver Mountain ski area overlooking the valley. Just to the west along Interstate 90 is the Cataldo Mission, Idaho's oldest building, also well worth a tour.

The major public campgrounds in the area are in the mountains north of the Silver Valley, north of the old towns of Murray and Prichard. Access to those communities and some distance beyond is paved. In between Pritchard and the campground, campers can use a Forest Service dump station.

This is more gorgeous mountain country, and it is a little more remote from the crowds than some of the campgrounds nearer Coeur d'Alene. These campgrounds are bases for fishing and hunting and for rafting or inner-tubing down the Coeur d'Alene River.

For more information:

Kellogg Chamber of Commerce
608 Bunker Avenue
Kellogg, ID 83837
(208) 784–0821
www.kellogg-id.org

Wallace Chamber of Commerce
8 East Idaho Street
Wallace, ID 83873
(208) 753–7151

Idaho Panhandle National Forests
3815 Schreiber Way
Coeur d'Alene, ID 83814
(208) 765–7223
www.fs.fed.us/ipnf/

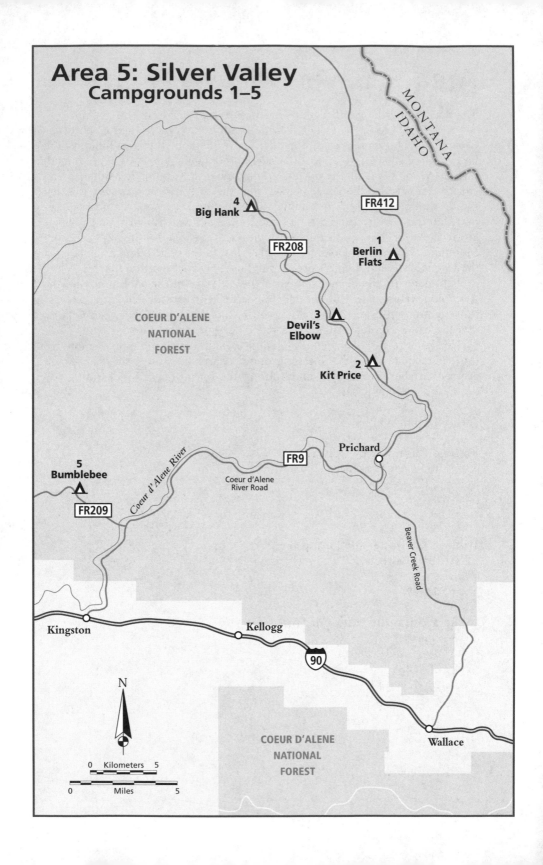

Area 5

		Town	Sites	Max. RV length	Electric	Picnic	Fire rings	Toilets	Showers	Water	Dump station	Disability access	Recreation	Can reserve	Fees ($)	Season	Stay limit (days)
1	Berlin Flats	Prichard	9	22		•	•	V		•		•	F		$	May–Oct.	14
2	Kit Price	Prichard	52	22		•	•	V		•		•	FH	•	$	May–Oct.	14
3	Devil's Elbow	Prichard	20	22		•	•	V		•		•	FH	•	$	May–Sept.	14
4	Big Hank	Prichard	30	22		•	•	V		•		•	FH		$	May–Oct.	14
5	Bumblebee	Kingston	25	16		•	•	V		•			FH	•	$$	May–Oct.	14

1 Berlin Flats

Location: North of Prichard
Sites: 9
Facilities: Drinking water (from hand pumps), fire rings, barrier-free access, vault toilets
Fee per night: $
Elevation: 2,600 feet
Road conditions: Paved, except for the last mile
Management: Forest Service, Coeur d'Alene River Ranger District, (208) 752–1221
Reservations: No
Activities: Fishing, picnicking, river floating
Season: May 25–October 15 (depending on weather)
Finding the campground: From Wallace drive the Beaver Creek Road 15 miles north to Prichard, then continue on Forest Road 208 14 miles north, and then turn right (northeast) onto Forest Road 412 (along Shoshone Creek) and continue for 7 miles.
The campground: Farthest northeast of this region's campgrounds, Berlin Flats is located next to the North Fork of the Coeur d'Alene River. Fishing, swimming, and inner-tubing down the river are all popular here. The forested location (the name notwithstanding) is less manicured here than in some other campgrounds in the region; this is the only campground in this region that doesn't have a resident campground host. This is a popular site, and though spaces are usually available on most weekends, it tends to fill up on holiday weekends.

2 Kit Price

Location: North of Prichard
Sites: 52 (reservations possible for 15)
Facilities: Drinking water, fire rings, barrier-free access, vault toilets
Fee per night: $
Elevation: 3,600 feet
Road conditions: Paved almost all the way

Management: Forest Service, Coeur d'Alene River Ranger District, (208) 752-1221
Reservations: For 15 of the sites, reservations can be made by calling (877) 444-6777 or visiting Web site www.reserveamerica.com.
Activities: Fishing, hiking, picnicking, river floating
Season: May 15–October 1 (depending on weather)
Finding the campground: From Wallace drive the Beaver Creek Road 15 miles north to Prichard, and then take FR 208 north for 11 miles.
The campground: This is the largest and most popular of the Prichard-area sites. Another of the pretty sites along the North Fork of the Coeur d'Alene River, it is one of the easiest to access and one of the largest, and it tends to be one of the more crowded during high season. It has pretty shaded spots and good river access.

3 Devil's Elbow

Location: North of Prichard
Sites: 20 (1 group site reservable)
Facilities: Drinking water, fire rings, barrier-free access, vault toilets
Fee per night: $
Elevation: 2,800 feet
Road conditions: Good and easy
Management: Forest Service, Coeur d'Alene River Ranger District, (208) 752-1221
Reservations: Only group site is reservable; call (877) 444-6777 or visit Web site www.reserveamerica.com.
Activities: Fishing, hiking, picnicking, river floating
Season: May 15–September 10 (depending on weather)
Finding the campground: From Wallace drive the Beaver Creek Road 15 miles north to Prichard, and then continue north on FR 208 for 14 miles.
The campground: One of the closer campgrounds to the Prichard area, Devil's Elbow has a large group site in an open meadow. The North Fork of the Coeur d'Alene River is nearby for floating and fishing.

4 Big Hank

Location: North of Prichard
Sites: 30
Facilities: Drinking water, fire rings, barrier-free access, vault toilets
Fee per night: $
Elevation: 2,600 feet
Road conditions: FR 208, on which much of the route here is taken, is paved.
Management: Forest Service, Coeur d'Alene River Ranger District, (208) 752-1221
Reservations: No
Activities: Fishing, hiking, picnicking, river floating
Season: May 25–October 15 (depending on weather)
Finding the campground: From Wallace drive the Beaver Creek Road 15

miles north to Prichard, and then drive 20 miles north on FR 208.

The campground: Located along the shallow North Fork of the Coeur d'Alene River, this area is thickly forested.

5 Bumblebee

Location: North of Kingston
Sites: 25
Facilities: Drinking water, fire rings, vault toilets
Fee per night: $$
Elevation: 2,200 feet
Road conditions: Paved to the campground
Management: Forest Service, Coeur d'Alene River Ranger District, (208) 769-3000
Reservations: Yes for group sites; call the ranger station.
Activities: Fishing, hiking, picnicking
Season: May 15-October 1
Finding the campground: From Wallace drive 19 miles west on I-90 to exit 43 (Kingston-Enaville), then 6 miles north on Forest Road 9 (the Coeur d'Alene River Road), and then turn left at Bumblebee Junction 3 miles west on Forest Road 209 (the Bumblebee Road).
The campground: Located in a dense woods next to Bumblebee Creek, this is a good place for pines and privacy, even from one's camping neighbors. It is the closest of the Silver Valley-area campgrounds to I-90, which means it gets substantial traffic. There are two loops, the northern being a group area that can be reserved, the southern split up into individual sites.

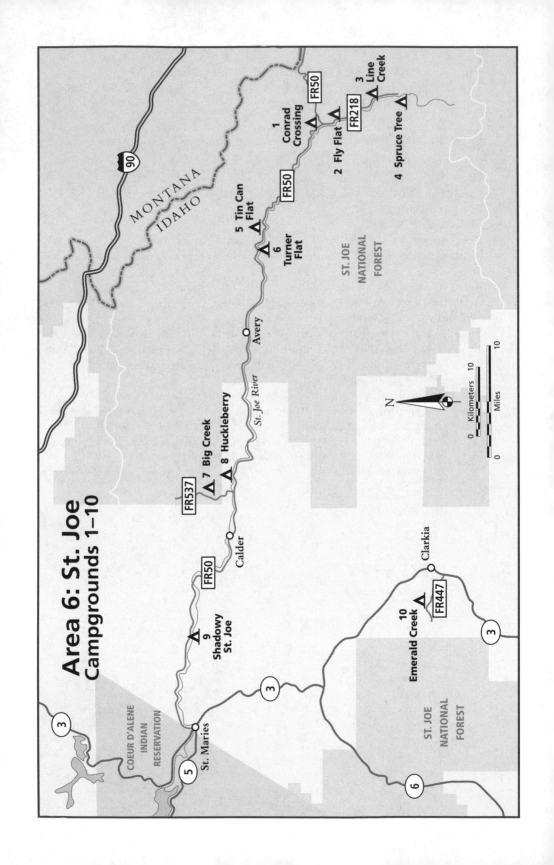

Area 6: St. Joe
Campgrounds 1–10

Area 6: St. Joe

They call it the Shadowy St. Joe (a book of local history was even given that title) because of all the trees overhanging the slow-moving river that dumps into Lake Coeur d'Alene. The country around it is not only off the interstate but even off any major highway at all: U.S. Highway 95, which many people use to access this area, is most of an hour's drive to the west. The only sizable town in the area is St. Maries, a timber mill community.

The campgrounds mostly lie east of St. Maries, along or near the St. Joe River and some of them close to the old Milwaukee Road railroad, built a century ago and dismantled in the 1980s. The ride from St. Maries to Montana along the remnants of this old route is one of the most spectacular in the state. The road has been paved in recent years beyond Avery all the way to Gold Summit, which is the Montana state line. (You can continue into Montana on gravel road.)

Much of this area still is logging country, and logging trucks are major users of the forest roads—and some of them move faster than you might guess and throw lots of gravel into the air. Give them a wide berth (as wide as you can, since many of these roads are narrow).

For more information:

St. Maries Chamber of Commerce
906 Main Avenue
St. Maries, ID 83861
(208) 245-3563

Idaho Panhandle National Forests
3815 Schreiber Way
Coeur d'Alene, ID 83814
(208) 765-7223
www.fs.fed.us/ipnf/

1 Conrad Crossing

Location: East of Avery
Sites: 8
Facilities: Drinking water, fire rings, vault toilets
Fee per night: None
Elevation: 3,300 feet
Road conditions: Paved to the campground
Management: Forest Service, St. Joe Ranger District, (208) 245-2531
Reservations: No
Activities: Fishing, hiking, picnicking
Season: June 1–October 31 (exact dates variable)
Finding the campground: From Avery drive 28 miles east on Forest Road 50 (the St. Joe River Road). Watch out for logging trucks!

Area 6

		Town	Sites	Max. RV length	Electric	Picnic	Fire rings	Toilets	Showers	Water	Dump station	Disability access	Recreation	Can reserve	Fees ($)	Season	Stay limit (days)
1	Conrad Crossing	Avery	8	16		•	•	V		•			FH			June–Oct.	14
2	Fly Flat	Avery	14	32		•	•	V		•			FHS			July–Oct.	14
3	Line Creek (Stock Camp)	Avery	9	35			•	V					FH		$	June–Oct.	14
4	Spruce Tree	Avery	9	35		•	•	V		•			FH			June–Oct.	14
5	Tin Can Flat	Avery	11	32		•	•	V		•			FH		$	June–Oct.	14
6	Turner Flat	Avery	11	32			•	V		•			FH		$	June–Oct.	14
7	Big Creek	Calder	8	30		•	•	V					FH			June–Oct.	14
8	Huckleberry	Calder	33	50	•	•	•	V		•	•		BFS		$$–$$$	April–Nov.	14
9	Shadowy St. Joe	St. Maries	14	45		•	•	V		•		•	BFS		$	May–Oct.	14
10	Emerald Creek	Clarkia	18	22		•	•	V		•			F		$	May–Oct.	14

The campground: This somewhat scattered forested campground is located partly on the river (three sites) and partly uphill and across the road (the other five). Conrad Crossing basically marks the end of the St. Joe River Road and the beginning of the St. Joe River; the mountain roads that fan out from here are challenging and steep. This pretty and remote country is only a few miles over the mountains from Montana; access to the Historic Montana Trail is located nearby.

2 Fly Flat

Location: East of Avery
Sites: 14
Facilities: Drinking water (hand pump), fire rings, vault toilets
Fee per night: None
Elevation: 3,200 feet
Road conditions: Almost all paved to the campground. Some of this is narrow and twisting road, however. Watch out for logging trucks!
Management: Forest Service, St. Joe Ranger District, (208) 245–2531
Reservations: No
Activities: Fishing, hiking, swimming
Season: July 1–October 31
Finding the campground: A few miles uphill and to the south from Conrad Crossing, along fast-running Copper Creek. From Avery drive east 29 miles on FR 50 (the St. Joe River Road) and then south 4 miles on Forest Road 218.
The campground: Thickly forested, this is one of the best spots for hikers, with two excellent trailheads (Peggy Creek and Fly Creek) located close by. A group picnic site is provided here.

3 Line Creek (Stock Camp)

Location: East of Avery
Sites: 9
Facilities: Fire rings, vault toilets, pull-through sites
Fee per night: $
Elevation: 3,800 feet
Road conditions: Paved to Conrad Crossing, then mildly rugged and steep in places; you're heading up into the mountains. The campsite marks the end of the line for hauling a horse trailer.
Management: Forest Service, St. Joe Ranger District, (208) 245-2531
Reservations: No
Activities: Fishing, hiking
Season: June 1–October 31 (depending on weather)
Finding the campground: From Avery drive east 29 miles on FR 50 (the St. Joe River Road), then 11 miles south on FR 218 (Red Ives Road).
The campground: This campground is basically designed for horses and the people who own them. The pull-through sites are well designed for horse trailers, and riding trails fan out from the campground area. Apart from toilets, there are no services (including water) here, though a creek does run nearby.

4 Spruce Tree

Location: East of Avery
Sites: 9
Facilities: Drinking water, fire rings, vault toilets, pull-through sites
Fee per night: None
Elevation: 3,750 feet
Road conditions: Partway paved, then about half the distance out of Avery; semirugged in places. Watch out for logging trucks!
Management: Forest Service, St. Joe Ranger District, (208) 245-2531
Reservations: No
Activities: Fishing, hiking, picnicking
Season: June 1–October 31 (depending on weather)
Finding the campground: From Avery drive east 29 miles on FR 50 (the St. Joe River Road), then 12 miles south on FR 218.
The campground: Located mainly in a mountain meadow with forests all around, this campground is located at the headwaters of the wild portion of St. Joe Wild and Scenic River—a terrific trout fishing river—and the St. Joe River Trailhead. Goes without saying that the countryside all around is some of the prettiest in the west. Three hours or more from the nearest incorporated city, you're well out in the wilds here—and ordinarily far away from the crowds; Spruce Tree is the most remote yet generally accessible by road campsite in this region. And staying here is free.

Tin Can Flat

Location: East of Avery
Sites: 11
Facilities: Drinking water, fire rings, vault toilets
Fee per night: $
Elevation: 2,900 feet
Road conditions: Mostly paved, with some Forest Service gravel road, mostly good and flat
Management: Forest Service, St. Joe Ranger District, (208) 245–2531
Reservations: No
Activities: Fishing, hiking, picnicking
Season: June 1–October 31 (depending on weather)
Finding the campground: From Avery drive 10 miles east on FR 50 (the St. Joe River Road). Watch out for logging trucks!
The campground: They call the St. Joe River the "Shadowy St. Joe" because of the overhanging trees, and none of the area campsites better reflects the nickname than this one. The evergreens and other trees crowd tightly around here, with the effect of emphasizing the adjacent river.

Turner Flat

Location: East of Avery
Sites: 11
Facilities: Drinking water, fire rings, vault toilets
Fee per night: $
Elevation: 2,800 feet
Road conditions: Paved to the campground
Management: Forest Service, St. Joe Ranger District, (208) 245–2531
Reservations: No
Activities: Fishing, hiking
Season: June 1–October 31 (depending on weather)
Finding the campground: Drive 9 miles east of Avery on FR 50 (the St. Joe River Road).
The campground: Set in a pleasant meadow area, this is a more varied campground than most in this area. There's one group site suitable for about fifteen people.

Big Creek

Location: East of Calder
Sites: 8
Facilities: Barrier-free access, fire rings, vault toilets
Fee per night: None
Elevation: 2,400 feet
Road conditions: Mostly flat riverside paved on the St. Joe River Road, then periodically worn and dusty gravel throughout. Beware those logging trucks!
Management: Forest Service, St. Joe Ranger District, (208) 245–2531

Reservations: No
Activities: Fishing, hiking, picnicking
Season: June 1–October 31
Finding the campground: From St. Maries drive 18 miles east on FR 50 (the St. Joe River Road) to Calder. At Calder cross the river and drive 5 miles east on the Northside Road (also called County Road 347, on the north side of the St. Joe River), then 3 miles northwest on Forest Road 537.

The campground: In this pretty and often sun-drenched mountain meadow campground well off the busy St. Joe River Road lies a story. It begins (as Cort Conley recounts in his book *Idaho for the Curious*) with Fred Herrick, a timber entrepreneur from Wisconsin, who salvaged timber after the massive 1910 fire ripped through this area. For a time his company was the largest independent timber producer in the inland Northwest, but the Great Depression wiped him out. His abandoned logging camp was turned into a Civilian Conservation Corps camp in the New Deal years, and those CCC workers built the foundation of the forest road system that today connects St. Maries to Avery and beyond; before then, only boat or railroad (the old Milwaukee Railroad followed the St. Joe River) travel was possible. With World War II, all was abandoned except for a local bar, but soon a notorious double murder closed even that; all the buildings were razed, and today's campground eventually was built. Most of today's campers have no idea how many ghosts abound in this quiet mountain setting.

8 Huckleberry

Location: East of Calder
Sites: 33
Facilities: Drinking water, dump station, fire rings, electric and water hookups, vault toilets, pets allowed
Fee per night: $$–$$$, depending on site
Elevation: 3,100 feet
Road conditions: Generally good and flat (but sometimes narrow) paved road
Management: Bureau of Land Management, Coeur d'Alene Field Office, (208) 769-5030
Reservations: Call (208) 245-2531
Activities: Boating, fishing, picnicking, swimming
Season: April 1–November 30
Finding the campground: From Calder drive 5 miles east on FR 50 (the St. Joe River Road) to the campground sign.

The campground: This relatively large and surprisingly "civilized" campground is designed for a variety of uses, from large RVs to tents. Highly unusual for a BLM facility, Huckleberry has electric and water hookups. Trailer pads are paved, and tent pads have gravel. This location on the St. Joe River draws plenty of fly fishermen; in season, it is a popular location for elk hunting, too.

9 Shadowy St. Joe

Location: East of St. Maries
Sites: 14
Facilities: Drinking water, fire rings, vault toilets, barrier-free access, boat dock
Fee per night: $
Elevation: 2,100 feet
Road conditions: Paved to the campground, gravel within
Management: Forest Service, St. Joe Ranger District, (208) 245–2531
Reservations: No
Activities: Boating, fishing, picnicking, swimming
Season: May 1–October 31
Finding the campground: From St. Maries drive 1 mile east on ID 3, then 10 miles east on the FR 50 (the St. Joe River Road); the campground is next to that road.
The campground: This is the St. Joe River campground closest to the city of St. Maries, and it is located where the river is slow, wide, and easy. It's a favorite for boating (there's a good boat dock here), river floating, and fishing. This is a great site for kids because of the play area and swimming opportunities. There's also a group picnic shelter. There are a few trees around, but mostly this is an open meadow site.

10 Emerald Creek

Location: Northwest of Clarkia
Sites: 18
Facilities: Drinking water, fire rings, vault toilets, river access
Fee per night: $
Elevation: 2,800 feet
Road conditions: Paved up to the forest road, then gravel
Management: Forest Service, St. Joe Ranger District, (208) 245–2531
Reservations: No
Activities: Fishing, picnicking, rock hunting
Season: May 15–October 1
Finding the campground: From Clarkia drive 5 miles northwest on Idaho Highway 3, then turn left at the sign for Emerald Creek Recreation Area and drive 6 miles southwest on Forest Road 447.
The campground: This area is garnet country; several businesses along ID 3 are based on mining and processing the mineral, sometimes seen as a red gemstone in polished form. Rock hounds will find this campground one of the most interesting in Idaho.

Area 7: Palouse

In Idaho, Latah County is best known as the home of the University of Idaho, the state's premier educational institution; the city of Moscow is an attractive university town (and located just 8 miles away from another much like it across the Washington border: Pullman, home of Washington State University). But Moscow and the Palouse rolling grain country around it are some distance from the area's public campgrounds.

Those are located off to the north and east, where the university has little obvious influence and where timber communities—Potlatch, Harvard, Troy, Bovill, Helmer, Deary—are the small centers of population. The land here is hilly, mountainous in places, and thickly forested.

Three of the campgrounds in this area are national forest campgrounds. Mention should be made of a probable fourth planned for availability to campers by 2004, near the city of Elk River. Extensive fossil beds are located there, and this campground may become a center for fossil hunters. The Oviatt Creek Fossil Beds (southwest of Elk River) already are a destination site for amateur paleontologists, who are allowed to search for and keep (a limited number of) fossils. Some of the best-preserved plant fossils in the world can be found here.

The fourth existing public campground area here, McCroskey State Park, is a special case, an unusual state park with a peculiar history.

For more information:

Moscow Chamber of Commerce
411 South Main Street
Moscow, ID 83843
(208) 882–1800
www.moscow.com

Idaho Panhandle National Forests
3815 Schreiber Way
Coeur d'Alene, ID 83814
(208) 765–7223
www.fs.fed.us/ipnf/

1 Little Boulder Creek

Location: East of Deary
Sites: 17
Facilities: Drinking water, fire rings, vault toilets, barrier-free access, pets allowed
Fee per night: $$
Elevation: 2,760 feet
Road conditions: Nearly all paved access, good gravel road for the last 3 miles

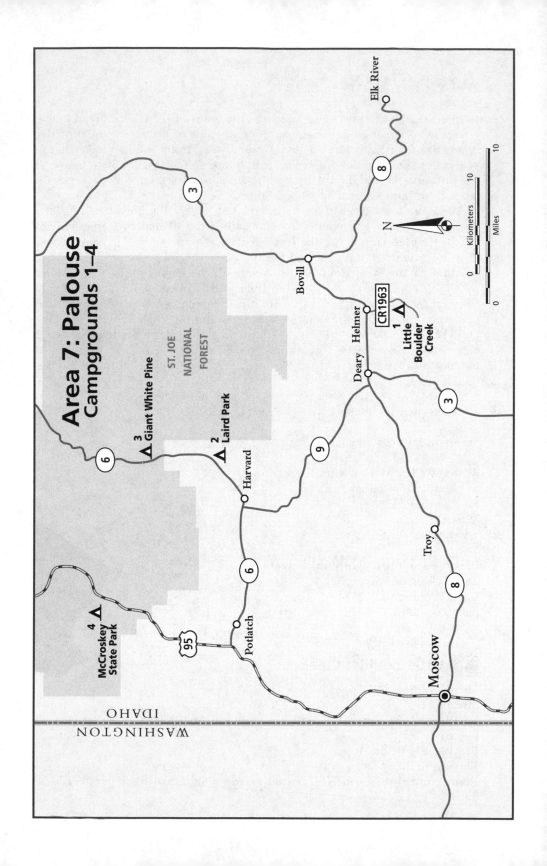

Area 7

		Town	Sites	Max. RV length	Electric	Picnic	Fire rings	Toilets	Showers	Water	Dump station	Disability access	Recreation	Can reserve	Fees ($)	Season	Stay limit (days)
1	Little Boulder Creek	Deary	17	35		•	•	V		•		•	F	•	$$	May–Sept.	14
2	Laird Park	Harvard	31	35		•	•	V		•		•	HS		$	May–Sept.	14
3	Giant White Pine	Harvard	14	30		•	•	V		•			FH		$	May–Sept.	14
4	McCroskey State Park	Potlatch	U	20				V					H	•	$$	April–Nov.	14

Management: Forest Service, Palouse Ranger District, (208) 875–1131
Reservations: No
Activities: Fishing, picnicking
Season: May 20–September 30
Finding the campground: From Deary drive 4 miles east on Idaho Highway 8, then 3 miles southeast on Latah County Road 1963.
The campground: The other two Forest Service campgrounds in the Palouse region are located close to highways, but Little Boulder Creek is a little more remote and consequently gets less traffic. Mostly forested, it's a pleasing spot for relaxing and for fishing. Campground hosts have been added here in recent years.

2 Laird Park

Location: East of Harvard
Sites: 31
Facilities: Drinking water, vault toilets, barrier-free access, playground, pets allowed
Fee per night: $
Elevation: 2,640 feet
Road conditions: Paved all the way into the campground
Management: Forest Service, Palouse Ranger District, (208) 875–1131
Reservations: No
Activities: Hiking, picnicking, swimming
Season: May 20–September 30
Finding the campground: From Harvard drive 3 miles northeast on Idaho Highway 6, then 1 mile southeast on Forest Road 447. Look for the sign for the campground.
The campground: The largest and most popular of the Forest Service campgrounds around the Palouse, Laird is also one of the most unusual because of one of its features—an "artificial dam." All dams are artificial, you say? Well, this one is installed and removed every spring and fall, specifically to create a swimming and recreation area for children. Part of this large campground is uphill amid the trees; the "artificial dam" is located down in a meadow bisected by the Palouse River. A campground host is available here in the summer.

The "artificial dam" at Laird Park in Latah County is removed each fall and replaced each spring. The campground is one of the most popular in north-central Idaho.

3 Giant White Pine

Location: North of Harvard
Sites: 14
Facilities: Drinking water, vault toilets, fire rings, pets allowed
Fee per night: $
Elevation: 2,800 feet
Road conditions: Paved to the campground
Management: Forest Service, Palouse Ranger District, (208) 875–1131
Reservations: No
Activities: Fishing, hiking, picnicking
Season: May 20–September 30
Finding the campground: From Harvard drive 7 miles north on ID 6; the campground entrance is on the highway.
The campground: White pines are found all around this part of north-central

Idaho, but this campground was named for one in particular—a giant white pine, the largest on record, nearly 200 feet tall. The tree died of disease in the late 1990s, and a sliver of it can still be found in the Forest Service ranger's office at Potlatch. The campground may lack that particular tree, but it still has plenty of others, which provide ample shade for the well-spaced camping spaces. The biggest draw now is the campground's strategic location as a trailhead, and a lot of day hikers use the campground.

4 McCroskey State Park

Location: North of Potlatch
Sites: Undetermined number
Facilities: Vault toilets
Fee per night: $$
Elevation: 4,300 feet at its highest peak, but widely variable
Road conditions: After leaving U.S. Highway 95, much of the road is narrow and gravel, sometimes twisting and steep, and definitely not recommended for trailers longer than 25 feet.
Management: Idaho Department of Parks and Recreation, (208) 443–6710
Reservations: Available via Web site www.idahoparks.org
Activities: Hiking
Season: April–November (depending on weather)
Finding the campground: From Potlatch drive 9 miles north on US 95 to the DeSmet turnoff, and then turn left (west) onto DeSmet Road to the park entrance. Camping is located at several sites along Skyline Drive, which runs through the park.
The campground: This is one of Idaho's most unusual camping areas, at the second-oldest state park. Virgil McCroskey owned land along the Washington-Idaho border and in the late 1940s offered to donate it to both states. Washington quickly accepted, but McCroskey had to convince the Idaho Legislature over a period of years to accept his donation on the Idaho side. When it finally did agree, it did so only on condition that McCroskey pay $500 a year for park upkeep (for fifteen years) and personally work on upkeep. McCroskey, remarkably, accepted the conditions and remained faithful to them until his death in 1970, at age ninety-three. That determination becomes more understandable when you see the area, which is filled with forests, mountain peaks, and an unusual presence that McCroskey himself described as ghostly. Today, it remains Idaho's least developed park. Skyline Drive is a little challenging and not recommended for larger RVs, and the three campground areas (scattered along Skyline) are decidedly primitive; vault toilets are just about the only nicety provided. If you're interested in roughing it and getting away from the crowd, though, McCroskey provides one of Idaho's finer remote experiences, while not far from a major highway.

Area 8: Clearwater

Drive along the rivers of north-central Idaho—the Clearwater and its equally scenic tributaries, the Potlatch, Lochsa, and Selway—and you have the very definition of a scenic byway. Most of these roads are not heavily used (though you should beware of the long trucks that sometimes barrel down U.S. Highway 12), and you can take a leisurely, winding drive through the lowlands of mountain country that features a new great picture every thirty seconds or so.

The Clearwater exits into the Snake River at Lewiston, the largest city in this area, which is where the Snake also leaves Idaho. That two-river system has given Idaho its only port; Lewiston also has the distinction of having been Idaho's first capital (in its territorial days) and has many sites still visible from its old days.

This part of Idaho has some of the state's most extensive history. On their Voyage of Discovery, Meriwether Lewis and William Clark led the first United States expedition into the area in 1805. It was one of the most difficult and hazardous parts of their journey, crossing into the state at the Lolo Pass and meandering downstream toward present-day Lewiston. A half-century later, this region was the site of the first permanent cities and towns in Idaho, after the discovery of gold near Pierce.

Drive up the river roads east of Lewiston, and between the small timber towns you'll see forested valleys and occasional open meadow areas. The lands are occupied more by deer, elk, otters, mink, beavers, and many more creatures than by humans, and when fishing season allows, several of the rivers are prime locations for steelhead angling. And at Orofino be sure to turn north for a tree-lined drive along the spectacular Dworshak Reservoir, which has excellent fishing, 54 miles of shoreline, and lots of camping locations.

The more adventurous will continue on into the backcountry beyond the Dworshak Reservoir, on the North Fork of the Clearwater River. Here lie a string of Forest Service campgrounds where fishing on the riverbanks is considered excellent. (All of these campgrounds are relatively primitive as well as strictly "pack it in, pack it out.")

For more information:

Lewiston Chamber of Commerce
2207 Main Street
Lewiston, ID 83501
(208) 743–3531
www.lewistonchamber.org

Clearwater National Forest
12730 U.S. Highway 12
Orofino, ID 83544
(208) 476–4541
www.fs.fed.us/r1/clearwater

Nez Perce National Forest
Route 2, Box 475
Grangeville, ID 83530
(208) 983–1950
www.fs.fed.us/r1/nezperce

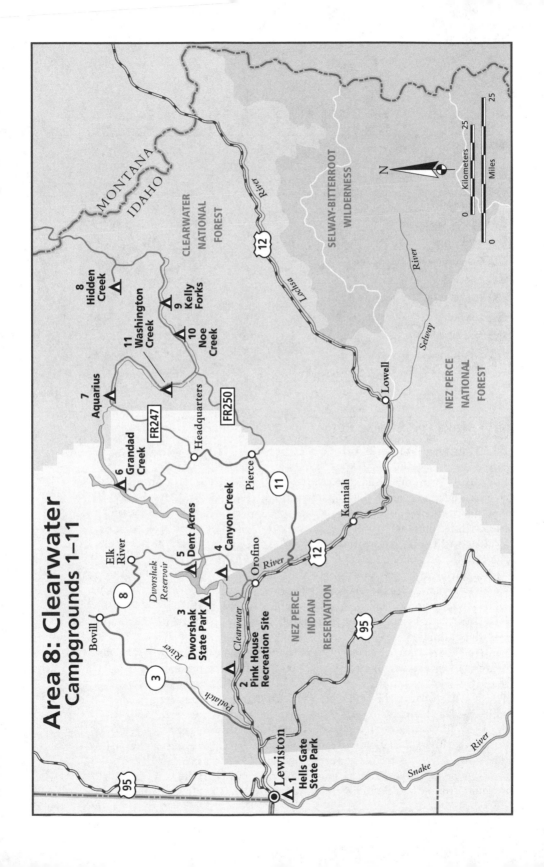

Area 8: Clearwater
Campgrounds 1–11

MONTANA
IDAHO

CLEARWATER NATIONAL FOREST

SELWAY-BITTERROOT WILDERNESS

NEZ PERCE NATIONAL FOREST

NEZ PERCE INDIAN RESERVATION

8 Hidden Creek

9 Kelly Forks

10 Noe Creek

11 Washington Creek

7 Aquarius

6 Grandad Creek

FR247

Headquarters

FR250

Lowell

Lochsa River

Selway River

12

11

Pierce

Kamiah

5 Dent Acres

4 Canyon Creek

Dworshak Reservoir

Elk River

Bovill

8

Dworshak State Park

3

River

2 Pink House Recreation Site

Orofino

Clearwater River

12

95

3

Potlatch River

Lewiston

1 Hells Gate State Park

95

Snake River

River

N

Kilometers   0   25
Miles   0   25

Area 8

	Town	Sites	Max. RV length	Electric	Picnic	Fire rings	Toilets	Showers	Water	Dump station	Disability access	Recreation	Can reserve	Fees ($)	Season	Stay limit (days)
1 Hells Gate State Park	Lewiston	93	60	•	•	•	F	•	•	•	•	BFHS	•	$$	Year-round	
2 Pink House	Orofino	15	40	•	•	•	F		•		•	BF		$$–$$$	Year-round	14
3 Dworshak State Park	Orofino	102	50	•	•	•	F	•	•	•	•	BFHS	•	$$	April–Oct.	
4 Canyon Creek	Orofino	17	22		•	•	V		•			BF	•		Spring–Fall	
5 Dent Acres	Orofino	50	35	•	•	•	F	•	•	•		BFHS	•	$$$	Spring–Fall	
6 Grandad Creek	Orofino	6			•	•	V					BF			Spring–Fall	14
7 Aquarius	Pierce	7	22		•	•	V		•			F		$	May–Sept.	14
8 Hidden Creek	Pierce	13	22		•	•	V		•			FH		$	May–Oct.	14
9 Kelly Forks	Pierce	14	32		•	•	V		•			FH		$	May–Oct.	14
10 Noe Creek	Pierce	6	22		•	•	V		•			FH		$	May–Oct.	14
11 Washington Creek	Pierce	23	32		•		V		•			FH		$	May–Sept.	14

1 Hells Gate State Park

Location: South of Lewiston
Sites: 93
Facilities: Drinking water, flush toilets, showers, fire rings, dump station, barrier-free access, electric hookups, fire rings, river access, playground
Fee per night: $$
Elevation: 760 feet
Road conditions: Paved through most of the campground; easy access from the city for all vehicles
Management: Idaho Department of Parks and Recreation, (208) 443–6710
Reservations: Available via Web site www.idahoparks.org
Activities: Boating, fishing, hiking, picnicking, swimming
Season: All year, technically; as a practical matter, about April through October (depending on weather)
Finding the campground: From downtown Lewiston drive toward the bridge to Clarkston, but before reaching it exit south on Snake River Avenue, then drive 4 miles south to the park.
The campground: This is a well-manicured area, resembling a cross between a city park and a private park. There isn't a lot of shade in most of the camping areas (though some have tree cover), but there is a great riverside view of the Snake River, just before it merges with the Clearwater at Lewiston and flows out of the state. This is also a good jumping-off point for boat trips south into the Hells Canyon area, which is 30 miles away; Hells Gate has a 100-slip marina. The park is popular with campers around north-central Idaho for its

convenience (it is close to the city, and has a store and other facilities) and even its social atmosphere. Fishing is popular, for trout and smallmouth bass mostly but also for steelhead. The natural atmosphere is a drawing point, too: Lewiston's low elevation makes it one of the warmest places in Idaho, which as a practical matter can result in a long camping season for places like Hells Gate. A dump station is available free of charge for campers.

2 Pink House Recreation Site

Location: West of Orofino
Sites: 15
Facilities: Drinking water, flush toilets, electric hookups, barrier-free access, lake access, pets allowed
Fee per night: $$ tents, $$$ RVs
Elevation: 900 feet
Road conditions: Paved to and inside the campground
Management: Bureau of Land Management, Cottonwood Field Office, (208) 962–3245
Reservations: Generally no, but for availability call (208) 962–3245.
Activities: Boating, fishing, picnicking
Season: All year
Finding the campground: From Orofino drive 3 miles west on US 12.
The campground: The campground setting as such isn't any big deal; the site is in an open, almost desertlike, plot of land with little shade. None of that probably matters much to the campers here, because this is very much a riverside site; a boat launch is located here and many of the campers have steelhead fishing ambitions. The Clearwater River close by is one of the premier steelhead fishing locations anywhere. Group facilities are available as well. Pink House does have a campground host. By the way, no one seems to know exactly why it's called Pink House.

3 Dworshak State Park

Location: Northwest of Orofino
Sites: 102
Facilities: Drinking water, flush toilets, showers, dump station, fire rings, electric and water hookups, barrier-free access, playground
Fee per night: $$
Elevation: 1,100 feet
Road conditions: Widely variable; the main routes are two lanes and paved, and most of the other roads are good gravel roads. Note, however, that the last 2 miles of the main camp road are paved but on a very steep 10 percent grade, so check your brakes before driving it, especially if you're hauling an RV.
Management: Idaho Department of Parks and Recreation, (208) 443–6710
Reservations: Available via Web site www.idahoparks.org
Activities: Boating, fishing, hiking, picnicking, swimming
Season: April 15–October 31

Finding the campground: From Orofino drive 3 miles west on Idaho Highway 7, then northwest on Clearwater County Road P-1 to Cavendish. Then turn right (east) on Freeman Creek Road and go 12 miles to the park.

The campground: The main camping area here is the 102-site Freeman Creek Campground, located on Dworshak Reservoir and next to a boat ramp. Fishing is popular here and there is even a fish-cleaning station at the campground. There are three main loops of campsites and three others dedicated to groups. About half of the sites here have water and electric hookups. The park also has an RV dump station. Besides all this there's Camp Three Meadows, a forested area featuring nine cabins and room for a bunch of RVs, specially designated for large groups (ranging from church groups to business retreats to large family reunions). It is located about 3.5 miles down a rugged dirt road from the Freeman site.

4 Canyon Creek

Location: North of Orofino
Sites: 17, mixed RV and tent-suitable
Facilities: Drinking water, vault toilets, fire rings, boat ramp, pets allowed
Fee per night: None
Elevation: 1,700 feet
Road conditions: Generally good mixed paved and gravel road, but sometimes narrow and winding
Management: Army Corps of Engineers; visitor center, (208) 476–1255
Reservations: No
Activities: Boating, fishing, picnicking
Season: Spring through fall, no specifically designated season
Finding the campground: From Orofino drive 11 miles north on the Orofino–Elk River Road along the Wells Bench and Eureka Ridge Road.
The campground: A fine lakeside campground, with a mix of developed and primitive sites, suitable for both RVs and tents. Pets are allowed but must be leashed.

5 Dent Acres

Location: North of Orofino
Sites: 50
Facilities: Drinking water, flush toilets, showers, dump station, fire rings, electric and water hookups, pull-through sites, playground
Fee per night: $$$
Elevation: 1,700 feet
Road conditions: Good paved and gravel to the campground; sometimes steep, narrow and winding, though, so drive carefully.
Management: Army Corps of Engineers; visitor center, (208) 476–1255
Reservations: Call (877) 444–6777 or visit Web site www.reserve america.com.
Activities: Boating, fishing, hiking, picnicking, swimming
Season: Spring through fall

Dworshak Dam backs up a large reservoir, which provides camping space for hundreds of campers at a time.

Finding the campground: From Orofino drive 20 miles north along the east side of Dworshak Reservoir, on the Orofino–Elk River Road; turn at the campground sign.

The campground: The main campground at the reservoir has a good boat launch and general facilities. A less-developed group site is located 3 miles away. As with many Army Corps sites, there is no specific season of use, but the campground does close when winter weather begins to impede access, and then it reopens in the spring.

6 Grandad Creek

Location: North of Orofino
Sites: 6
Facilities: Fire rings, vault toilets
Fee per night: None
Elevation: 1,800 feet
Road conditions: Gravel mountain roads, sometimes narrow and twisting,

and sometimes challenging for larger vehicles. Bring your RV.
Management: Army Corps of Engineers; visitor center, (208) 476–1255
Reservations: No
Activities: Boating, fishing, picnicking
Season: Spring to fall, varying according to weather and road conditions
Finding the campground: From Orofino drive northeast on Idaho Highway 11 to Headquarters, the old timber town, and then 28 miles farther north on Silver Creek Road; or, from Headquarters take Beaver Creek Road and the Grandad turnoff in 17 miles. Either way, check your mileage and take note of landmarks; as the Army Corps notes, "There are many miles of gravel road and no signs."
The campground: These are primitive sites with no drinking water, but the remote location (which can discourage some drivers) keeps the crowds down. The site is shady and forested, with mountains all around. A one-lane boat launch allows for easy boating and fishing in the Dworshak Reservoir. The nearest phone is an hour or more away (don't expect much action on your cell phone up here), but some CB radio channels are monitored.

7 Aquarius

Location: North of Pierce
Sites: 7
Facilities: Drinking water, vault toilets, fire rings, pets allowed
Fee per night: $
Elevation: 1,700 feet
Road conditions: Paved to the campground
Management: Forest Service, North Fork Ranger Station, (208) 476–4541
Reservations: No
Activities: Fishing, picnicking
Season: May 31–September 8
Finding the campground: From Orofino drive northeast on ID 11 to Headquarters and then 25 miles north on Forest Road 247.
The campground: Aquarius is shady and forested and right next to the North Fork of the Clearwater River, just a few miles east of the point where it widens into the Dworshak Reservoir. When driving from Pierce, this is the first of several campgrounds you'll see along the North Fork of the Clearwater River. Kelly Forks, Noe Creek, and Washington Creek are still more miles to the northeast. (Aquarius is the only one in this area you can reach without leaving paved road.) Fishing is prized here, and hiking trails are scattered all around the campground. Several new sites have recently been added.

8 Hidden Creek

Location: Northeast of Pierce
Sites: 13
Facilities: Drinking water, vault toilets, fire rings, pets allowed
Fee per night: $
Elevation: 1,400 feet

Road conditions: From Pierce, paved to French Mountain (about halfway, a few miles east of Aquarius campground), then rugged and sometimes water-worn lane-and-a-half-wide gravel road
Management: Forest Service, North Fork Ranger Station, (208) 476–4541
Reservations: No
Activities: Fishing, hiking, picnicking
Season: May 31–October 31
Finding the campground: From Pierce drive 1 mile south on ID 11 and then 55 miles northeast on Forest Road 250.
The campground: One of the best remote places to enjoy the North Fork of the Clearwater River, and the fishing and hiking that come with it—far beyond the relatively crowded reservoir area. Deep into the Clearwater forests, this is a relatively primitive but attractive camping location.

9 Kelly Forks

Location: Northeast of Pierce
Sites: 14
Facilities: Drinking water, vault toilets, fire rings, pets allowed
Fee per night: $
Elevation: 1,350 feet
Road conditions: From Pierce, paved to French Mountain (about halfway), then rugged and sometimes waterworn lane-and-a-half-wide gravel road
Management: Forest Service, North Fork Ranger Station, (208) 476–4541
Reservations: No
Activities: Fishing, hiking, picnicking
Season: May 31–October 31
Finding the campground: From Pierce drive 1 mile south on ID 11 and then 47 miles northeast on FR 250.
The campground: This is the farthest east of the North Fork campgrounds, the most remote, the most work to get to—and often the one with the greatest solitude. The riverside location is priceless, and the fishing and hiking are both excellent—but, yeah, that's true of all the North Fork campgrounds. Even in that class, though, Kelly Creek is considered something special. The creek here (of the same name) has been listed nationally as a Blue Ribbon trout stream—one of the very best in Idaho. For the serious angler, the extra few miles of dusty and washboarded gravel roads are worth the effort.

10 Noe Creek

Location: Northeast of Pierce
Sites: 6
Facilities: Drinking water, vault toilets, fire rings, pets allowed
Fee per night: $
Elevation: 1,400 feet
Road conditions: From Pierce, paved to French Mountain (about halfway), then rugged and sometimes waterworn (and dusty, when not wet) lane-and-a-half-wide gravel road
Management: Forest Service, North Fork Ranger Station, (208) 476–4541

Reservations: No
Activities: Fishing, hiking, picnicking
Season: May 31–October 31
Finding the campground: From Pierce drive 1 mile south on ID 11 and then 40 miles northeast on FR 250.
The campground: In the shade of Pot Mountain to the north, this is yet another fine North Fork campground, an excellent launch point for fishing and hiking.

---

11 Washington Creek

Location: Northeast of Pierce
Sites: 23
Facilities: Drinking water, vault toilets, pets allowed
Fee per night: $
Elevation: 1,400 feet
Road conditions: From Pierce, paved to French Mountain (about halfway), then rugged and sometimes waterworn land-and-a-half-wide gravel road
Management: Forest Service, North Fork Ranger Station, (208) 476–4541
Reservations: No
Activities: Fishing, hiking, picnicking
Season: May 31–September 8
Finding the campground: From Pierce drive 1 mile south on ID 11, then 39 miles northeast on FR 250, and then 6 miles northeast on Forest Road 247.
The campground: A middle choice among the string of North Fork campgrounds, about midway between Aquarius and Noe Creek—the first one you hit after leaving pavement. Like the others, this is a good staging ground for fishing.

Area 9: Wilderness

If you're determined to escape the pull of civilization as thoroughly as you can, you can do no better anywhere in the United States—excepting only parts of Alaska—than in Idaho's wilderness. Idaho has five wilderness areas, but about seven-eighths of their total land area is in north-central Idaho, in the Selway-Bitterroot Wilderness Area to the north and the Frank Church–River of No Return Wilderness Area immediately to the south. They are administered mainly by U.S. Forest Service offices. A third smaller wilderness area, the Gospel Hump, sits just to the west of the Frank Church.

These are special areas, where vast spaces contain no sign of human habitation, places where people can come and visit and look but not stay—and not leave behind any trace they were there. Excepting some remote airplane landing strips, motor vehicles of all sorts are banned from the wilderness areas.

Since this guide includes campgrounds that are accessible by car, that means the campgrounds listed here are not actually inside the wilderness areas, though they do come close to them, and they certainly are plenty remote. Several of them offer a truly unique opportunity: to drive along a narrow strip of land, called the Magruder Corridor, which is all that separates two large wilderness areas (the Selway-Bitterroot to the north and the Frank Church–River of No Return to the south). The Magruder Corridor is not for the faint of heart: Portions of this narrow gravel road are very steep and heavily rock-strewn. But it is a trip to remember for a lifetime.

Moose and deer contemplate a salt block—currently under control of the moose—in the Frank Church–River of No Return Wilderness Area, near Big Creek. (Photo by Linda Watkins)

Remember that you're leaving pavement far behind in traveling to most of these places. Do check ahead for road and other conditions, and prepare carefully. But don't let that discourage you. These campgrounds come as close as you might ever get to the real, untrammeled, wild Idaho.

For more information:

Nez Perce National Forest
Frank Church–River of No Return Wilderness Area
Selway-Bitterroot Wilderness Area
Route 2, Box 475
Grangeville, ID 83530
(208) 983–1950
www.fs.fed.us/r1/nezperce

---

1 Indian Creek

Location: Near the Montana border
Sites: 12
Facilities: Vault toilets, fire rings, pets allowed
Fee per night: $
Elevation: 3,000 feet
Road conditions: Paved from Darby to the Idaho line at Nez Perce Pass, then narrow gravel and often steep—its exact condition is widely variable according to weather. High-clearance vehicles are recommended; RVs may be OK, but check with the ranger station first.
Management: Forest Service, Elk City/Red River Ranger District, (208) 842–2255
Reservations: No
Activities: Fishing, hiking, picnicking
Season: June 15–October 30
Finding the campground: This Magruder Corridor campground is best reached from Darby, Montana. From that city, drive 4 miles south on U.S. Highway 93, then 14 miles southwest on Ravalli County Road 473, then 37 miles west on Forest Road 468 (in Idaho), and then 5 miles north on Forest Road 223 (along the Selway River).
The campground: In 1978 a college student named Pete Fromm spent the winter at Indian Creek campground, watching over the local Forest Service facilities. He described that winter, unforgettably, in the book *Indian Creek Chronicles: A Winter in the Bitterroot Wilderness* (St. Martin's Press, 1993). Today's visitor will arrive in the summer, not the winter, but otherwise may find the area similar to Fromm's description. The camp is located at the confluence of Indian Creek and the Selway River; a fish hatchery was built here in 1964 (this was what Fromm was mainly sent to oversee). Indian Creek is located in the deep folds of valleys in the Sawtooth Range. This is a very primitive jumping-off spot for hunters and fishermen, with almost no services available. Don't expect drinking water here (other than what you might try from the creek, with a proper filter). This is almost as remote as it gets.

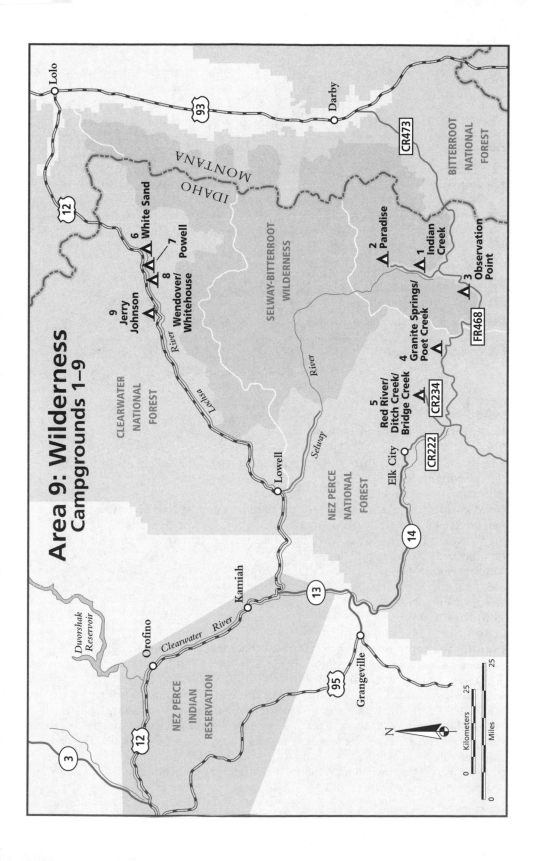

Area 9: Wilderness
Campgrounds 1–9

Area 9

		Town	Sites	Max. RV length	Electric	Picnic	Fire rings	Toilets	Showers	Water	Dump station	Disability access	Recreation	Can reserve	Fees ($)	Season	Stay limit (days)
1	Indian Creek	Darby, MT	12	22		•	•	V					FH		$	June–Oct.	14
2	Paradise	Darby, MT	11	16			•	V					FH		$	June–Oct.	14
3	Observation Point	Darby, MT.	U				•	V					FH			June–Oct.	14
4	Granite Springs/ Poet Creek	Elk City	8			•	•	V		•			FH		$	June–Oct.	14
5	Red River/ Ditch Creek/ Bridge Creek	Elk City	48	16		•	•	V					F			June–Oct.	14
6	White Sand	Lolo, MT	7	32		•	•	V		•		•	FS		$$	June–Sept.	14
7	Powell	Lolo, MT	35	40	•	•	•	V		•		•	F	•	$$	June–Sept.	14
8	Wendover/ Whitehouse	Lolo, MT	40	32		•	•	V		•		•	F		$	June–Sept.	14
9	Jerry Johnson	Lolo, MT	15	22		•	•	V		•			FH		$$	June–Sept.	14

2 Paradise

Location: Near the Montana border
Sites: 11
Facilities: Vault toilets, fire rings, picnic tables, pets allowed
Fee per night: $
Elevation: 3,060 feet
Road conditions: Paved from Darby to the Idaho line at Nez Perce Pass, then narrow gravel and often steep—its exact condition is widely variable according to weather. High-clearance vehicles are recommended; RVs may be OK, but check with the ranger station first.
Management: Forest Service, Elk City/Red River Ranger District, (208) 842–2255
Reservations: No
Activities: Fishing, hiking
Season: June 15–October 30
Finding the campground: From Darby, Montana, drive 4 miles south on US 93, then 14 miles southwest on Ravalli CR 473, then 37 miles west on FR 468, and then 11 miles north on FR 223.
The campground: Paradise is literally at the end of the road (a spur of the Magruder Corridor), bumping up against—and almost surrounded by—the Selway-Bitterroot Wilderness. This is obviously a great launch site for hiking explorations into that wilderness, and several hiking trails are available. Horse stock facilities are available, too, and so are meat racks—an indication of how popular (very) this site is with hunters. (During the end of camping season this campground is sometimes filled with hunters.) If you can get there early

enough (after May 15 but before the end of July), you may be able to get a permit to float one of the most remote stretches of river in Idaho, the 47 miles of the Selway River from Paradise to Selway Falls. A Forest Service administrative office is also located nearby. No drinking water is available.

3 Observation Point

Location: Near the Montana border
Sites: Variable; none designated
Facilities: Vault toilets, fire rings, pets allowed
Fee per night: None
Elevation: 7,620 feet
Road conditions: Paved from Darby to the Idaho line at Nez Perce Pass, then narrow gravel and often steep—its exact condition is widely variable according to weather. High-clearance vehicles are recommended; RVs may be OK, but check with the ranger station first.
Management: Forest Service, Elk City/Red River Ranger District, (208) 842–2255
Reservations: No
Activities: Fishing, hiking
Season: June 15–October 30
Finding the campground: From Darby, Montana, drive 4 miles south on US 93, then 14 miles southwest on Ravalli CR 473, and then 44 miles west on FR 468.
The campground: Observation Point, about midway on the Magruder Corridor between Elk City, Idaho, and Darby, Montana, is one of the highest-elevation campgrounds in Idaho, and—as its name suggests—a place of vast views, taking in most of the southern Bitterroot Mountains.

4 Granite Springs/Poet Creek

Location: East of Elk City
Sites: 8 (4 at each campground)
Facilities: Drinking water (Granite Springs only), vault toilets, fire rings, picnic tables, pets allowed
Fee per night: $
Elevation: 3,000 feet
Road conditions: This gravel and dirt road is narrow and steep, especially the westernmost 8 miles, which climb steeply into the mountains, and on the mountainside winding downhill just west of Poet Creek, and then again just east of that campground. High-clearance vehicles are recommended; RVs may be OK, but check with the ranger station first.
Management: Forest Service, Elk City/Red River Ranger District, (208) 842–2255
Reservations: No
Activities: Fishing, hiking, picnicking
Season: June 15–October 30
Finding the campgrounds: From Elk City take Idaho Highway 14 about 5

miles south. Turn on Idaho County Road 222 and drive generally east (the road twists and turns) for about 8 miles before reaching FR 468 (the Magruder Corridor); turn east. The campgrounds are about 20 miles down the road.

The campgrounds: These campgrounds lie on the Magruder Corridor, with Granite Springs straddling it and Poet Creek (the more remote of the two) just north of the road. Both are well set up for horseback riding, with stock facilities in the area. Expect generally primitive conditions, however, and be prepared to pack in your own water (along with most everything else you need).

5 Red River/Ditch Creek/Bridge Creek

Location: East of Elk City
Sites: 48
Facilities: Fire rings, vault toilets
Fee per night: None (though Red River has charged in the past, and fees may be imposed again in coming years)
Elevation: 4,100 feet
Road conditions: Paved to the Red River Forest Road 234 cutoff, then narrow gravel to the campgrounds; the gravel roads are well maintained by Idaho County.
Management: Forest Service, Elk City/Red River Ranger District, (208) 842–2255
Reservations: No
Activities: Fishing, picnicking
Season: June 1–October 31
Finding the campgrounds: From Elk City drive 3 miles southwest on ID 14, then go 14 miles southeast on Idaho CR 222, and then turn left onto Idaho County Road 234 and drive 6 miles northeast.
The campgrounds: These popular campgrounds have lost some of their former looks, since disease and other problems led the Forest Service to chop down a lot of trees in this area that had become diseased and threatened to topple over onto a camper. So don't expect much shade. On other hand, the recreational assets are intact: fishing on several streams and hunting for deer, elk, and bear. These campgrounds sometimes fill up when hunting season arrives in the fall. These are good sites for tents or small RVs, but (though there's no formal ban or restriction) those over about 30 feet may have difficulty getting into and around the campgrounds. The sites have no drinking water, so bring plenty of your own.

6 White Sand

Location: Southwest of Lolo, Montana
Sites: 7
Facilities: Drinking water, vault toilets, fire rings, barrier-free access, pets allowed
Fee per night: $$
Elevation: 6,400 feet

Road conditions: Paved except the last mile; conditions on the 1-mile gravel road vary according to weather, but the drive is easy.
Management: Forest Service, Moose Creek (Kooskia) Ranger District, (208) 926–4250
Reservations: No
Activities: Fishing, picnicking, swimming
Season: June 1–September 30
Finding the campground: From Lolo, Montana, drive 43 miles west on U.S. Highway 12 and then 1 mile south on Elk Summit Road.
The campground: Most of the campgrounds on the Lochsa River are located directly on US 12; White Sand is one of the few located off the road, about a mile away. Just a couple of miles east of Powell, where supplies can be purchased, this is a good creekside—rather than riverside—camping site.

7 Powell

Location: Southwest of Lolo, Montana
Sites: 35
Facilities: Drinking water, vault toilets, electric and water hookups, fire rings, pull-through sites, barrier-free access, pets allowed
Fee per night: $$ (depending on hookups)
Elevation: 2,800 feet
Road conditions: Paved to the campground
Management: Forest Service, Moose Creek (Kooskia) Ranger District, (208) 926–4250
Reservations: Call (877) 444–6777 or visit Web site www.reserveamerica.com.
Activities: Fishing, picnicking
Season: June 1–September 30
Finding the campground: From Lolo, Montana, drive 44 miles southwest on US 12.
The campground: This campground on the Lochsa River is the only public campground on the US 12 corridor that has hookups, including electric power— rare for a Forest Service campground almost anywhere.

8 Wendover/Whitehouse

Location: Southwest of Lolo, Montana
Sites: 40 (27 at Wendover, 13 at Whitehouse)
Facilities: Drinking water, vault toilets, fire rings, barrier-free access, pets allowed
Fee per night: $
Elevation: 4,400 feet
Road conditions: Paved to the campground
Management: Forest Service, Moose Creek (Kooskia) Ranger District, (208) 926–4250
Reservations: No
Activities: Fishing, picnicking

Season: June 1–September 30
Finding the campgrounds: From Lolo, Montana, drive 48 miles southwest on US 12.
The campgrounds: These two adjacent and very similar campgrounds on the Lochsa River are tucked deep in the forested draws of high mountains—you get direct sunlight in much of this area only during the middle of the day. The river is in one of its prettiest passages here, wide but still dramatically rumbling. More important to many of the campers here is the easy hiking access to the north side of the Selway-Bitterroot Wilderness Area, whose boundary is just a few miles south. Whitehouse Campground is named not for a building but for Army Private Joseph Whitehouse. A member of the Lewis and Clark expedition, he was one of five participants to write a journal about it.

9 Jerry Johnson

Location: Southwest of Lolo, Montana
Sites: 15
Facilities: Drinking water, vault toilets, fire rings, pets allowed
Fee per night: $$
Elevation: 5,600 feet
Road conditions: Paved nearly to the campground, though there are some steep spots to slow down an RV
Management: Forest Service, Moose Creek (Kooskia) Ranger District, (208) 926–4250
Reservations: No
Activities: Fishing, hiking, picnicking
Season: June 1–September 15
Finding the campground: From Lolo, Montana, drive 56 miles southwest on US 12.
The campground: One of the many campgrounds on the Lochsa River and one of the few on its north shore, this campground is located close to the Powell campground, so services and supplies are readily available. The Jerry Johnson campground is mostly shaded and gives campers some room to spread out. Jerry Johnson was a fur trapper who lived in a cabin near the present campground site. It was a frequent stopping point for hunting parties in the area.

Area 10: Camas Prairie

Not all of this area is prairie. To the west lies the deep gorge of the Snake River where it forms borders with Oregon and Washington and constitutes the northern part of Hells Canyon. To the east lie the deep valleys cut by the Clearwater River and its tributaries, which split some of the landforms into distinctive pieces. (By the way, one of the largest of these streams, Lawyer Creek, is so named not because it is twisted and crooked—as some cynics might suggest—but instead after a respected leader of the Nez Perce Tribe.)

The center of this region, however, is a large plains area, centered on the city of Grangeville, which mostly is a service center for grain farmers but also is a recreation jumping-off point. Around the sides of this plain, however, are some spectacular vistas and glorious campgrounds. Deer and elk and a wide variety of birds often are seen here. This little-known (outside of Idaho) area also is home to a surprising number of attractions, from the St. Gertrude's Museum outside Cottonwood to the state park at Winchester.

For more information:

Grangeville Chamber of Commerce
Highway 95 and Pine Street
Grangeville, ID 83530
(208) 983–0460

Nez Perce National Forest
Frank Church–River of No Return Wilderness Area
Selway-Bitterroot Wilderness Area
Route 2, Box 475
Grangeville, ID 83530
(208) 983–1950
www.fs.fed.us/r1/nezperce

1 Pine Bar

Location: South of Cottonwood
Sites: 6
Facilities: Drinking water, vault toilets, fire rings, river access, pets allowed
Fee per night: $$
Elevation: 2,900 feet
Road conditions: Gravel road, generally wide and well maintained
Management: Bureau of Land Management, Cottonwood Field Office, (208) 962–3245
Reservations: Call (208) 962–3245.
Activities: Boating, fishing, hiking, picnicking, swimming
Season: All year
Finding the campground: From Cottonwood drive 11 miles south on Graves Creek Road.

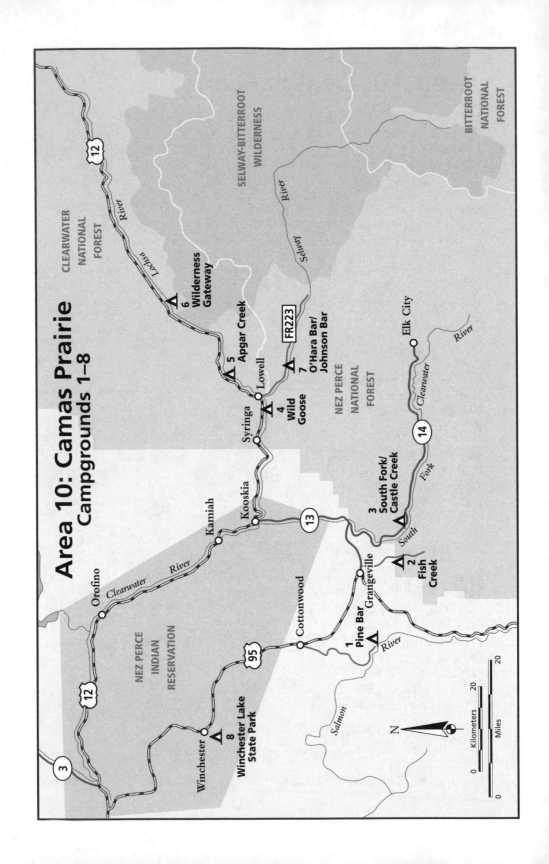

Area 10

	Town	Sites	Max. RV length	Electric	Picnic	Fire rings	Toilets	Showers	Water	Dump station	Disability access	Recreation	Can reserve	Fees ($)	Season	Stay limit (days)
1 Pine Bar	Cottonwood	7			•	•	V		•			BFHS	•	$$	Year-round	14
2 Fish Creek	Grangeville	8	16		•	•	V					F		$	June–Sept.	14
3 South Fork/ Castle Creek	Grangeville	18	22		•	•	V		•	•		FS	•	$	June–Oct.	14
4 Wild Goose	Kooskia	6	22		•	•	V		•		•	F		$$	May–Oct.	14
5 Apgar Creek	Kooskia	7	22		•	•	V		•		•	F	•	$	May–Oct.	14
6 Wilderness Gateway	Kooskia	91	40		•	•	F,V		•	•	•	FHS	•	$$	May–Oct.	14
7 O'Hara Bar/ Johnson Bar	Kooskia	41	20		•	•	V		•			BFS	•	$$	May–Oct.	14
8 Winchester Lake	Winchester	73	60	•	•	•	F,V		•	•	•	BFH	•	$$–$$$	Year-round	

The campground: This is a desert canyon location, right on the Lower Salmon River with steep-sloped mountains all around. Fishing and hiking are popular here, and several beaches accommodate swimmers and sun worshippers, but the focus is on boating. This is a favorite location for putting in to the Lower Salmon River. A wide range of craft, including rafts, kayaks, and jet boats, make their way into the water here.

2 Fish Creek

Location: South of Grangeville
Sites: 8
Facilities: Drinking water, fire pits, vault toilets
Fee per night: $ (this may change)
Elevation: 3,800 feet
Road conditions: Paved to the campground
Management: Forest Service, Clearwater Ranger District, (208) 983–1963
Reservations: No (except for a pavilion)
Activities: Fishing, picnicking
Season: June–September
Finding the campground: From downtown Grangeville, look on the main street for the sign to Forest Road 221, and follow it about 7 miles south.
The campground: Located in a pretty mountain meadow, the camping sites here are a mix of tree covered and open air. Hiking trails can be found nearby, and in the winter this campground turns into a popular trailhead for cross-country skiers. A substantial dispersed camping area (informally called the Girl Scout camp, after a development that existed there years ago) is also close by.

3 | South Fork/Castle Creek

Location: East of Grangeville
Sites: 16 (8 at each campground)
Facilities: Drinking water, dump station, vault toilets, fire rings
Fee per night: $
Elevation: 3,300 feet
Road conditions: Paved to the campground
Management: Forest Service, Elk City/Red River Ranger District, (208) 842–2255
Reservations: Call (877) 444–6777 or visit Web site www.reserveamerica.com.
Activities: Fishing, picnicking, swimming
Season: June 1–October 1
Finding the campgrounds: From Grangeville, drive 9 miles south on Idaho Highway 13 and then 6.5 miles east on Idaho Highway 14.
The campgrounds: ID 14, which runs from the Grangeville-Kooskia Idaho Highway 13 to the town of Elk City, has a string of campgrounds in a woodsy national forest valley, all along the South Fork of the Clearwater River, with mountains towering on almost all sides. South Fork and Castle Creek are the first two that visitors coming from Grangeville or Kooskia will encounter, and they are two of the most attractive, buried in woods close by the highway but (for the most part) effectively shielded from traffic and the external world.

⁞ | Wild Goose

Location: East of Kooskia, between Syringa and Lowell
Sites: 6
Facilities: Drinking water, vault toilets, fire rings, barrier-free access, pets allowed
Fee per night: $$
Elevation: 1,250 feet
Road conditions: Paved to the campground
Management: Forest Service, Moose Creek (Kooskia) Ranger District, (208) 926–4250
Reservations: No
Activities: Fishing, picnicking
Season: May 25–October 10
Finding the campground: From Kooskia drive 20 miles east on US 12, just past the small community of Syringa.
The campground: Normal Forest Service amenities are available in this pretty valley location on the Middle Fork of the Clearwater River. Anglers pile in here during key points in the fishing season.

5 | Apgar Creek

Location: East of Kooskia and northeast of Lowell
Sites: 7

The South Fork and Castle Creek Campgrounds lie in the valley folds along the South Fork of the Clearwater River.

Facilities: Drinking water, vault toilets, fire rings, barrier-free access, pets allowed
Fee per night: $
Elevation: 1,250 feet
Road conditions: Paved; road is winding but relatively flat and closely tracks the river.
Management: Forest Service, Moose Creek (Kooskia) Ranger District, (208) 926-4250
Reservations: Call (877) 444-6777 or visit Web site www.reserveamerica.com.
Activities: Fishing, picnicking
Season: May 25-October 10
Finding the campground: From Kooskia drive 29 miles east (a couple of miles past Lowell) on US 12.
The campground: Apgar Creek is the most downstream of the Lochsa River campgrounds, which stretch from Lowell to the Montana line. Apgar is a small site but has a pleasing river location and good amenities, including drinking water.

6 Wilderness Gateway

Location: East of Kooskia and northeast of Lowell
Sites: 91 (23 reservable)
Facilities: Drinking water, flush and vault toilets, fire rings, barrier-free access, dump station, playground, pull-through sites, pets allowed
Fee per night: $$
Elevation: 1,400 feet
Road conditions: Paved to the campground
Management: Forest Service, Moose Creek (Kooskia) Ranger District, (208) 926–4250
Reservations: Call (877) 444–6777 or visit Web site www.reserveamerica.com.
Activities: Fishing, hiking, picnicking, swimming
Season: May 25–October 10
Finding the campgrounds: From Kooskia drive 49 miles east-northeast on US 12.
The campground: This is the largest campground on the Lochsa River and the only one on the US 12 corridor located across the river from the highway. (A good, sturdy bridge provides access). The large campground has four loops. Of these, the D loop (farthest back from the river) is geared toward people who want to bring horses for a ride. True to its name, Wilderness Gateway is close by the northern border of the Selway-Bitterroot Wilderness Area.

7 O'Hara Bar/Johnson Bar

Location: East of Kooskia and southeast of Lowell
Sites: 41 (34 in O'Hara, 7 in Johnson Bar)
Facilities: Drinking water (O'Hara only), fire rings, vault toilets
Fee per night: $
Elevation: 1,250 feet
Road conditions: Paved almost to the entrance to the campgrounds
Management: Forest Service, Moose Creek (Kooskia) Ranger District, (208) 926–4250
Reservations: Call (877) 444–6777 or visit Web site www.reserveamerica.com.
Activities: Boating, fishing, picnicking, swimming
Season: May 24–October 1
Finding the campgrounds: From Kooskia drive 24 miles east on US 12, then 7 miles southeast on Forest Road 223, and then 1 mile south on Forest Road 651.
The campgrounds: O'Hara is the only public campground among the many in the Selway River Corridor with on-site water availability, and by far the largest. Located on O'Hara Creek (which converges with the Selway River here) in a forested area, this campground was recently renovated, and a 1-mile interpretative tour explains how that was done. O'Hara Bar is located close to the border of the Selway-Bitterroot Wilderness Area. Johnson Bar, which is located on the other side of O'Hara Creek, is similar except for water availability and smaller size.

8 Winchester Lake State Park

Location: West of Winchester
Sites: 73 summer, 23 winter
Facilities: Drinking water, electric and water hookups, dump station, flush and vault toilets, showers, fire rings, pets allowed
Fee per night: $–$$$
Elevation: 2,600 feet
Road conditions: Paved up to the campground and partly within it; good gravel roads throughout
Management: Idaho Department of Parks and Recreation, Winchester Lake State Park, (208) 924–7563
Reservations: Available via Web site www.idahoparks.org
Activities: Boating, fishing, hiking, picnicking
Season: All year, technically; as a practical matter, about May 1 through October 31 (depending on weather)
Finding the campground: From Winchester drive 1 mile west from the U.S. Highway 95 business loop; follow the signs to the campground area on the west side of the lake.
The campground: The park generally extends through the forested hills around Winchester Lake, which at 103 acres is one of the largest in north-central Idaho. The park was created in 1969 out of land purchased by the state from a timber company. The lake is regularly stocked with rainbow trout, and fishing is popular as a result. (Don't try running a motor on your boat, however; they're prohibited on this smallish lake.) Several camping loops are located on the west side of the lake. A boat launch is nearby, and nature trails run all the way around the lake. Of the 73 camping sites available in the summer, 50 have electric and water hookups; none of the 23 winter units are so equipped. An unusual provision of Winchester is "yurt camping." The park maintains a collection of yurts, domelike structures (similar in design to those in China and Mongolia) with doors and windows and furniture inside. The yurts can be rented year-round.

Area 11: Lower Salmon

Travelers through Idaho on U.S. Highway 95 know this area as the region where they can follow the Salmon River in western Idaho on paved road. That translates to an area just east of Riggins north, along a twisting river path, up to the town and mountain pass of White Bird, the site of a famous 1877 battle in which the Nez Perce Indians defeated the U.S. Army.

Off US 95, there is roadless wilderness in this area—the Gospel Hump—but also a great deal of national forest land, which determined campers can explore in their vehicles (preferably of the four-wheel-drive variety). The landscape is mountainous, forested in many places, but similar to desert in others. This is a very popular river rafting area, but boaters who are less than very experienced should hire a boating guide to take them down the river.

For more information:

Salmon River Chamber of Commerce
P.O. Box 289
Riggins, ID 83549
(208) 464–2212
www.rigginsidaho.com

Nez Perce National Forest
Frank Church–River of No Return Wilderness Area
Selway-Bitterroot Wilderness Area
Route 2, Box 475
Grangeville, ID 83530
(208) 983–1950
www.fs.fed.us/r1/nezperce

1 Seven Devils/Windy Saddle

Location: Southwest of Riggins
Sites: 15 (10 at Seven Devils, 5 at Windy Saddle)
Facilities: Vault toilets, fire rings, pets allowed
Fee per night: $
Elevation: 1,800 feet
Road conditions: After US 95, this is a rugged drive on one-lane gravel road strewn with water holes, washboards, and much dust. Not recommended for RVs.
Management: Forest Service, Slate Creek Ranger Station, (208) 839–2211
Reservations: No
Activities: Fishing, hiking, picnicking
Season: July–October (depending on weather)
Finding the campgrounds: From Riggins drive 4 miles south on US 95, then turn right and go 17 miles southwest on Forest Road 517 (trailers not recommended).

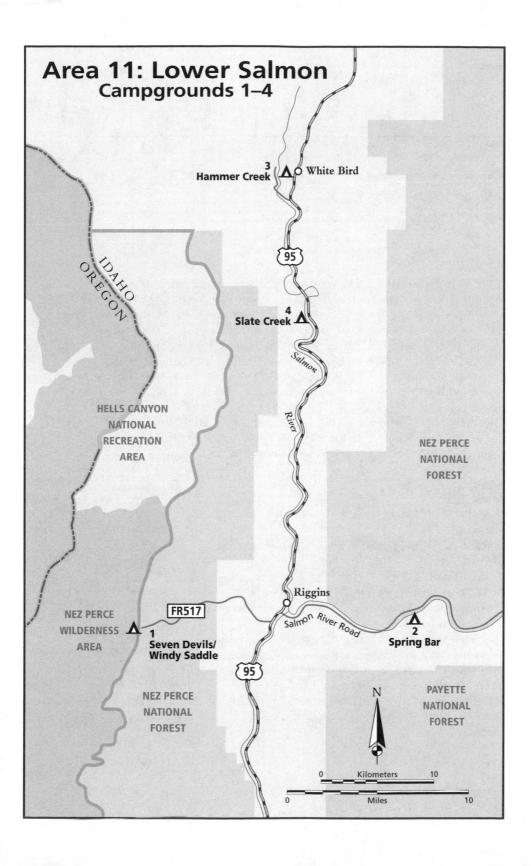

Area 11: Lower Salmon
Campgrounds 1–4

IDAHO
OREGON

3
Hammer Creek ▲△○ White Bird

95

4
Slate Creek ▲

Salmon

River

HELLS CANYON
NATIONAL
RECREATION
AREA

NEZ PERCE
NATIONAL
FOREST

Riggins

NEZ PERCE
WILDERNESS
AREA

FR517

▲ **1**
Seven Devils/
Windy Saddle

Salmon River Road

▲ **2**
Spring Bar

95

NEZ PERCE
NATIONAL
FOREST

N

PAYETTE
NATIONAL
FOREST

0   Kilometers   10

0   Miles   10

Area 11

	Town	Sites	Max. RV length	Electric	Picnic	Fire rings	Toilets	Showers	Water	Dump station	Disability access	Recreation	Can reserve	Fees ($)	Season	Stay limit (days)
1 Seven Devils/ Windy Saddle	Riggins	15			•	•	V					FH		$	July–Oct.	14
2 Spring Bar	Riggins	14	20		•	•	V		•			BFS		$	April–Oct.	14
3 Hammer Creek	White Bird	8	26		•	•	F		•	•		BFS		$$	Year-round	14
4 Slate Creek	White Bird	6	21		•	•	F		•	•		BFS		$$	Year-round	14

The campgrounds: Because of the challenges accessing this area, these campgrounds (which are less than a mile apart) are recommended for tenting or similar camping, rather than RVing. There are rewards for getting here, though, and it is popular with serious backcountry enthusiasts in Idaho. This is one of the campgrounds in the Hells Canyon Recreation Area, and from here—high up in the Seven Devils—you get a view that reaches well into three states (Idaho, Oregon, and Washington). These are rare sites that combine spectacular views with pleasant, forested locations. A long trail (the Snake River National Recreation Trail) along the high ridges of the Seven Devils runs through (both north and south) the campgrounds. Four camping sites are set up for horseback riders and stock. There's no water available locally, so bring your own. Both campgrounds have been expanded recently.

2 Spring Bar

Location: East of Riggins
Sites: 14
Facilities: Drinking water, vault toilets, fire rings
Fee per night: $
Elevation: 1,800 feet
Road conditions: Paved to the campground
Management: Forest Service, Slate Creek Ranger Station, (208) 839–2211
Reservations: No
Activities: Boating, fishing, picnicking, swimming
Season: April 1–October 31
Finding the campground: From Riggins drive 1 mile south on US 95 and then 10 miles east on Salmon River Road along the Salmon River.
The campground: Pleasant riverside campsites are available along the Salmon River Road east of Riggins. This is a good place to boat along the Salmon River.

Salmon River area near Riggins

3 Hammer Creek

Location: West of White Bird
Sites: 8
Facilities: Drinking water, flush toilets, fire rings, dump station, pull-through sites, river access, pets allowed
Fee per night: $$
Elevation: 2,250 feet
Road conditions: Paved nearly to the campground
Management: Bureau of Land Management, Cottonwood Field Office, (208) 962–3245
Reservations: Call (208) 962–3245.
Activities: Boating, fishing, picnicking, swimming
Season: All year (though usually not advisable after midfall)
Finding the campground: From White Bird drive 1.5 miles south on US 95, and then follow the signs 1.5 miles west.

The campground: Hammer Creek is a nice riverside site in the shadow of the White Bird Pass and close to the small city of White Bird, where supplies are available. River craft put-in launching is easily available here, along with beaches and swimming areas.

4 Slate Creek

Location: South of White Bird
Sites: 6
Facilities: Drinking water, flush toilets, fire rings, dump station, pull-through sites, river access, pets allowed
Fee per night: $$
Elevation: 2,250 feet
Road conditions: Paved to the campground
Management: Bureau of Land Management, Cottonwood Field Office, (208) 962–3245
Reservations: Call (208) 962-3245.
Activities: Boating, fishing, picnicking, swimming
Season: All year
Finding the campground: From White Bird drive 10 miles south on US 95, and then turn left at the campground exit.
The campground: Slate Creek is another Little Salmon River riverside site, somewhat exposed to the sun but directly next to the river. Boating and swimming are possible here, and limited hiking—with berry picking an option in season.

Southwest Idaho

Area 12: Seven Devils

Of all Idaho's place-name juxtapositions, the most striking must be the Seven Devils Mountains towering over Hells Canyon. The latter is the deepest gorge in Idaho and, say some who measure these things, the deepest in North America. The Seven Devils are not Idaho's highest peaks, but they are high enough; drive on the modestly maintained roads in the deepest backcountry here, and you'll more than likely run across snow even in midsummer. You may also find the remnants of a copper mining boom (one of the tiny communities back in the mountains here is called Cuprum) that went bust a century ago.

There are two ways down into Hells Canyon from these mountains. One is Idaho Highway 71 from the town of Cambridge, the preferred "gateway to Hells Canyon." The more adventurous route—for the truly daring and for those with the right kind of vehicle—is the Kleinschmidt Grade, a narrow, winding, torturous gravel road literally running down the side of Hells Canyon, scary enough to give shivers even to the locals. (About half of the way from Council to the grade, which is to say from Council to the tiny community of Bear, was paved in 2002.) Take your pick.

To the east of these spectacles are two broad plains, each striking in its own way. The Council and Indian Valley area marks one of the upper reaches of the Weiser River, and it remains one of Idaho's less-explored pretty places despite the presence of U.S. Highway 95, which runs through it. North of this area, the Meadows Valley is a small world unto itself, a bowl surrounded by high peaks all around and fed by a water system unusually generous in Idaho terms. Meadows Valley also features hot springs and other resort attractions.

There are public campgrounds (as well as some private ones) in each of the three parts of this region. Most of the public campgrounds in this area are in the Payette National Forest, and no reservations can be made for any of its campgrounds. Although some of these campgrounds are within the New Meadows Ranger District, that district doesn't manage campgrounds; the McCall Ranger District handles the task.

For more information:

Council Chamber of Commerce
P.O. Box 507
Council, ID 83612
(208) 253–4851

Payette National Forest
P.O. Box 1026
McCall, ID 83638
(208) 634–0700
www.mccall.net/pnf

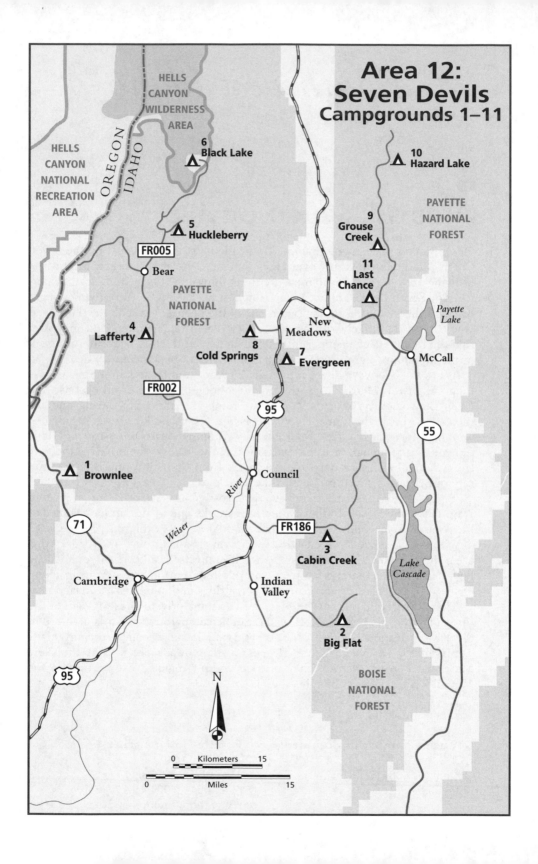

Area 12:
Seven Devils
Campgrounds 1–11

HELLS CANYON WILDERNESS AREA

OREGON IDAHO

HELLS CANYON NATIONAL RECREATION AREA

6 Black Lake ⛺

⛺ **10 Hazard Lake**

PAYETTE NATIONAL FOREST

⛺ **5 Huckleberry**

FR005

○ Bear

9 Grouse Creek ⛺

PAYETTE NATIONAL FOREST

11 Last Chance ⛺

4 Lafferty ⛺

⛺ **8 Cold Springs**

New Meadows

⛺ **7 Evergreen**

Payette Lake

○ McCall

FR002

95

55

⛺ **1 Brownlee**

○ Council

River

71

Weiser

FR186

⛺ **3 Cabin Creek**

Lake Cascade

Cambridge ○

○ Indian Valley

95

⛺ **2 Big Flat**

BOISE NATIONAL FOREST

N

0 — Kilometers — 15

0 — Miles — 15

Area 12

	Town	Sites	Max. RV length	Electric	Picnic	Fire rings	Toilets	Showers	Water	Dump station	Disability access	Recreation	Can reserve	Fees ($)	Season	Stay limit (days)
1 Brownlee	Cambridge	11	16		•	•	V		•			FH		$$	May–Oct.	14
2 Big Flat	Council	13	45		•	•	V					F		$	May–Oct.	14
3 Cabin Creek	Council	12	22		•	•	V		•			FH		$$	May–Oct.	14
4 Lafferty	Council	8	22		•	•	V		•			F		$	May–Oct.	14
5 Huckleberry	Council	8	16		•	•	V		•			FH		$	June–Oct.	14
6 Black Lake	Council	4			•	•	V		•		•	FHS		$	July–Sept.	14
7 Evergreen	Council	12	22		•	•	V		•			F		$	June–Sept.	14
8 Cold Springs	New Meadows	33	22		•	•	V		•			BFS		$$	May–Oct.	14
9 Grouse Creek	New Meadows	7	16		•	•	V		•			BFHS		$	July–Sept.	14
10 Hazard Lake	New Meadows	12	22		•	•	V		•			BFHS		$	July–Sept.	14
11 Last Chance	New Meadows	28	45		•	•	V		•		•	FH		$	June–Oct.	14

1 Brownlee

Location: Northwest of Cambridge
Sites: 11
Facilities: Drinking water, vault toilets, fire rings, pets allowed
Fee per night: $$
Elevation: 4,240 feet
Road conditions: Paved highway to the campground turnoff, then easy-to-drive one-lane gravel road the remaining mile-plus
Management: Forest Service, Weiser Ranger District, (208) 549-4200
Reservations: No
Activities: Fishing, hiking, picnicking
Season: May 15–October 31
Finding the campground: From Cambridge drive 16.6 miles northwest on ID 71 just past the point where the road starts to descend into Hells Canyon, and then turn right and drive 1 mile east on Forest Road 044.
The campground: Brownlee is a very thickly forested campground, about 10 miles above Hells Canyon—which isn't at all visible from here. Forest Service staffers say Brownlee gets less use than might be expected, given its proximity to Hells Canyon. One reason may be that the Idaho Power campgrounds down in the canyon offer more amenities (utility hookups, for instance); Brownlee is a typical, relatively primitive, Forest Service campground. And the woodsy setting doesn't match up with the austere feel of the canyon. But this campground still is one of the best in the region. The woods are thick and

gorgeous, the canopy ample without being darkening. The road in is one-lane gravel but an easy drive for most any vehicle. The fast, burbling Brownlee Creek runs through the campground, next to a number of pads. A Forest Service guard station is located less than a mile from the campground on the entrance road, should help be needed. The site pads are nicely worn down. Finally, the site is historic. Around 1900 the small mining community of Heath arose where the campground now is, and silver and copper were mined and smelted. What's left of Heath today isn't even a ghost town, but a few artifacts (including one wooden tool that was used in the mining-smelting process) still stand around the campground and are protected by the Forest Service.

2 Big Flat

Location: Southeast of Council
Sites: 13
Facilities: Drinking water (maybe), vault toilets, fire rings, pets allowed
Fee per night: $
Elevation: 4,080 feet
Road conditions: Progressively rougher, narrow, and twisting road as you head up into the mountains
Management: Forest Service, Council Ranger District, (208) 253–0100
Reservations: No
Activities: Fishing, picnicking
Season: May 30–October 30
Finding the campground: From Council drive 9 miles south on US 95 to Indian Valley, then continue south on the Indian Valley Road another mile toward the C. Ben Ross Reservoir, and then turn east on the Little Weiser River Road.
The campground: Located on the Little Weiser River, this is a very remote mountain campground, with modestly forested cover. Drinking water may or may not be available; you'd be wise to carry in your own.

3 Cabin Creek

Location: Southeast of Council
Sites: 12
Facilities: Drinking water, vault toilets, fire rings, pets allowed
Fee per night: $$
Elevation: 4,160 feet
Road conditions: Beyond US 95 the mountain Forest Road 186 is narrow (a lane and a half at most) and sometimes rugged.
Management: Forest Service, Council Ranger District, (208) 253–0100
Reservations: No
Activities: Fishing, hiking, picnicking
Season: May 25–October 31
Finding the campground: From Council drive on US 95 south 4 miles (to the bottom of Mesa Hill), and then go 10 miles east on FR 186 into the mountains.

The campground: A pleasant mountain site; unlike some others in this region, drinking water is available (accounting for the higher cost).

4 Lafferty

Location: Northwest of Council
Sites: 8
Facilities: Drinking water, vault toilets, fire rings, pull-through sites, pets allowed
Fee per night: $
Elevation: 4,300 feet
Road conditions: The forest road to (and beyond) Lafferty was paved in 2002, so the conditions are excellent.
Management: Forest Service, Council Ranger District, (208) 253-0100
Reservations: No
Activities: Fishing, picnicking
Season: May 25–October 31
Finding the campground: From Council drive 24 miles northwest on Forest Road 002 (the Hornet Creek Road).
The campground: This small woodsy campground has been reopened since its renovation in 2002.

5 Huckleberry

Location: Northwest of Council
Sites: 8
Facilities: Drinking water, vault toilets, fire rings, pets allowed
Fee per night: $
Elevation: 6,500 feet
Road conditions: Paved to Bear; after that, the forest roads are narrow gravel and dirt, OK for passenger vehicles by midsummer. Snow hangs around late in some of these elevations, so drive carefully.
Management: Forest Service, Council Ranger District, (208) 253-0100
Reservations: No
Activities: Fishing, hiking, picnicking
Season: June 1–October 31
Finding the campground: From Council drive 30 miles northwest on FR 002 (the Hornet Creek Road), then 5 miles northeast on Forest Road 105, and then 1 mile east on Forest Road 110.
The campground: Here's the place to stay if you want to get high up in the Seven Devils and well away from town (about 35 miles from Council). Ironically, Huckleberry does sit amid an old (turn of the last century) mining district, where copper was energetically extracted for about a decade. Only traces of all that remain now. The Seven Devils area is both high (you'll be well over 6,000 feet in most of it) and thinly maintained; the narrow mountain gravel roads are often muddy, owing to the late presence of snow (sometimes into June). Hiking and fishing are both good here.

6 Black Lake

Location: North of Council
Sites: 4
Facilities: Drinking water, vault toilets, fire rings, barrier-free access, pets allowed
Fee per night: $
Elevation: 4,600 feet
Road conditions: The forest roads are paved to Bear but become progressively more challenging after that and very rough by the time you get to the campground. High-clearance and sturdy motor vehicles are recommended; RVs and trailers are not.
Management: Forest Service, Council Ranger District, (208) 253–0100
Reservations: No
Activities: Fishing, hiking, picnicking, swimming
Season: Late July–September
Finding the campground: From Council drive Forest Road 002 (the Hornet Creek Road) to Bear, then switch to FR 005 just past the Bear Guard Station, then take Forest Road 112 to the campground—about 40 miles (and about three hours) in all from Council.
The campground: Not found on most listings of public campgrounds, this is one of the more remote and primitive in the Seven Devils (and in the Hells Canyon National Recreation Area, which is saying something). This campground is at the edge of the Hells Canyon Wilderness Area, a useful jumping-off point for hiking into that part of the backcountry. Black Lake, good for swimming and fishing, is within easy walking distance from the campground.

7 Evergreen

Location: North of Council
Sites: 12
Facilities: Drinking water, vault toilets, fire rings, pets allowed
Fee per night: $
Elevation: 3,800 feet
Road conditions: Paved to the campground
Management: Forest Service, Council Ranger District, (208) 253–0100
Reservations: No
Activities: Fishing, picnicking
Season: June 1–September 10
Finding the campground: From Council drive 14 miles north on US 95.
The campground: This campground was closed in 2002 for a renovation project; the bridge that provides the only entrance to the campground needed work. It will remain closed for overnight use until the repair funds are provided. Day-use walking across the bridge is permitted, and tenting probably can be done in the area.

8 Cold Springs

Location: West of New Meadows
Sites: 33
Facilities: Drinking water, vault toilets, fire rings, pets allowed
Fee per night: $$ (group)
Elevation: 4,800 feet
Road conditions: Beyond the highway, wide (two-lane) forest gravel road, but badly washboarded in places
Management: Forest Service, McCall Ranger District, (208) 634-0400
Reservations: No (except for the group sites; call the McCall Ranger District)
Activities: Boating, fishing, picnicking, swimming
Season: May 1-October 31
Finding the campground: From New Meadows drive on US 95 southwest 8 miles (at the Tamarack area), then 2.5 miles west on Forest Road 089, and then 1 mile west of Forest Road 091.
The campground: The Lost Valley Reservoir is well named, since it gets relatively little attention. The lake area is as pretty as the better-known water bodies in the area, though, and the camping areas around it are nicely developed. Cold Springs is group-oriented; the entry area has a large parking lot area, and the group sites here can be reserved. Individual sites also are available. Boating and fishing are good in the nearby reservoir (which is a healthy hike away), and hikers can enjoy berry picking in the mountain woods.

9 Grouse Creek

Location: East of New Meadows
Sites: 7 (6 available for trailers)
Facilities: Drinking water, vault toilets, fire rings, pets allowed
Fee per night: $
Elevation: 6,500 feet
Road conditions: After the highway, the road is mostly good and flat forest road.
Management: Forest Service, McCall Ranger District, (208) 634-0400
Reservations: No
Activities: Boating, fishing, hiking, picnicking, swimming
Season: July 1-September 30
Finding the campground: From New Meadows drive 6 miles east on Idaho Highway 55 (to Goose Creek Summit) and then 9 miles north on Forest Road 257 (the Brundage Mountain Road).
The campground: This is a high mountain site with some good mountain trails for hikers. The area is popular with skiers and is located not far from Brundage Mountain Ski Area.

10 Hazard Lake

Location: Northeast of New Meadows
Sites: 12
Facilities: Drinking water, vault toilets, fire rings, pets allowed
Fee per night: $
Elevation: 7,040 feet
Road conditions: Rugged as it climbs into the mountains—take a sturdy backcountry vehicle up here.
Management: Forest Service, McCall Ranger District, (208) 634-0400
Reservations: No
Activities: Boating, fishing, hiking, picnicking, swimming
Season: July 1–September 30
Finding the campground: From New Meadows drive 6 miles east on ID 55, then 19 miles north on FR 257, and then 1 mile north on Forest Road 259.
The campground: This is one of the highest-elevation campgrounds in southwestern Idaho, which means its season starts late; snow tends to stick above 7,000 feet well into the summer. These particular mountains rise high above Meadows Valley, and you do get some great views. The campground is Forest Service—basic but well maintained.

11 Last Chance

Location: East of New Meadows
Sites: 28
Facilities: Drinking water, vault toilets, fire rings, barrier-free access, pets allowed
Fee per night: $
Elevation: 4,600 feet
Road conditions: After the highway, the forest road is narrow, steep, washboarded, and twisty, and it has steep drop-offs to the side down to the creek. If you can survive that, you'll be amused to see that the campground itself is paved! (The forest road beyond the campground is, ominously, marked as NARROW STEEP ROAD; your author did not engage it to learn more.)
Management: Forest Service, McCall Ranger District, (208) 634-0400
Reservations: No
Activities: Fishing, hiking, picnicking
Season: June 1–October 31
Finding the campground: From New Meadows drive 4 miles east on ID 55, and then 2 miles north on Forest Road 453.
The campground: For the brave souls who roll through the challenging roads, this campground will come as a fine reward. It is well maintained, has a great location next to roaring Goose Creek (which is plenty audible throughout the site), and is looked over by a resident host during the summer. There's a great hiking trail along and across the creek up to a waterfall. The hike is several miles and there are some steep stretches, but it's well worth the effort.

Area 13: Heartland

The Middle Fork of the Payette River and the South Fork of the Salmon River have their points of origin not far apart, in some of the highest Idaho country. Toward the west of it is a populated area called the Long Valley, and from the Long Valley vacationers reach some of the most popular campgrounds in Idaho.

The Long Valley is narrow and runs north to south, defined largely by its cities—McCall, Cascade, and Donnelly—and by the large bodies of water to its southwest (the Cascade Reservoir, generally referred to as Lake Cascade) and northeast (Payette Lake). Both are among the favored vacation and second-home locations for many people in the Boise area. Public and private campgrounds are abundant near these bodies of water, but farther away, deep in the national forests around the valley, campers can find plenty of other opportunities as well.

In such high country, the winters are solidly snowy (and McCall even hosts an annual Ice Festival each February), but the summertime activities run the gamut, from fishing—very popular in most of the streams here—and swimming and boating to hiking and all kinds of camping and animal watching.

The area could be transformed if a massive resort project, called Westrock and on the drawing boards for some years, comes to fruition in the Donnelly area. For the time being, however, the Long Valley area remains, if not undiscovered among Idahoans, at least not yet a major national destination.

This area is split between two national forests: the Payette to the north and east (including McCall), and the Boise to the south and west (including Cascade).

For more information:

McCall Chamber of Commerce
McCall, ID 83638
(208) 634-7631
www.mccall-idchamber.org

Payette National Forest
P.O. Box 1026
McCall, ID 83638
(208) 634-0700
www.mccall.net/pnf

Boise National Forest
1249 South Vinnell Way
Boise, ID 83709
(208) 373-4100
www.fs.fed.us/r4/boise

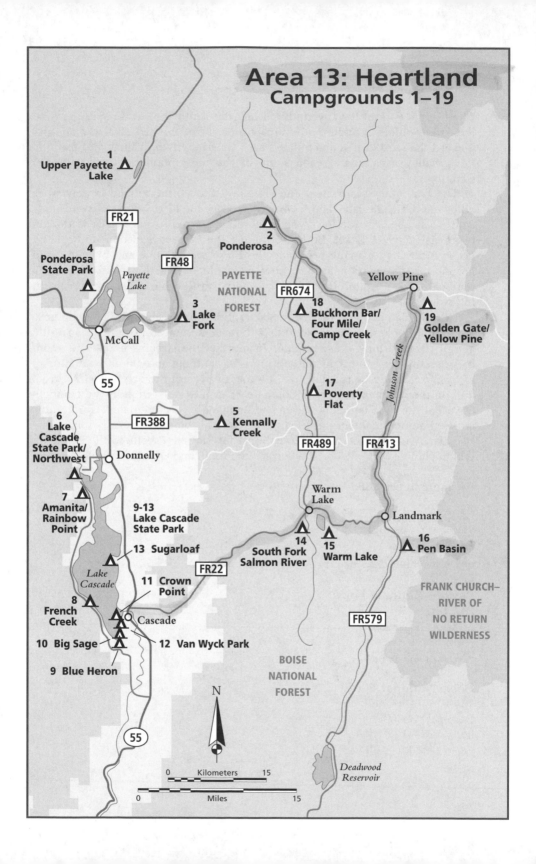

Area 13

	Town	Sites	Max. RV length	Electric	Picnic	Fire rings	Toilets	Showers	Water	Dump station	Disability access	Recreation	Can reserve	Fees ($)	Season	Stay limit (days)
1 Upper Payette Lake	McCall	19	22		•	•	V		•			BFHS		$	June–Oct.	14
2 Ponderosa	McCall	14	20		•	•	V		•			FHS		$	May–Nov.	14
3 Lake Fork	McCall	9	22		•	•	V		•			FH		$	June–Oct.	14
4 Ponderosa State Park	McCall	130	30	•	•	•	F,V	•	•	•		BFHS	•	$	May–Oct.	14
5 Kennally Creek	Donnelly	11	26		•	•	V		•			FH		$	June–Sept.	14
6 Lake Cascade State Park/ Northwest	Cascade	127	30		•	•	V		•		•	BFHS	•	$$–$$$	May–Sept.	
7 Amanita/ Rainbow Point	Donnelly	22	22		•	•	V		•			BFHS	•	$$	May–Sept.	14
8 French Creek	Cascade	21	30		•	•	V		•			BF	•	$$	May–Sept.	14
9 Lake Cascade Park/Blue Heron	Cascade	70	32		•	•	V		•		•	BFHS	•	$–$$	May–Oct.	
10 Lake Cascade Park/Big Sage	Cascade	U	32		•	•	V				•	BHS		$	May–Oct.	
11 Lake Cascade Park/Crown Point	Cascade	38	30		•	•	V		•			BFHS	•	$$	May–Oct.	
12 Lake Cascade Park/Van Wyck	Cascade	62	32		•	•	V		•		•	BFHS	•	$$	May–Oct.	
13 Lake Cascade Park/Sugarloaf	Cascade	42	32		•	•	V		•		•	BFHS	•	$$	May–Oct.	
14 South Fork Salmon River	Cascade	11	30		•	•	V		•			F		$	May–Sept.	14
15 Warm Lake	Cascade	50	30		•	•	V		•			BFS	•	$$–$$$	May–Sept.	14
16 Pen Basin	Cascade	6	22			•	V					F		$	June–Oct.	14
17 Poverty Flat	Cascade	10	25		•	•	V				•	FH		$	March–Nov.	14
18 Buckhorn Bar/ Four Mile/Camp Creek	McCall	20	22		•	•	V		•		•	FHS		$	June–Sept.	14
19 Golden Gate/ Yellow Pine	Yellow Pine	23	22			•	V					F		$	June–Oct.	14

1 Upper Payette Lake

Location: Northeast of McCall
Sites: 19
Facilities: Drinking water, vault toilets, fire rings, pull-through sites, pets allowed
Fee per night: $
Elevation: 5,560 feet

Road conditions: Paved to within a couple of miles of the campground
Management: Forest Service, McCall Ranger District, (208) 634–0400
Reservations: No
Activities: Boating, fishing, hiking, picnicking, swimming
Season: June 20–October 1
Finding the campground: From McCall drive 18.5 miles northeast on Forest Road 021, then follow signs to the campground, about 2 miles.
The campground: Upper Payette Lake is the much smaller and lesser-known lake upstream from the Lower Payette Lake on which McCall sits. This is higher mountain territory and just as pretty.

2 Ponderosa

Location: Northeast of McCall
Sites: 14
Facilities: Drinking water, vault toilets, fire rings, pets allowed
Fee per night: $
Elevation: 4,000 feet
Road conditions: Rugged dirt and gravel, mostly one lane
Management: Forest Service, Krassel Ranger District, (208) 634–0600
Reservations: No
Activities: Fishing, hiking, picnicking, swimming
Season: May 15–November 15
Finding the campground: From McCall drive 31 miles northeast on Forest Road 048.
The campground: This is a high mountain camp located at the Secesh River. Fishing is good here, and so is horseback riding; a horse camp is located close by.

3 Lake Fork

Location: Northeast of McCall
Sites: 9
Facilities: Drinking water, vault toilets, fire rings, pets allowed
Fee per night: $
Elevation: 5,600 feet
Road conditions: Good near McCall, then rough gravel, narrow, and steep after a few miles
Management: Forest Service, McCall Ranger District, (208) 634–0400
Reservations: No
Activities: Fishing, hiking, picnicking
Season: June 15–October 15 (depending on weather)
Finding the campground: From McCall drive 9.5 miles east on FR 048.
The campground: A fairly ordinary Forest Service campground located in the mountains east of McCall. Hikers will enjoy several of the trails running through the campground.

4 Ponderosa State Park

Location: Northeast of McCall
Sites: 130
Facilities: Drinking water, electric hookups, dump station, showers, flush and vault toilets, fire rings, pull-through sites, pets allowed
Fee per night: $$$
Elevation: 5,500 feet
Road conditions: Paved all through campground; some sites for the disabled have paved pads as well.
Management: Idaho Department of Parks and Recreation, (208) 634–2164
Reservations: Call (208) 634–2164 (during summer, after which it reverts to first come, first served) or available via Web site www.idahoparks.org.
Activities: Bicycling, boating, fishing, hiking, picnicking, swimming
Season: May 30–October 15 (or until the snow falls, whichever comes first)
Finding the campground: From downtown McCall, where Idaho Highway 55 turns left at the Hotel McCall, take Lakeside Road north along Payette Lake about 3 miles to the park.
The campground: One of the plushest and one of the larger (and one of the more expensive) public campgrounds in Idaho, Ponderosa has a little bit of everything. It is both richly wooded and full of great views out on Lower Payette Lake. Trails from here abound, for both hikers and bicyclists. A covered shelter is available for group picnics. Note also the nearby lookout, to which you can bike or drive and which provides excellent views of the whole lake area.

5 Kennally Creek

Location: East of Donnelly
Sites: 11 (9 suitable for trailers)
Facilities: Drinking water, vault toilets, fire rings, pull-through sites, pets allowed
Fee per night: $
Elevation: 5,620 feet
Road conditions: Can be rough and narrow one-lane headed up into the mountains
Management: Forest Service, McCall Ranger District, (208) 634–0400
Reservations: No
Activities: Fishing, hiking, picnicking
Season: June 1–September 30
Finding the campground: From Donnelly drive 3 miles north on ID 55 and then 19 miles east on Forest Road 388.
The campground: Located next to Kennally Creek, this campground is a relatively undiscovered gem. It has a good complement of amenities. Horseback riding is easily accommodated here, as is hiking; several trails are based nearby.

6 Lake Cascade State Park/Northwest

Location: On Lake Cascade
Sites: 127
Facilities: Drinking water, barrier-free access, fire rings, lake access, vault toilets, pets allowed
Fee per night: $$-$$$
Elevation: 4,900 feet
Road conditions: Paved up to, and generally within, the campgrounds (coming from Donnelly). If you arrive from the south (from the Cascade side of the reservoir), there's a rough stretch of about 10 miles of gravel road to contend with.
Management: Idaho Department of Parks and Recreation, Lake Cascade State Park, (208) 382-6544
Reservations: Available via Web site www.idahoparks.org
Activities: Boating, fishing, hiking, picnicking, swimming
Season: May 15-September 10
Finding the campgrounds: From ID 55 at Donnelly, take West Roseberry Road west to the Cascade Reservoir, and once there follow the signs south on the West Mountain Road south to the campgrounds.
The campgrounds: These five campgrounds—Poison Creek, West Mountain, Buttercup, Curlew, and Huckleberry—are all bunched closely together, several of them separated only by a fence and a name, and they are almost identical in appearance and services. Generally, they are well-manicured parks with some planted trees and bushes and mowed lawns, not forested (the way the nearby Forest Service campgrounds, such as Amanita, are). The trade-off is modern facilities (these are mostly relatively new campgrounds) and a terrific view of Cascade Reservoir, looking across to Donnelly and the farmland and mountains beyond. Hiking trails are generally available through the area. Note that the Curlew site, unlike the others, is a tents-only campground.

7 Amanita/Rainbow Point

Location: Southwest of Donnelly
Sites: 22
Facilities: Drinking water, vault toilets, fire rings
Fee per night: $$
Elevation: 5,000 feet
Road conditions: Paved to the campground
Management: Forest Service, Cascade Ranger District, (208) 382-7400
Reservations: Call (877) 444-6777 or visit Web site www.reserveamerica.com.
Activities: Boating, fishing, hiking, picnicking, swimming
Season: May 15-September 15
Finding the campgrounds: From Donnelly drive 4.8 miles southwest on Valley County Road 422.
The campgrounds: Amanita and Rainbow Point, which are next door to each other, are located in between the open-meadowed and well-manicured Lake Cascade State Park sites but are nothing like them: These are much more like

standard, woodsy, more rugged Forest Service campgrounds. There's good forest cover, and the site has a homey, well-used but well-maintained feel. In between the trees there is that great view over the reservoir (especially in the afternoon when the sunlight hits the eastern shore, and it shines like a surreal object). Amanita and Rainbow Point do have small beach areas and some good opportunities for hiking.

8 French Creek

Location: Southwest of Cascade, on the west side of Cascade Reservoir
Sites: 21
Facilities: Drinking water, vault toilets, fire rings
Fee per night: $$
Elevation: 5,000 feet
Road conditions: Paved
Management: Forest Service, Cascade Ranger District, (208) 382-7400
Reservations: Call (877) 444-6777 or visit Web site www.reserveamerica.com.
Activities: Boating, fishing, picnicking
Season: May 15–September 15 (depending on weather)
Finding the campground: From Cascade drive 4 miles south on Lake Shore Drive, then 5 miles west and north on Forest Road 422.
The campground: A shady, woodsy park (similar to Amanita and Rainbow Point farther north), which seems to have a very stable group of campers who return on a regular basis. French Creek runs through the grounds and empties into Cascade Reservoir here.

9 Lake Cascade State Park/Blue Heron

Location: On Lake Cascade
Sites: 70
Facilities: Drinking water, lake access, vault toilets, pets allowed, fire rings, barrier-free access
Fee per night: $–$$
Elevation: 4,900 feet
Road conditions: Paved to the campground
Management: Idaho Department of Parks and Recreation, Lake Cascade State Park, (208) 382-6544
Reservations: Available via Web site www.idahoparks.org
Activities: Boating, fishing, hiking, picnicking, swimming
Season: May 1–October 15
Finding the campground: Drive south of Cascade 3.2 miles on Cascade Reservoir Road.
The campground: Blue Heron is located just south of Big Sage and similar to the five state park campgrounds on the northwest side of the reservoir: well-kept lawns and an open view, looking out toward the west (instead of toward the east). This is a good place for boating and just hanging out next to the reservoir. Be aware that Blue Heron allows for overnight camping but the nearby Cabarton site, which looks similar, does not.

10 Lake Cascade State Park/Big Sage

Location: On Lake Cascade
Sites: Number undetermined
Facilities: Drinking water, vault toilets, fire rings, barrier-free access, lake access, pets allowed
Fee per night: $
Elevation: 4,900 feet
Road conditions: From Cascade, paved to the campground
Management: Idaho Department of Parks and Recreation, Lake Cascade State Park, (208) 382–6544
Reservations: No
Activities: Boating, hiking, picnicking, swimming
Season: May 1–October 15
Finding the campground: Drive south of Cascade (from the golf course 1 mile west of ID 55) 2.9 miles on Cascade Reservoir Road.
The campground: This is a new site, opened in 2002 and barely developed; unlike the other state park sites in this area, there is no manicured lawn. It is considered an "undeveloped" dispersal camping site. The location is nice, though: an unobstructed spot on the beach of Cascade Reservoir. No camping is allowed below the high-water mark.

11 Lake Cascade State Park/Crown Point

Location: On Lake Cascade
Sites: 38
Facilities: Drinking water, lake access, vault toilets, fire rings, pets allowed
Fee per night: $$
Elevation: 4,900 feet
Road conditions: Mostly paved, with a few hundred yards of gravel (and gravel within the campground); that stretch is steep and washboarded but mercifully brief.
Management: Idaho Department of Parks and Recreation, Lake Cascade State Park, (208) 382–6544
Reservations: Available via Web site www.idahoparks.org
Activities: Boating, fishing, hiking, picnicking, swimming
Season: May 1–October 15
Finding the campground: From Cascade start to head out of town north on ID 55, but turn left (west) at the Cascade Dam spillway and head up the hill; the campground is less than a mile from either the highway or the town below.
The campground: Close to Cascade (and therefore convenient), Crown Point does have one of the best views of any of the reservoir campgrounds: up on a hill, looking down over the lake. (Most of the individual campsites, however, don't have such a direct view.) The campground is an outgrowth of the Idaho Power Company Cascade project, a dam located adjacent to the campground.

12 Lake Cascade State Park/Van Wyck

Location: At Cascade
Sites: 62
Facilities: Drinking water, barrier-free access, fire rings, river access, vault toilets, pets allowed
Fee per night: $$
Elevation: 4,900 feet
Road conditions: Paved all the way
Management: Idaho Department of Parks and Recreation, Lake Cascade State Park, (208) 382-6544
Reservations: Available via Web site www.idahoparks.org
Activities: Boating, fishing, hiking, picnicking, swimming
Season: May 1–October 15
Finding the campground: Driving along ID 55 through the north side of Cascade, the road veers right as it heads out of town; just prior to that, at the Howdy gas and convenience stop, turn left (west) on the Old State Highway (it is so marked). Drive up over the hill, past the Cascade medical center, and toward the reservoir; the campground is on the right as you get there.
The campground: This park area abuts the city of Cascade; a residential area overlooks the park, the beach, and the reservoir. The state park looks a little like a city park. It is well maintained (like the other state campgrounds in the area) and a pleasant and convenient lakeside location for family recreation. It is not a place to get away from civilization; the area can become quite crowded and busy. Headquarters for Lake Cascade State Park are located within walking distance up the hill to the north.

13 Lake Cascade State Park/Sugarloaf

Location: North of Cascade, on Cascade Reservoir
Sites: 42
Facilities: Drinking water, barrier-free access, river access, vault toilets, pets allowed
Fee per night: $$
Elevation: 4,900 feet
Road conditions: Mostly paved from ID 55 to the reservoir
Management: Idaho Department of Parks and Recreation, Lake Cascade State Park, (208) 382-6544
Reservations: Available via Web site www.idahoparks.org
Activities: Boating, fishing, hiking, picnicking, swimming
Season: May 1–October 15
Finding the campground: Drive 8.8 miles north of Cascade on ID 55, turn left at the campground sign, driving west (there is no road name), and continue 2 miles to the reservoir.
The campground: Sugarloaf is an open-air and well-developed water's edge campground, favored by boaters and anglers headed out to Cascade Reservoir.

4 South Fork Salmon River

Location: Northeast of Cascade
Sites: 11
Facilities: Drinking water, vault toilets, fire rings
Fee per night: $
Elevation: 5,200 feet
Road conditions: Paved nearly to the campground
Management: Forest Service, Cascade Ranger District, (208) 382–7400
Reservations: No
Activities: Fishing, hiking, picnicking
Season: May 15–September 15
Finding the campground: From Cascade take ID 55 north 1 mile and then drive 22 miles east on Forest Road 022 (the Warm Lake Road).
The campground: This one shares a host with Warm Lake Campground, and it has similar services, but it is more heavily wooded and doesn't have the Warm Lake waterfront. It does have a nice location near the South Fork of the Salmon River and is good for fishing and hiking.

5 Warm Lake

Location: East of Cascade
Sites: About 50
Facilities: Drinking water, pull-through sites, vault toilets, fire rings
Fee per night: $$–$$$
Elevation: 6,800 feet
Road conditions: Paved up to the campgrounds, but there are some steep climbs and plenty of twists and turns.
Management: Forest Service, Cascade Ranger District, (208) 382–7400; Warm Lake Lodge and Resort, (208) 632–3553; North Shore Lodge and Resort, (208) 632–2000
Reservations: Call (877) 444-6777, or visit Web site www.reserveamerica.com, or call the lodges.
Activities: Boating, fishing, picnicking, swimming
Season: May 15–September 15
Finding the campground: From Cascade drive 1 mile north on ID 55 and then 26 miles northeast on FR 022 (the Warm Lake Road).
The campground: No, it isn't especially warm; this is a high mountain lake, good for a brisk swim, even in late summer, or for sunning oneself on the beach. Warm Lake has two complexes of campgrounds, one based around Warm Lake Lodge and the other around North Shore Lodge; the two are little more than a mile apart. These two lodges have supplies and operate cabins as well as campgrounds, all on land leased from the Forest Service. (The post office is located at Warm Lake Lodge.) In addition, the Forest Service operates two campgrounds of its own near the lodge properties, with hosts situated at both. Shoreline Campground is located near North Shore Lodge. It isn't on the shoreline and despite the numerous trees in the area (lodgepoles) feels like an open-air site; it is oriented mostly to groups. Warm Lake Campground is

The view at Warm Lake, west of Cascade, at one of the boat docks. Camping opportunities are located most of the way around the lake.

located across the road from the Warm Lake Lodge, has more forest cover, and is geared toward individual stays. The campgrounds here do take reservations, and you probably should avail yourself of them if you want to stay here: Warm Lake is popular with Boise-area visitors. You should know, too, that this area is popular not only with people: Bears occasionally are spotted wandering through the grounds, so take appropriate precautions.

16 Pen Basin

Location: East of Cascade
Sites: 6
Facilities: Vault toilets, fire rings
Fee per night: $
Elevation: 6,700 feet
Road conditions: Paved to Landmark, rough gravel south of there
Management: Forest Service, Cascade Ranger District, (208) 382-7400
Reservations: No

Activities: Fishing
Season: June 15–October 15 (depending on weather)
Finding the campground: From Cascade drive 2 miles northeast on ID 55, then turn right (east) and drive east 33 miles on the FR 022 (Warm Lake Road) to Landmark, and then go 3 miles south (toward Deadwood Reservoir) on Forest Road 579.
The campground: Can't find Landmark on a map? That's OK, because even by Idaho backcountry standards it's no community: It's the point where the paved Warm Lake Road (which runs east from Cascade) comes to a stop and hits a T with the gravel road that runs north to Yellow Pine (along Johnson Creek) and south to Deadwood Reservoir. Pen Basin is a few miles south of Landmark, in the Deadwood Reservoir direction. This is a pretty, but pretty primitive, wooded camp site. Bring your own drinking water; there's none here.

17 Poverty Flat

Location: Northeast of Cascade
Sites: 10 (4 of them walk-in only)
Facilities: Vault toilets, fire rings, barrier-free access
Fee per night: $
Elevation: 5,200 feet
Road conditions: Paved most of the way, but don't expect to speed here. The Warm Lake Road is good paved highway, but while the South Fork Road is paved for its first 8 miles, it is mostly one lane (and twisting and steep in places) and after that rugged gravel forest road.
Management: Forest Service, Krassel Ranger District, (208) 634–0600
Reservations: No
Activities: Fishing, hiking, picnicking
Season: March 1–November 30 (depending on weather)
Finding the campground: From Cascade take ID 55 north 1 mile, then drive 24 miles east on FR 022 (the Warm Lake Road), and then about 10 miles north on Forest Road 489 (the South Fork Road).
The campground: Superb fishing opportunities make Poverty Flats the most popular of the four Forest Service campgrounds in the South Fork of the Salmon River area (away from Long Valley and Warm Lake). There are good facilities (hitching racks) for horseback riding here, too, but no drinking water; this is roughing-it backwoods camping. Like the other campgrounds in this area (Four Mile, Camp Creek, and Buckhorn), this remote site is more popular with tenters who are there for fishing than with RVers who have to struggle to get there.

18 Buckhorn Bar/Four Mile/Camp Creek

Location: Northeast of McCall
Sites: 20
Facilities: Drinking water, vault toilets, fire rings, barrier-free access, pets allowed
Fee per night: $

Elevation: 6,800 feet

Road conditions: Paved most of the way, but don't expect to speed through here. The Warm Lake Road is good paved highway, but while the South Fork Road is paved for its first 8 miles, it is mostly one lane (and twisting and steep in places), and after that it becomes rugged gravel forest road.

Management: Forest Service, Krassel Ranger District, (208) 634-0600

Reservations: No

Activities: Fishing, hiking, picnicking, swimming

Season: June 1–September 15 (depending on weather)

Finding the campgrounds: From McCall drive 30 miles northeast on Forest Road 048, then 7 miles south on Forest Road 674.

The campgrounds: These three remote campgrounds located near each other on the South Fork of the Salmon River (roughly north of Warm Lake, and northeast of Cascade) are more popular with tenters who are there for fishing than with RVers who have to struggle to get there. None of these sites is especially heavily used, and those who brace the roads to get here will find a serene backcountry experience. The fishing in this area can be spectacular, and a large portion of those who show up here (mostly to tent, since RVing is not especially easy) are serious anglers.

19 Golden Gate/Yellow Pine

Location: South of Yellow Pine

Sites: 23

Facilities: Vault toilets, fire rings

Fee per night: $

Elevation: 7,000 feet

Road conditions: Rough, rugged, narrow, twisting, and occasionally steep— fun if you've got a sturdy, high-clearance vehicle, nerve-racking otherwise

Management: Forest Service, Cascade Ranger District, (208) 382-7400

Reservations: No

Activities: Fishing

Season: June 1–October 15 (depending on weather)

Finding the campgrounds: From Yellow Pine drive 2 miles south on Forest Road 413 (Johnson Creek Road).

The campgrounds: These campgrounds are located in partly shaded meadows just a couple of miles south of the town of Yellow Pine on the Johnson Creek Road. These are remote and primitive sites. Expect no potable water source here; pack everything in and out.

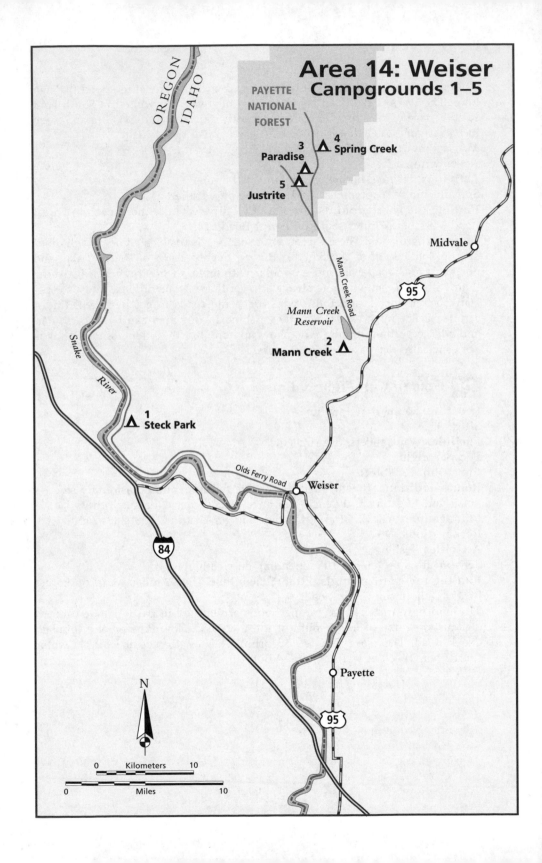

Area 14: Weiser
Campgrounds 1–5

OREGON
IDAHO

PAYETTE
NATIONAL
FOREST

3 ▲ **4** Spring Creek
Paradise ▲

5 ▲
Justrite

Midvale ○

Mann Creek Road

95

Mann Creek
Reservoir

2 ▲
Mann Creek

Snake

River

1 ▲
Steck Park

Olds Ferry Road Weiser ○

84

Payette ○

N

95

0   Kilometers   10

0   Miles   10

Area 14: Weiser

Above the Hells Canyon area on the Snake River, the river gouges less deeply, less spectacularly, into the landscape. The river and lands around it are not flat plains but look closer in harmony; hills, rather than mountains or flat plains, are the rule. The region around the city of Weiser follows this pattern—occasional mountains but rolling hills more ordinarily.

Besides the irrigation farming that marks so much of this area, bird hunting and fishing are important to the people locally and to many of the visitors who come here. The landscape may be less dramatic than in some parts of Idaho, but the recreational opportunities are no less real. Boating, swimming, hiking—possibilities for all abound, especially along the Snake River to the west and in the foothill regions to the east.

There are numerous festivals and arts events in this area through the year, the most popular of all being the Old Time Fiddlers Festival at Weiser, a national-level contest held every June.

Most of the public lands in this area are managed by the Bureau of Land Management, rather than the Forest Service, so there are some differences in the campgrounds here compared to those in other areas. The Forest Service lands here are in the Payette National Forest, which does not take reservations for its campgrounds.

For more information:

Weiser Chamber of Commerce
8 East Idaho Street
Weiser, ID 83672
(208) 549-0452
www.fiddlercontest.com

Payette Chamber of Commerce
700 Center Avenue
Payette, ID 83661
(208) 642-2362

1 Steck Park

Location: West of Weiser
Sites: 21 (16 RV-capable)
Facilities: Drinking water, vault toilets, lake access, fire rings, dump station, pets allowed
Fee per night: $$
Elevation: 2,100 feet
Road conditions: Paved nearly to the campground
Management: Bureau of Land Management, Four Rivers Field Office, (208) 384-3300
Reservations: No
Activities: Boating, fishing, hiking, picnicking

Area 14

	Town	Sites	Max. RV length	Electric	Picnic	Fire rings	Toilets	Showers	Water	Dump station	Disability access	Recreation	Can reserve	Fees ($)	Season	Stay limit (days)
1 Steck Park	Weiser	21	25		•	•	V		•	•		BFHS		$$	April–Oct.	14
2 Mann Creek	Weiser	4+	32		•	•	V		•			BFHS		$	April–Oct.	14
3 Paradise	Weiser	7	20		•	•	V					F			June–Oct.	14
4 Spring Creek	Weiser	14	45		•	•	V		•			FH		$	June–Oct.	14
5 Justrite	Weiser	8	20			•	V					F			June–Oct.	14

Season: April 1–October 30

Finding the campground: From Weiser drive 22 miles northwest on Olds Ferry Road to Brownlee Reservoir (on the Snake River).

The campground: Steck Park has lower and upper camping areas. The lower campground, the older area, is closer to the river and more shaded; the other a little higher. There are several pull-through camping sites. This is a boating and fishing paradise; fishing for smallmouth bass, catfish, and crappie is considered to be prime. There are two boat launches at the campground. Most of the camping sites have a good view of Brownlee Reservoir. A campground host is on-site.

2 Mann Creek

Location: Northwest of Weiser

Sites: 4, plus additional tent spaces

Facilities: Drinking water, vault toilets, fire rings, lake access, pets allowed

Fee per night: $

Elevation: 3,600 feet

Road conditions: Mostly good gravel roads

Management: Bureau of Reclamation, Boise District, (208) 365–2682

Reservations: No, but call (208) 365–2682 to check availability.

Activities: Boating, fishing, hiking, picnicking, swimming

Season: April 1–October 30

Finding the campground: From Weiser drive 10 miles north on U.S. Highway 95, then turn left onto the Mann Creek Reservoir Road, which climbs several miles into the hills west of Weiser.

The campground: This is one of the many southwest Idaho camping sites oriented toward boaters. The grounds are located in an open meadow next to Mann Creek, partially shaded by several deciduous trees. It sometimes gets busy on the weekends when boaters pile in.

▌ Paradise

Location: Northwest of Weiser
Sites: 7
Facilities: Vault toilets, fire rings, pets allowed
Fee per night: None
Elevation: 4,100 feet
Road conditions: Moderately rugged dirt and gravel road; call the ranger district for current conditions.
Management: Forest Service, Weiser Ranger District, (208) 549–4200
Reservations: No
Activities: Fishing, picnicking
Season: June 1–October 31
Finding the campground: From Weiser drive 12.5 miles north on US 95 and then 10 miles north on Washington County/Forest Road 009.
The campground: Paradise is very much like Justright—almost undeveloped, but pleasant mountain country for those seeking distance from society. Bring your own water.

▌ Spring Creek

Location: Northwest of Weiser
Sites: 14
Facilities: Drinking water, vault toilets, fire rings, barrier-free access, pets allowed
Fee per night: $$
Elevation: 4,800 feet
Road conditions: Plan some time—an hour, say—traveling here on the periodically rugged gravel forest road.
Management: Forest Service, Weiser Ranger District, (208) 549–4200
Reservations: No
Activities: Fishing, hiking, picnicking
Season: June 1–October 31
Finding the campground: Drive 12.5 miles north on US 95 and then 11.5 miles north on C/FR 009.
The campground: Generally regarded as the gem among the campgrounds in the Weiser area and the one with the prettiest setting, Spring Creek is also the most developed—and carries the largest camping fee. Unlike most other campgrounds in this area, Spring Creek has a resident host. Several good hiking trails branch out from here. The campground has been developed for barrier-free accessibility.

5 Justrite

Location: Northwest of Weiser
Sites: 8
Facilities: Vault toilets, fire rings, pets allowed
Fee per night: None
Elevation: 4,000 feet
Road conditions: Moderately rugged dirt and gravel road; call the ranger district for current conditions.
Management: Forest Service, Weiser Ranger District, (208) 549–4200
Reservations: No
Activities: Fishing
Season: June 1–October 31
Finding the campground: From Weiser drive 12.5 miles north on US 95 and then 13 miles northwest on C/FR 009.
The campground: Justrite is almost undeveloped—close to dispersal camping—and virtually a widening of the forest road. Four of the campsites do have tables. Its location up in the mountains is pretty enough, for those interested in roughing it. Bring your own water.

Area 15: Gem

The Emmett Valley—actually, a part of the Payette River Valley in the area of the city of Emmett—used to be the scene of vast apple orchards. Many of them are gone now, as Emmett increasingly becomes a bedroom community for the city of Boise. But outdoor opportunities are still plentiful in the neighborhood; you just have to drive a few miles out of town.

There is the Montour area, for one, a wooded riverside location still so popular that it serves as an annual gathering point for powwows conducted by Idaho's Indian tribes. Others lie farther north near the relatively remote community of Ola.

It may look like simple farming country, but there's more to this area than a first inspection will reveal. There are apple festivals in the area, and in early July the Montour area is home to a three-day statewide Indian powwow. Patience and continued exploration will reward the persistent traveler.

For more information:

Gem County Chamber of Commerce
120 North Washington Avenue
Emmett, ID 83617
(208) 365-3485
www.emmettid.com

Boise National Forest
1249 South Vinnell Way
Boise, ID 83709
(208) 373-4100
www.fs.fed.us/r4/boise

---

1 Montour

Location: East of Emmett and south of Montour
Sites: 17
Facilities: Drinking water, dump station, fire rings, vault toilets
Fee per night: $
Elevation: 3,000 feet
Road conditions: Paved all the way, including inside the campground; the roads are flat valley roads.
Management: Bureau of Reclamation, (208) 365-2682
Reservations: No
Activities: Hiking, picnicking
Season: April 1–October 30
Finding the campground: From Emmett drive 12 miles northeast on Idaho Highway 52 to the "Triangle" area where the road to Ola heads north and the road to Montour (to the right) heads south. Take the Montour Road south a couple of miles, just past the old community of Montour (which was relocated

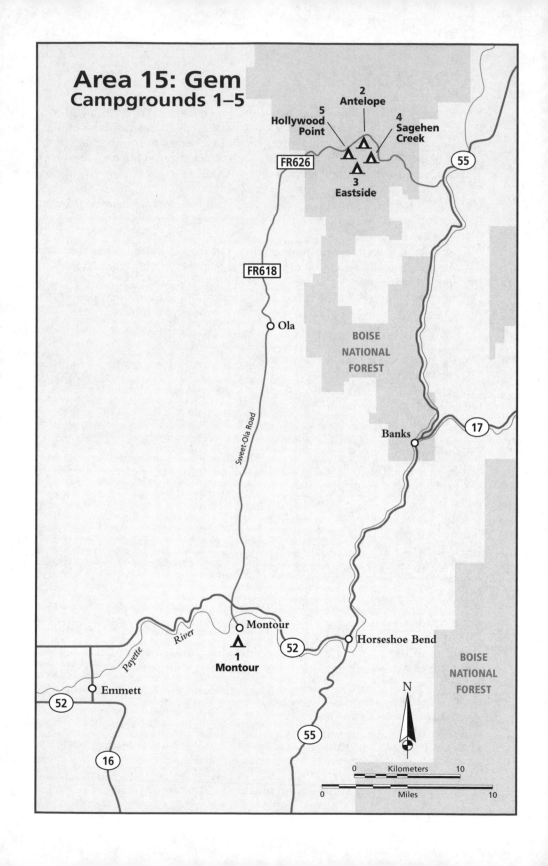

Area 15: Gem
Campgrounds 1–5

5
Hollywood
Point

2
Antelope

4
Sagehen
Creek

FR626

3
Eastside

FR618

55

Ola

BOISE
NATIONAL
FOREST

Banks

17

Sweet-Ola Road

Montour

52

Horseshoe Bend

BOISE
NATIONAL
FOREST

1
Montour

Payette
River

N

Emmett

52

16

55

0   Kilometers   10

0   Miles   10

Area 15

	Town	Sites	Max. RV length	Electric	Picnic	Fire rings	Toilets	Showers	Water	Dump station	Disability access	Recreation	Can reserve	Fees ($)	Season	Stay limit (days)
1 Montour	Montour	17	32		•	•	V		•	•		H		$	April–Oct.	
2 Antelope	Ola	20	32		•	•	V		•			BFH	•	$	May–Sept.	14
3 Eastside	Ola	6	32		•	•	V		•		•	BFH	•	$	May–Sept.	14
4 Sagehen Creek	Ola	15	32		•	•	V		•		•	BFH	•	$	May–Sept.	14
5 Hollywood Point	Ola	6	22		•	•	V		•			BFH		$	May–Sept.	14

here after the 1924 construction of the nearby Black Canyon Dam) to the campground sign.

The campground: This is a standard Bureau of Reclamation "manicured" campground, with mowed lawn (kept green with a sprinkler system), chain-link fence all around, and a gate that is closed at night. Dogs are allowed on leashes. A dump station is available. Most sites are pleasantly shaded. For many visitors the draw here is the Montour Wildlife Recreation Area, which stretches out to the north, northeast, and west of the campground. (Farmland lies to the south.) Bird hunting is allowed in some areas (except in "safety zones"), but bird-watchers will find this region a paradise, too: California quail, rink-necked pheasant, and gray partridge are abundant types here. Pheasants from game farms are released here as well on the opening day of hunting season. A state fishery may eventually be developed here, too.

2 Antelope

Location: Northeast of Ola
Sites: 20
Facilities: Drinking water (hand pump), river access, pull-through sites, fire rings, vault toilets, pets allowed
Fee per night: $
Elevation: 4,800 feet
Road conditions: The road is paved to Ola. From there it is sometimes rough forest gravel road, which in places hugs the sides of mountains. It is passable for most passenger vehicles, but a call to the ranger's office is a good idea for those unfamiliar with backcountry driving.
Management: Forest Service, Emmett Ranger District, (208) 365–7000
Reservations: Call (877) 444–6777 or visit Web site www.reserveamerica.com.
Activities: Boating, fishing, hiking, picnicking
Season: May 25–September 30
Finding the campground: From Emmett drive about 12 miles east on ID 52 to the Triangle intersection; turn left (north) and drive 20 miles on Sweet-Ola Road to Ola. From Ola drive 10 miles northeast on Forest Road 618, then about 8 miles northeast on Forest Road 626.

The campground: This is one of the more popular campgrounds in the Sage-hen area, which on the map lies north of Ola and west of Smith's Ferry—though you'd have a hard time being sure of that after twisting around on the mountain roads connecting those two places. Antelope is close by a small reservoir—boating is made easy with a boat launch and ramp here—and located in a forested basin area. The most popular activity here, though, is fishing; the aforementioned reservoir is annually stocked with trout by the state Department of Fish and Game. The campground is also a good staging area for elk, deer, and bear hunting. Several hiking trails are available. Three wells (with hand pumps) provide drinking water, but this is a standard Forest Service campground, which means amenities are relatively spartan. This campground has an on-site host.

3 Eastside

Location: Northeast of Ola
Sites: 6
Facilities: Drinking water, barrier-free access, fire rings, river access, vault toilets, pets allowed
Fee per night: $
Elevation: 4,800 feet
Road conditions: The road is paved to Ola. From there it is sometimes rough forest gravel road, which in places hugs the sides of mountains. It is passable for most passenger vehicles, but a call to the ranger's office is a good idea for those unfamiliar with backcountry driving.
Management: Forest Service, Emmett Ranger District, (208) 365–7000
Reservations: Call (877) 444–6777 or visit Web site www.reserveamerica.com.
Activities: Boating, fishing, hiking, picnicking
Season: May 25–September 30
Finding the campground: From Emmett drive about 12 miles east on ID 52 to the Triangle junction; turn left (north) and drive 20 miles on Sweet-Ola Road to Ola. From Ola drive 10 miles northeast on FR 618, then 9 miles northeast on FR 626.
The campground: Eastside is less than a mile from and similar to Antelope (it also is located next to a reservoir), except that boating is less practical; small boats are allowed on the reservoir. It is an equally prized fishing and hunting location, however, and has good wheelchair access.

4 Sagehen Creek

Location: Northeast of Ola
Sites: 15
Facilities: Drinking water, vault toilets, fire rings, barrier-free access, river access, pets allowed
Fee per night: $
Elevation: 4,800 feet

Road conditions: The road is paved to Ola. After that, the sometimes rough gravel road in places hugs the sides of mountains and is occasionally steep. It is passable for most passenger vehicles, but a call to the ranger's office is a good idea for those unfamiliar with backcountry driving.
Management: Forest Service, Emmett Ranger District, (208) 365–7000
Reservations: Call (877) 444–6777 or visit Web site www.reserveamerica.com.
Activities: Boating, fishing, hiking, picnicking
Season: May 25–September 30
Finding the campground: From Emmett drive about 12 miles east on ID 52 to the Triangle intersection; turn left (north) and drive 20 miles on Sweet-Ola Road to Ola. From Ola drive 10 miles northeast on FR 618, then around 9 miles northeast on FR 626.
The campground: This is the largest and possibly most popular of the Sagehen campgrounds. It has an on-site host, and the campground is managed by a concessionaire—which can mean more services provided than usual for Forest Service campgrounds. Sagehen has a boat ramp and dock for easy access to the reservoir; the site is well developed for wheelchair access. There is also beach space at the reservoir. As in the other campgrounds in this area, there's easy access to an extensive hiking trail system.

5 Hollywood Point

Location: Northeast of Ola
Sites: 6
Facilities: Drinking water, vault toilets, fire rings, river access, pets allowed
Fee per night: $
Elevation: 4,800 feet
Road conditions: The road is paved to Ola. From there the forest gravel road in places hugs the sides of mountains and switches back and forth along the mountainsides. It is passable for most passenger vehicles, but a call to the ranger's office is a good idea for those unfamiliar with backcountry driving.
Management: Forest Service, Emmett Ranger District, (208) 365–7000
Reservations: No
Activities: Boating, fishing, hiking, picnicking
Season: May 10–September 16
Finding the campground: From Emmett drive about 12 miles east on ID 52 to the Triangle junction; turn left (north) and drive 20 miles on Sweet-Ola Road to Ola. From Ola drive 10 miles northeast on FR 618, then 10 miles northeast on FR 626.
The campground: This is another of the pretty Sagehen area campgrounds, close by Antelope and Eastside, with similar amenities and recreational possibilities.

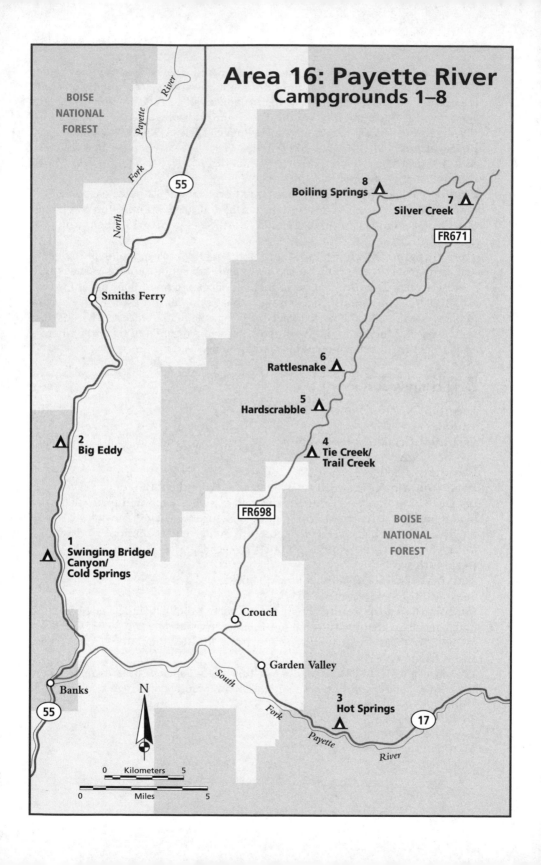

Area 16: Payette River
Campgrounds 1–8

BOISE
NATIONAL
FOREST

Payette River

North Fork

55

8 Boiling Springs

7 Silver Creek

FR671

Smiths Ferry

6 Rattlesnake

5 Hardscrabble

2 Big Eddy

4 Tie Creek/
Trail Creek

FR698

BOISE
NATIONAL
FOREST

1 Swinging Bridge/
Canyon/
Cold Springs

Crouch

Garden Valley

Banks

55

N

South Fork

Payette

3 Hot Springs

River

17

0 Kilometers 5

0 Miles 5

Area 16: Payette River

In Idaho, "driving along the Payette River" or "rafting the Payette" could mean many things, because the Payette is a very large river system with many branches (one that, in turn, flows into the Snake River near the city of Payette). But in practice it usually means the area tracking along Idaho Highway 55 from around Horseshoe Bend north to Banks and on to Smith's Ferry. Along much of this stretch, the North Fork of the Payette is a wild, fast-moving, serious white-water stream. Some of it is a great travel experience for the most casual boater, while other sections would be highly dangerous for all but the most experienced. If you want adventure in water travel, you can find something along the Payette to suit your tastes. (Hiring a guide for the trip is usually advisable.)

The river is only part of the story of this area, though. The forested mountains conceal a wealth of camping locations and an abundance of recreation opportunities. The area is popular with Boise-area residents, so camping spaces can be hard to get after midafternoon on summer Fridays. The more spectacular opportunities await, in many cases, as you roll away from pavement and climb out of the Long Valley into the mountains all around.

For more information:

Greater Garden Valley Chamber of Commerce
P.O. Box 10
Garden Valley, ID 83622
(208) 462-5003
www.gvchamber.org

Boise National Forest
1249 South Vinnell Way
Boise, ID 83709
(208) 373-4100
www.fs.fcd.us/r4/boise

1 Swinging Bridge/Canyon/Cold Springs

Location: North of Banks
Sites: 22 (11 in Swinging Bridge, 6 in Canyon, 5 in Cold Springs)
Facilities: Drinking water, vault toilets, fire rings, pets allowed
Fee per night: $
Elevation: 4,000 feet
Road conditions: Paved up to the campground (which is adjacent to ID 55); gravel in the campground
Management: Forest Service, Emmett Ranger District, (208) 365-7000
Reservations: Available for Swinging Bridge only. Call (877) 444-6777 or visit Web site www.reserveamerica.com.
Activities: Fishing, picnicking

Area 16

	Town	Sites	Max. RV length	Electric	Picnic	Fire rings	Toilets	Showers	Water	Dump station	Disability access	Recreation	Can reserve	Fees ($)	Season	Stay limit (days)
1 Swinging Bridge/ Canyon/Cold Springs	Banks	22	22		•	•	V		•			F	•	$	May–Nov.	14
2 Big Eddy	Banks	4	25		•	•	V					F		$	May–Nov.	14
3 Hot Springs	Garden Valley	8	35		•	•	V		•		•	F	•	$$	May–Sept.	14
4 Tie Creek/ Trail Creek	Garden Valley	17	22		•	•	V		•			FH		$	May–Oct.	14
5 Hardscrabble	Garden Valley	6	24		•	•	V					F		$	May–Sept.	14
6 Rattlesnake	Garden Valley	11	22		•	•	V					F		$$	April–Oct.	14
7 Silver Creek	Garden Valley	5	22		•	•	V		•			FH		$	June–Sept.	14
8 Boiling Springs	Garden Valley	7	22		•	•	V		•			FH		$	May–Oct.	14

Season: May 15–November 1

Finding the campgrounds: From Banks drive 8 to 9 miles north on ID 55. All three campgrounds are on the west side of the highway, and all have CAMPGROUND 1000 FEET AHEAD signs to warn you the entrance is around the next turn.

The campgrounds: These three nearly identical sites all cling to the side of the forested mountains to the immediate west of ID 55; the Payette River (usually in full white-water mode here) is on the other side of the highway. Inside the campgrounds you get some sense of the traffic roaring by, but these sites, hilly and pleasantly shaded, are nicely designed to shield campers from the worst of the highway impact. Hiking and fishing are easily engaged here; trails lead up the mountains for stout walkers. Which one to try? Recommendation here is Swinging Bridge, the largest of the three, which has the prettiest setting and for which reservations can be made. (Reality check: There is not, at least presently, any swinging bridge near the like-named campground.)

2 Big Eddy

Location: North of Banks
Sites: 4
Facilities: Vault toilets, fire rings, pets allowed
Fee per night: $
Elevation: 4,400 feet
Road conditions: Paved up to the campground (which is adjacent to ID 55); gravel in the campground
Management: Forest Service, Emmett Ranger District, (208) 365–7000

Reservations: No
Activities: Fishing, picnicking
Season: May 6–November 6
Finding the campground: From Banks drive 15 miles north on ID 55.
The campground: Of the four campgrounds on ID 55 between Banks and Smith's Ferry (the other three are Canyon, Cold Springs, and Swinging Bridge), Big Eddy is the only one on the river side of the highway. That sounds awfully exposed, with the highway traffic roaring by on one side and the river roaring down below. But thanks to some shrewd design, this shady and hilly patch of ground feels more remote than it is. This is a good spot for some white-water river fishing and even better as an access point for white-water kayaking, for which the Big Eddy area is an epicenter. Bring your own drinking water; Big Eddy has none.

3 Hot Springs

Location: East of Garden Valley
Sites: 8 (including 3 group sites)
Facilities: Drinking water (well with hand pump), vault toilets, fire rings, barrier-free access, river access, pets allowed
Fee per night: $$
Elevation: 3,200 feet
Road conditions: Paved up to and into the campground. Idaho Highway 17 is one of Idaho's newest paved highways.
Management: Forest Service, Emmett Ranger District, (208) 365–7000
Reservations: Call (877) 444–6777 or visit Web site www.reserveamerica.com.
Activities: Fishing, picnicking
Season: May 15–September 30
Finding the campground: From Garden Valley drive 2 miles east on ID 17; enter the campground from the highway.
The campground: From the Banks-Lowman Highway (more recently, ID 17), you see Hot Springs as a large parking lot stuck incongruously in the woods; this is one of the newer campgrounds in the area. But it has two distinct assets that are evident on close inspection. One is the South Fork of the Payette River, which roars just across the highway from the campground; this place is a favorite for boaters to put into the river. (Kayaks and rafts sometimes seem to reach traffic-jam levels.) The other is the hot springs themselves, located nearby. Fishing (especially for rainbow trout) and hunting also are activities for which Hot Springs is a good jumping-off point. The campground has an on-site manager. Six of the sites are pull-throughs.

4 Tie Creek/Trail Creek

Location: North of Garden Valley
Sites: 17
Facilities: Drinking water (well with hand pump), vault toilets, fire rings, river access, pets allowed
Fee per night: $

Elevation: 3,300 feet (Trail Creek 3,800 feet)
Road conditions: From Garden Valley the road turns to gravel and dirt. It is reasonably well maintained, but this is forest mountain road winding next to the Middle Fork of the Payette River, so expect no fast travel.
Management: Forest Service, Emmett Ranger District, (208) 365–7000
Reservations: No
Activities: Fishing, picnicking
Season: May 1–October 25
Finding the campgrounds: From Garden Valley drive 2.5 miles west on ID 17 and then north on Forest Road 698 for 11 miles (Tie Creek) or 19 miles (Trail Creek).
The campgrounds: The river flows fast here, and the sightseeing—of nearby mountains—is spectacular. Hunting and fishing both are popular pastimes. Both Tie Creek and Trail Creek are managed by concessionaires, so when you get there some services may be added beyond those listed here.

5 Hardscrabble

Location: East of Garden Valley
Sites: 6
Facilities: River access, vault toilets, fire rings, pets allowed
Fee per night: $
Elevation: 3,400 feet
Road conditions: From Garden Valley the road turns to gravel and dirt. It is reasonably well maintained, but this is forest mountain road winding next to the Middle Fork of the Payette River, so expect no fast travel.
Management: Forest Service, Emmett Ranger District, (208) 365–7000
Reservations: No
Activities: Fishing, picnicking
Season: May 15–September 30
Finding the campground: From Garden Valley drive 2.5 miles west on ID 17 and then 11 miles north on FR 698.
The campground: A relatively small campground with just a half-dozen spaces, Hardscrabble is another of those pretty riverside locations with excellent fishing and hunting possibilities. Be sure to pack in your own water, since none is available on-site. The campground is managed by concessionaires.

6 Rattlesnake

Location: North of Garden Valley
Sites: 11
Facilities: Vault toilets, fire rings, pull-through sites, pets allowed
Fee per night: $$
Elevation: 3,800 feet
Road conditions: From Garden Valley the road turns to gravel and dirt. It is reasonably well maintained, but this is forest mountain road winding next to the Middle Fork of the Payette River, so expect no fast travel.
Management: Forest Service, Emmett Ranger District, (208) 365–7000

Reservations: No
Activities: Fishing, picnicking
Season: April 1–October 30
Finding the campground: From Garden Valley drive 2.5 miles west on ID 17 and then 18 miles north on FR 698.
The campground: The Middle Fork of the Payette River runs past this campground, and the forested setting can't be beat. Fishing is reputedly excellent in the river in this region, and hunting for deer and elk is popular, too. The campground is well equipped for RVs, and a covered "pavilion" recreation building is available. But Rattlesnake has had some hard times. In 1988 a massive storm blew down most of the old-growth forest cover in the area and some of the facilities. The Forest Service rehabilitated the campground in 2002. Rattlesnake is managed by concessionaires. Hand-pump water is available, but the Forest Service recommends not drinking it and instead bringing your own.

7 Silver Creek

Location: North of Garden Valley
Sites: 5
Facilities: Drinking water (well with hand pump), vault toilets, fire rings, pets allowed
Fee per night: $
Elevation: 3,150 feet
Road conditions: From Garden Valley the road turns to gravel and dirt. It is reasonably well maintained, but this is forest mountain road winding next to the Middle Fork of the Payette River, so expect no fast travel.
Management: Forest Service, Emmett Ranger District, (208) 365–7000
Reservations: Call (877) 444–6777 or visit Web site www.reserveamerica.com.
Activities: Fishing, hiking, picnicking
Season: June 1–September 30
Finding the campground: From Garden Valley drive 2.5 miles west on ID 17, then 19 miles north on FR 698, and then 7 miles northeast on Forest Road 671.
The campground: One of the smallest campgrounds in the area, Silver Creek is well known among regional anglers for the fine rainbow trout fishing from the banks of the Middle Fork of the Payette River. It's also known for the nearby private resort and swimming facility (the Silver Creek Plunge) and for a fire lookout building close by.

8 Boiling Springs

Location: East of Garden Valley
Sites: 7
Facilities: Drinking water (well with hand pump), vault toilets, fire rings, pets allowed
Fee per night: $
Elevation: 4,000 feet

Road conditions: From Garden Valley the road turns to gravel and dirt. It is reasonably well maintained, but this is forest mountain road winding next to the Middle Fork of the Payette River, so expect no fast travel.

Management: Forest Service, Emmett Ranger District, (208) 365–7000

Reservations: No

Activities: Fishing, hiking, picnicking

Season: May 20–October 31

Finding the campground: From Garden Valley drive 10 miles east on ID 17 and then 23 miles north on FR 698.

The campground: One of the more remote campgrounds in the region, Boiling Springs is also closest to the wildlife and one of the best for hunting and fishing. The forest mountain scenery is as good as it gets. An artesian water system provides the drinking water here. A hiking trail goes upriver about a half mile from the campground to an old ranger station; high-temperature hot springs are located near it.

Area 17: Lowman

Lowman is a little less remote than it once was, with the opening of the Banks-Lowman Highway (Idaho Highway 17) in the mid-1990s. That route had earlier been available only as a treacherous gravel road, and the other way to Lowman—from the Boise area—was the slow, steep, switchback-laden route from Idaho City. (From the east, Lowman is an hour from Stanley and a couple of hours from the Sun Valley and Ketchum area.)

The Lowman area is well worth the drive. The eastern branch of the Payette River has one of the prettiest parts of southwest Idaho, and a growing number of vacation homes are turning up on the riverside. Almost all of the square mileage of this mountainous area is national forest, and most of it is excellent hiking territory; the river and creeks here are prime fishing areas. This area is almost as popular in the winter, when cross-country skiers roam over well-groomed paths.

There is another attraction, too: hot springs. This region of Idaho, reaching from Boise in the west to beyond Stanley in the area, has plenty of geologic ferment, and hot springs can be found all over. Most of the campgrounds in or near the Lowman district have hot springs or are not far from you. Travel along Idaho Highway 21 in this region, and you'll see several just off the highway.

For more information:

Boise National Forest
1249 South Vinnell Way
Boise, ID 83709
(208) 373–4100
www.fs.fcd.us/r4/boise

---

1 Pine Flats

Location: West of Lowman
Sites: 29
Facilities: Drinking water (hand pumps), vault toilets, fire rings, pull-through sites, pets allowed
Fee per night: $$
Elevation: 3,800 feet
Road conditions: Paved to the campground and within
Management: Forest Service, Lowman Ranger District, (208) 259–3361
Reservations: No
Activities: Fishing, picnicking
Season: May 20–September 30
Finding the campground: From Lowman drive west on ID 17 for 5 miles; enter the campground from the highway.

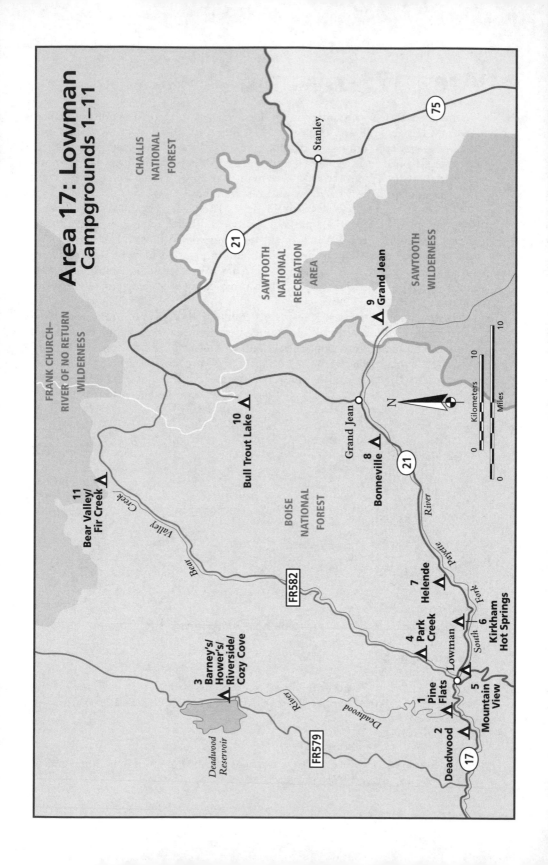

Area 17: Lowman
Campgrounds 1–11

Area 17

	Town	Sites	Max. RV length	Electric	Picnic	Fire rings	Toilets	Showers	Water	Dump station	Disability access	Recreation	Can reserve	Fees ($)	Season	Stay limit (days)
1 Pine Flats	Lowman	29	40		•	•	V		•			F		$	May–Sept.	14
2 Deadwood	Lowman	6	22			•	V		•			BFH		$$	May–Sept.	14
3 Barney's/Hower's/ Riverside/ Cozy Cove	Lowman	31	30		•	•	V		•			F		$	July–Sept.	14
4 Park Creek	Lowman	26	32		•	•	V		•			F	•	$$	May–Sept.	14
5 Mountain View	Lowman	13	32		•	•	V		•			F	•	$$	May–Sept.	14
6 Kirkham Hot Springs	Lowman	16	32		•	•	V		•			F	•	$	May–Sept.	14
7 Helende	Lowman	10	30		•	•	V		•			F	•	$$	May–Sept.	14
8 Bonneville	Lowman	22	30		•	•	V		•		•	BFH	•	$	July–Sept.	14
9 Grand Jean	Grand Jean	6	22		•	•	V		•			FH		$$$	June–Sept.	14
10 Bull Trout Lake	Lowman	32	60		•	•	V		•			BFH	•	$	July–Sept.	14
11 Bear Valley/ Fir Creek	Lowman	15	30		•	•	V					BFH			July–Sept.	14

The campground: This is a good family campground with ample shade and room for children to play—but a couple of its best assets call for a cautionary note for parents. First, the South Fork of the Payette River is close by and rumbles pleasantly, but it's down a steep hill, which can be a treacherous climb, and the river runs fast here—this is not a place for swimming (though experienced boaters will be attracted). Second, natural hot springs can be found about a half mile downriver, but be careful of these: The Forest Service warns that they are extremely hot and can cause burns. If you're thinking of bathing here, check it out very cautiously first.

2 Deadwood

Location: West of Lowman
Sites: 6
Facilities: Drinking water (hand pumps), vault toilets, fire rings, pull-through sites, pets allowed
Fee per night: $$
Elevation: 3,700 feet
Road conditions: Paved throughout
Management: Forest Service, Lowman Ranger District, (208) 259–3361
Reservations: No
Activities: Boating, fishing, picnicking
Season: May 20–September 30

Finding the campground: From Lowman drive west on ID 17 for 8 miles. The campground is north of the highway.

The campground: Mainly, this campground is heaven for rafters and boaters, for both put in and take out, since Deadwood sits at the confluence of the Deadwood River (the Deadwood Reservoir is upstream) and the South Fork of the Payette River. There's also a 26-mile Deadwood Ridge Trail, which runs all the way to the reservoir. The campground itself is nothing special, not a place to hang around, but serious recreationists will find it a useful starting point.

3 Barney's/Hower's/Riverside/Cozy Cove

Location: North of Lowman
Sites: 34 (9 in Barney's, 8 in Hower's, 8 in Riverside, 9 in Cozy Cove)
Facilities: Vault toilets, fire rings, pets allowed
Fee per night: $
Elevation: 5,400 feet
Road conditions: The forest road away from ID 21 is rough gravel, often one lane, and slow going.
Management: Forest Service, Lowman Ranger District, (208) 259-3361
Reservations: No
Activities: Fishing, picnicking
Season: July 1–September 30
Finding the campgrounds: From Lowman drive northeast on ID 21 for 36 miles and then turn left (west) onto Forest Road 198 (the Bear Valley Road) and drive 14 miles. Turn right (generally continuing west) on Forest Road 579 (the Landmark-Stanley Road) and drive until it ends on Forest Road 555. Turn left (south) and continue 7 miles to the campground area.

The campgrounds: These four similar campgrounds are bunched together on the east side of Deadwood Reservoir, a remote but popular camping location. No services are provided at any of these campgrounds, but they make up for all this with their pristine setting and a fine lakeside location. The area has the scenery of Redfish or Warm Lakes without the crowds and the semiurban development. Cozy Cove, the southernmost, is also the largest and has a boat ramp, plus a great view of Wild Buck Peak visible through the lodgepole pines. The heaviest use, and the most competition for spaces, probably is at the Riverside on the north end of the lake, which is a favorite for fishing. Several hand pumps have been added to the campgrounds, but bringing your own water is advised.

4 Park Creek

Location: East of Lowman
Sites: 26
Facilities: Drinking water, vault toilets, fire rings, pull-through sites, pets allowed
Fee per night: $
Elevation: 4,300 feet
Road conditions: Paved to the campground

Management: Forest Service, Lowman Ranger District, (208) 259-3361
Reservations: Call (877) 444-6777 or visit Web site www.reserveamerica.com.
Activities: Fishing, picnicking
Season: May 20-September 30
Finding the campground: From Lowman drive 4 miles northeast on ID 21; enter the campground from the highway.
The campground: This is one of the few campgrounds in the area designed as a group site (for up to 200 people). Its location is on the hillside overlooking the South Fork of the Payette River. Get there early, because this campground often fills on summer weekends and holidays.

5 Mountain View

Location: East of Lowman
Sites: 13 (8 reservable)
Facilities: Drinking water, vault toilets, fire rings, pull-through sites, pets allowed
Fee per night: $$
Elevation: 3,800 feet
Road conditions: Paved to the campground and throughout
Management: Forest Service, Lowman Ranger District, (208) 259-3361
Reservations: Call (877) 444-6777 or visit Web site www.reserveamerica.com.
Activities: Fishing, picnicking
Season: May 20-September 30
Finding the campground: From Lowman drive 6 miles east on ID 21.
The campground: This well-developed area has pedestal grills and paved pads—uptown features for a Forest Service campground. It's just off ID 21, but most of the sites are far enough away to obscure the road traffic; a parking lot at the lower end, above the South Fork of the Payette River, is sometimes a gathering place for groups of campers. Mountain View is pleasantly shady and well designed to give campers a little room. This campground often fills up on summer weekends.

6 Kirkham Hot Springs

Location: East of Lowman
Sites: 16 (some reservable)
Facilities: Drinking water (hand pump), vault toilets, fire rings, pull-through sites, barrier-free access, pets allowed
Fee per night: $
Elevation: 3,300 feet
Road conditions: Paved to the campground
Management: Forest Service, Lowman Ranger District, (208) 259-3361
Reservations: Call (877) 444-6777 or visit Web site www.reserveamerica.com.
Activities: Fishing, picnicking
Season: May 20-September 30
Finding the campground: From Lowman drive 4.2 miles east on ID 21.

The campground: This is a nearly unshaded campground, with trees nearby but providing little cover; camping use here is less than in other nearby campgrounds such as Bonneville and Helende. The main draw here is the hot springs.

Helende

Location: East of Lowman
Sites: 10 (6 sites reservable)
Facilities: Drinking water (hand pump), vault toilets, fire rings, pets allowed
Fee per night: $$
Elevation: 4,200 feet
Road conditions: Paved highway up to the campground; some paving within the campground
Management: Forest Service, Lowman Ranger District, (208) 259-3361
Reservations: Call (877) 444-6777 or visit Web site www.reserveamerica.com.
Activities: Fishing, picnicking
Season: May 20–September 30
Finding the campground: From Lowman drive 9 miles east on ID 21.
The campground: The ponderosa pine stands provide rich cover at this hilly campground, located within easy walking distance of the South Fork of the Payette River. This campground sometimes fills up early on summer weekends.

Bonneville

Location: North of Lowman
Sites: 22 (14 sites reservable)
Facilities: Drinking water (hand pump), pull-through sites, vault toilets, fire rings, barrier-free access, pets allowed
Fee per night: $
Elevation: 4,700 feet
Road conditions: Paved up to the campground turnoff; gravel within
Management: Forest Service, Idaho City Ranger District, (208) 259-3361
Reservations: Call (877) 444-6777 or visit Web site www.reserveamerica.com.
Activities: Boating, fishing, hiking, picnicking
Season: July 1–September 30
Finding the campground: From Lowman drive 18 miles northeast on ID 21.
The campground: Most campgrounds seem to be located in lower areas, in draws; Bonneville is located up, above ID 21, on a bluff. There's still plenty of shade, courtesy of the Douglas fir and ponderosa pine, and there's water, courtesy of Warm Springs Creek (but there's also drinking water). One of the main draws here, as in so many Lowman-area campsites, is the hot springs located close by (a quarter mile north, on Warm Springs Creek). This campground is well developed for wheelchair access.

9 Grand Jean

Location: At Grand Jean, between Lowman and Stanley
Sites: Variable; ordinarily, 6 developed camping sites
Facilities: Drinking water, vault toilets, fire rings, pets allowed
Fee per night: $$$
Elevation: 5,060 feet
Road conditions: Paved highway, then about 7 miles on Grand Jean Road, a rough dirt road with some steep areas and some close drop-offs next to the South Fork of the Payette River (drive carefully, and scout out this road before bringing in your big RV).
Management: Forest Service, Lowman Ranger District, (208) 259–3361; Sawtooth National Recreation Area, (208) 727–5000
Reservations: No
Activities: Fishing, hiking, picnicking
Season: June 15–September 15
Finding the campground: The Grand Jean area is off ID 21 between Stanley and Lowman. From Lowman drive 26 miles northeast on ID 21 and then drive 7 miles east on Grand Jean Road.
The campground: The private Sawtooth Lodge and swimming pool area here are popular with Boise-area residents, and the nearby campground, with its fine location near the South Fork of the Payette River, gets plenty of attention, too. In common with many campgrounds in this region, there are hot springs in the area; some are too hot for use, but others are refreshing natural spas. Grand Jean also has access to several mountain hiking trails, including Big Meadows, Sawtooth Lake, and Baron Lakes. It is also a good jumping-off point for the Sawtooth Wilderness Area, the border of which is just a few miles south.

10 Bull Trout Lake

Location: Northeast of Lowman
Sites: 32 (most reservable)
Facilities: Drinking water, vault toilets, fire rings, pets allowed; group and equestrian sites available
Fee per night: $
Elevation: 7,000 feet
Road conditions: Paved highway, then sometimes washboarded gravel for 2 miles into the campground
Management: Forest Service, Idaho City Ranger District, (208) 259–3361
Reservations: Call (877) 444–6777 or visit Web site www.reserveamerica.com.
Activities: Boating, fishing, hiking, horseback riding, picnicking
Season: July 1–September 30
Finding the campground: From Lowman drive 35 miles northeast on ID 21 and then 2 miles southwest on Forest Road 520.

The campground: Bull Trout Lake is located next door to the campground, and fishing there is so popular that this campground is often one of the first to fill up in the summer. Get there early! The campground actually has a variety of recreation options, including horseback riding (in a specific area and on nearby trails) and hiking.

---

11 Bear Valley/Fir Creek

Location: North of Lowman
Sites: 15 (10 in Bear Valley, 5 in Fir Creek)
Facilities: Vault toilets, fire rings, pets allowed
Fee per night: None
Elevation: 6,400 feet
Road conditions: Rugged forest road, often one and one-half lanes wide
Management: Forest Service, Lowman Ranger District, (208) 259-3361
Reservations: No
Activities: Boating, fishing, hiking, picnicking
Season: July 1–September 30
Finding the campgrounds: From Lowman drive 36 miles northeast on ID 21 and then 12 miles north on the Cape Horn turnoff.
The campgrounds: These mountain campgrounds, within a couple of miles of each other, are on Bear Valley Creek (Bear Valley is at that creek's confluence with Elk Creek), and canoeists often use the campground as a staging area for their expeditions. The Elk Creek Forest Service guard station is nearby. Lodgepole pines cover the area and provide shade. There are no services at either campground, so bring your own drinking water and supplies.

Area 18: Boise Basin

There are four "Boises" to know in southwest Idaho. One is the city, the state's capital city and its largest. The others are off to its northeast, out of the valley and up in the mountains. Boise County is named for the Boise River, which runs through it (as well as through the city of Boise), and the Boise River Basin.

The Boise River Basin was one of Idaho's first mining boom areas, the focus of frantic mining and other activities for more than 10,000 people during the Civil War era. But unlike most gold mining boom communities from that era, the Boise Basin didn't die out completely. The main community there, Idaho City, is much smaller but very much alive and a wonderful stop for visitors looking for a sense of what the Old West was like. The main street in town still looks (if you mentally eliminate the motor vehicles) a lot like it did so many years ago. The little community of Placerville, a few miles away on a gravel road, is also worth a look. As you drive around the Boise Basin, you'll see massive piles of rocks—the remnants of the placer mining in the area, most of it more than a century old.

For all that human habitation, most of the land in the Boise Basin is managed by the Boise National Forest, and the campgrounds it manages are among the most popular with people in the Boise valley. Get there early.

For more information:

Idaho City Chamber of Commerce
180 Main Street
Idaho City, ID 83631
(208) 392–4148
www.idahocitychamber.com

Boise National Forest
1249 South Vinnell Way
Boise, ID 83709
(208) 373–4100
www.fs.fed.us/r4/boise

1 Neinmeyer

Location: Northeast of Boise
Sites: 8
Facilities: Vault toilets, fire rings, tables
Fee per night: None
Elevation: 4,600 feet
Road conditions: Beyond Idaho Highway 21 this is gravel road whose condition varies from time to time. Prone to washboards, much of it is flat and well graded, usually. But a call ahead may be advisable.
Management: Forest Service, Idaho City Ranger District, (208) 259–3361
Reservations: No

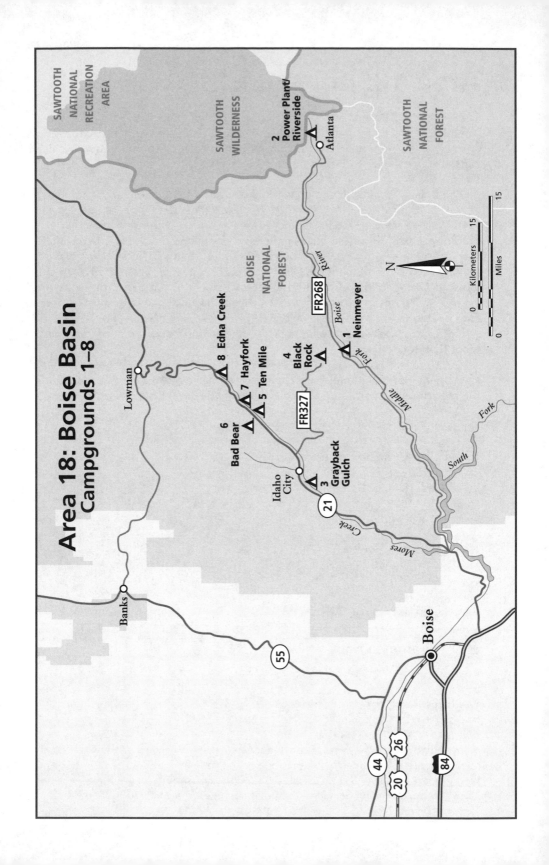

Area 18: Boise Basin
Campgrounds 1–8

Area 18

	Town	Sites	Max. RV length	Electric	Picnic	Fire rings	Toilets	Showers	Water	Dump station	Disability access	Recreation	Can reserve	Fees ($)	Season	Stay limit (days)
1 Neinmeyer	Atlanta	8	22		•	•	V					F			May–Oct.	14
2 Power Plant/ Riverside	Atlanta	24	22		•	•	V		•			FH			June–Oct.	14
3 Grayback Gulch	Idaho City	20	30		•	•	V		•			FS	•	$$	May–Oct.	14
4 Black Rock	Idaho City	11	22		•	•	V		•			FS	•	$	June–Oct.	14
5 Ten Mile	Idaho City	15	22		•	•	V		•			FH		$$	June–Oct.	14
6 Bad Bear	Idaho City	6	22		•	•	V		•			FH		$$	June–Oct.	14
7 Hayfork	Idaho City	7	22		•	•	V		•			F	•	$	June–Oct.	14
8 Edna Creek	Idaho City	9	24		•	•	V		•			FH		$	June–Oct.	14

Activities: Fishing, picnicking
Season: May 25–October 1
Finding the campground: From Boise drive northeast on ID 21 (Warm Springs Avenue) to Lucky Peak Reservoir; turn east at Spring Shores on Forest Road 268 (the road to Atlanta), and continue about 35 miles to the campground.
The campground: The camping area overlooks the Middle Fork of the Boise River, a prime fishing location, and the sites are under cover of ponderosa pine. The campground has no drinking water, so pack your own.

2 Power Plant/Riverside

Location: Northeast of Boise
Sites: 24
Facilities: Drinking water, vault toilets, fire rings
Fee per night: None
Elevation: 5,700 feet
Road conditions: Beyond ID 21 this is gravel road whose condition varies from time to time. Prone to washboards, much of it is flat and well graded, usually. But a call ahead may be advisable.
Management: Forest Service, Idaho City Ranger District, (208) 259–3361
Reservations: No
Activities: Fishing, hiking, picnicking
Season: June 1–October 1
Finding the campground: From Boise drive northeast on ID 21 (Warm Springs Avenue) to Lucky Peak Reservoir; turn east at Spring Shores on FR 268 (the road to Atlanta), and continue about 60 miles to Atlanta. The campground is 1.5 miles northeast of Atlanta on FR 268.
The campground: Getting there is a serious trek into the backcountry, but the rewards are many. The camping site is in a wooded and meadows area

close to the Middle Fork of the Boise River, a great fishing area, and close as well to hot springs and to the lively little community of Atlanta. There are stories behind the real power plant after which this campground is named, too, since the dam on the river near Atlanta has been a power generator for decades. Watch for wildlife under the red fir and ponderosa pine. There is also another Atlanta-area campground called Riverside, where the same conditions generally apply.

3 Grayback Gulch

Location: South of Idaho City
Sites: 20
Facilities: Drinking water, vault toilets, fire rings
Fee per night: $$
Elevation: 4,000 feet
Road conditions: Paved except for the entrance to the campground
Management: Forest Service, Idaho City Ranger District, (208) 259–3361
Reservations: Call (877) 444–6777 or visit Web site www.reserveamerica.com.
Activities: Fishing, picnicking, swimming
Season: May 1–October 31
Finding the campground: From Idaho City drive 2.4 miles south on ID 21, and then look for the sign to the campground on the east side of the road.
The campground: This is a "family" camping site, oriented toward groups— and in some sites multifamily groups. (There are fifteen single-family units and three multifamily units.) Camping is comfortably spread out under the tall ponderosa pines.

4 Black Rock

Location: Northeast of Idaho City
Sites: 11
Facilities: Drinking water, vault toilets, fire rings
Fee per night: $
Elevation: 5,300 feet
Road conditions: Dusty gravel road but generally kept in good condition, passable for RVs
Management: Forest Service, Idaho City Ranger District, (208) 259–3361
Reservations: Call (877) 444–6777 or visit Web site www.reserveamerica.com.
Activities: Fishing, picnicking, swimming
Season: June 1–October 15
Finding the campground: From Idaho City drive 2 miles northeast on ID 21 and then 18 miles east on Forest Road 327.
The campground: As one of the campgrounds within an easy drive from Boise (it's 37 miles from Boise to Idaho City), this one tends to fill up early on weekends, so plan accordingly. It's a pretty wooded camping area, like most in this region. Although well off the highway, this is a well-developed campground, with concrete cooking areas and a water system.

5 Ten Mile

Location: Northeast of Idaho City
Sites: 15
Facilities: Drinking water (from hand pumps), vault toilets, fire rings, picnic tables, recycling bins
Fee per night: $$, but $$$ for multifamily units
Elevation: 5,000 feet
Road conditions: Paved two-lane highway to the campground, but sometimes treacherous in winter
Management: Boise National Forest, Idaho City Ranger District, (208) 259–3361
Reservations: No
Activities: Fishing, hiking, picnicking, scenic walks and drives
Season: June–October
Finding the campground: From Idaho City drive 9.1 miles northeast on ID 21.
The campground: Despite its name, the Ten Mile campground is located a little over 9 miles northeast of Idaho City. Although located adjacent to ID 21, the campground feels shielded from the roadway traffic (which ordinarily is not very busy anyway). Ten Mile is split almost evenly in two parts; the entry gates face each other across the highway. This is forested mountain country, with plenty of ponderosa pine and Douglas fir cover. The campsites are well spaced from each other. There are no hookups. RVs are allowed, but trailer length is limited to 22 feet. Ten Mile Creek and Mores Creek form part of the border for the campground, and fishing is allowed in the area.

6 Bad Bear

Location: Northeast of Idaho City
Sites: 6
Facilities: Drinking water (from hand pumps), vault toilets, fire rings, picnic tables, recycling bins
Fee per night: $$, but $$$ for multifamily units
Elevation: 5,200 feet
Road conditions: Paved two-lane highway to the campground, but sometimes treacherous in winter
Management: Boise National Forest, Idaho City Ranger District, (208) 259–3361
Reservations: No
Activities: Fishing, hiking, picnicking, scenic walks and drives
Season: June–October
Finding the campground: From Idaho City drive northeast on ID 21 about 9.3 miles; enter the campground from the highway.
The campground: This is a small campground, meaning—given its location near the Boise metro area—it is quieter and less crowded than some. Camping sites are a little farther away from ID 21 than are those at the nearby Ten Mile

campground, though access still is close. It is backed up against hillsides, and Bad Bear Creek bubbles against the back of it. Several fine hiking trails take off from the campground. The area is wooded—mainly with Douglas fir and ponderosa pine—and mountainous, so while hikes in the area are rewarding, they also are for the energetic.

7 Hayfork

Location: Northeast of Idaho City
Sites: 7
Facilities: Drinking water, vault toilets, fire rings
Fee per night: $$–$$$ (sometimes more for larger groups)
Elevation: 5,200 feet
Road conditions: Paved highway up to the campground
Management: Forest Service, Idaho City Ranger District, (208) 259–3361
Reservations: Call (877) 444–6777 or visit Web site www.reserveamerica.com.
Activities: Fishing, picnicking
Season: June 1–October 15
Finding the campground: From Idaho City drive 10 miles northeast on ID 21.
The campground: Look at this as a good possibility if you're camping with a lot of people—about fifty or so. That's what this campground is intended for, but individuals can use it as well when groups aren't there. Reservations are strongly advised.

8 Edna Creek

Location: North of Idaho City, halfway to Lowman
Sites: 9
Facilities: Drinking water, vault toilets, fire rings, pull-through sites, equestrian campground
Fee per night: $
Elevation: 5,400 feet
Road conditions: Good paved highway all the way up, but watch for the switchbacks.
Management: Forest Service, Idaho City Ranger District, (208) 259–3361
Reservations: No
Activities: Fishing, hiking, picnicking
Season: June 1–October 15
Finding the campground: From Idaho City drive 18 miles northeast on ID 21.
The campground: This is a simple, well-designed, forested campsite located near the Whoop-em-up ski area, with Whoop-em-up Creek running through the grounds and Edna Creek running nearby. It is adjacent to ID 21, however, and the traffic on that road is very much visible and audible. Three of the campsites are for groups.

Area 19: Southwest

The southwest corner of Idaho—which includes the cities of Boise, Nampa, and Caldwell and points south and west to the Oregon and Nevada borders—is large and varied, well worth exploring, and almost devoid of public campgrounds.

The Boise-Nampa-Caldwell area is Idaho's major urban area, where more than a third of Idaho's residents live. Recreation opportunities close in are plentiful, from skiing at Bogus Basin in the mountains overlooking Boise to floating the Boise River that cuts through town. Boise is the center of many events and activities, such as the River Festival each June, and it has an expanding nightlife as well. Boise has numerous private campgrounds, and several can be found outside of that city throughout the area.

Less than an hour south of the city lie the remote Owyhee Mountains, site of one of Idaho's earliest and most spectacular mining booms. Thousands of people poured into the Silver City area deep in the Owyhees (that name is said to be a corruption of *Hawaii*), and for several decades late in the nineteenth century, precious metals were extracted. But the area fell into decline throughout the next century, and Silver City remains today as something akin to a ghost town, though some weekend residents do occupy some of the old buildings there, and a few businesses—including a revival of an old hotel—service the tourists who stop to visit.

One of the two formal public campgrounds in the area is located in the mountains east of Silver City. But many people camp at remote locations across the Owyhees, a vast region managed mainly by the Bureau of Land Management and containing very few human residents. It is popular among hikers and among enthusiasts of remote rivers. The Owyhee Canyonlands is not one of the most easily accessible parts of Idaho, but those interested in desert rivers consider it to be among the most spectacular in the nation.

One entry here, located in the middle of the Boise metro area, falls into a gray area. The On the River RV Park is operated by a private business but located on Ada County property, next door to the Western Idaho Fairgrounds (at Garden City), which is owned and operated by Ada County.

For more information:

Bureau of Land Management
1387 Vinnell Way
Boise, ID 83705
(208) 373-4000

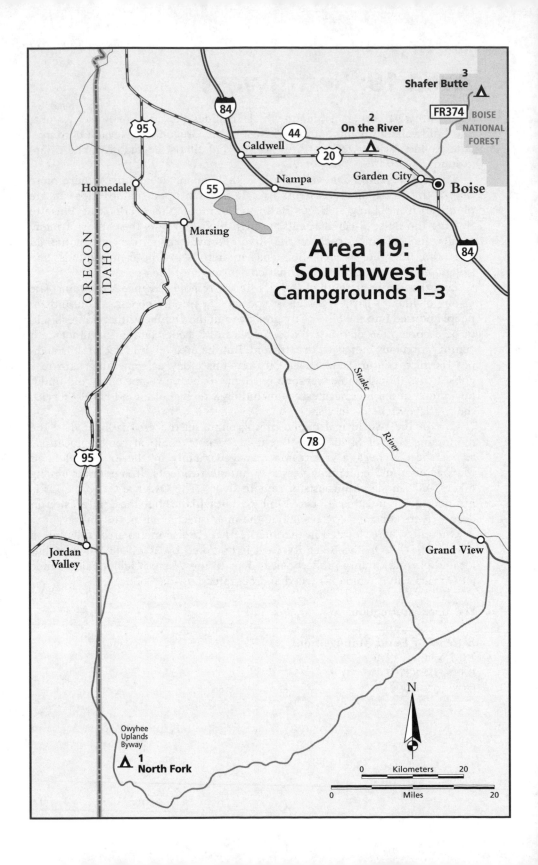

3
Shafer Butte △

FR374 BOISE
NATIONAL
FOREST

84

44   2
On the River

Caldwell   20   △

Nampa   Garden City   ● Boise

95

Homedale ●

55

● Marsing

84

Area 19:
Southwest
Campgrounds 1–3

Snake

78

River

95

Jordan
Valley ●   Grand View ●

OREGON | IDAHO

Owyhee
Uplands
Byway
△ 1
North Fork

N

0   Kilometers   20

0   Miles   20

Area 19

	Town	Sites	Max. RV length	Electric	Picnic	Fire rings	Toilets	Showers	Water	Dump station	Disability access	Recreation	Can reserve	Fees ($)	Season	Stay limit (days)
1 North Fork	Jordan Valley, OR	7	16			•	V					FH			April–Oct.	7
2 On the River	Boise	100	40	•	•	•	F	•	•	•	•	FHS	•	$$$	April–Oct.	
3 Shafer Butte	Boise	7	22		•	•	V			•		H	•	$$	June–Oct.	14

1 North Fork

Location: South of Jordan Valley, Oregon
Sites: 7
Facilities: Vault toilets, fire rings
Fee per night: None
Elevation: 3,250 feet
Road conditions: Time to crank up the four-wheel drive. Once you leave U.S. Highway 95, you're on rugged gravel and dirt road, and in this country the ride on such pathways tends to be rugged. Make sure you have high clearance and a spare tire, and allow plenty of time to cover those 30 miles.
Management: Bureau of Land Management, Owyhee Field Office, (208) 384–3300
Reservations: No
Activities: Fishing, hiking
Season: April 15–October 31
Finding the campground: The best access is through Jordan Valley, Oregon, which is about 32 miles south of Marsing on US 95. From Jordan Valley drive generally south on Deep Creek Road, the Owyhee Uplands Byway, for 27 miles.
The campground: Here's a true desert canyon campground, tucked in the canyon of the North Fork of the Owyhee River. Camping, picnicking, and hiking are favored here. There's a seven-day camping limit. Be aware before setting out that you're well upward of an hour from supplies—including drinking water, which the campground does not have—and civilization.

2 On the River

Location: Garden City, north of Boise
Sites: 100
Facilities: Drinking water, utility hookups (including electric and cable), laundry, barbecue area, flush toilets, showers, fire rings, dump station, barrier-free access, propane available
Fee per night: $$$
Elevation: 3,250 feet

Road conditions: Mostly paved (all paved up to the campground); some spots within this urban campground are gravel.
Management: Ada County/private
Reservations: Call (208) 375–7432.
Activities: Fishing, hiking, picnicking, swimming
Season: April 15–October 31
Finding the campground: From the downtown area of Boise, take U.S. Highway 20/26 northwest for 4 miles as it turns into Chinden Boulevard. At Glenwood Boulevard turn right and drive 1 mile to the campground.
The campground: The manager says this isn't even a gray area—this campground is private, and operated without governmental involvement. It looks and feels and is set up like a fully modern, private-style campground, oriented mainly toward—but not limited to—visitors to or exhibitors at the Western Idaho Fairgrounds, which is located next door. (During the weeks of the fair in August, this campground generally is booked far in advance.) However, it is located on Ada County land (which is leased), and the county informally considers it a county campground. In appearance, it is partly sunny, partly shady, in a nicely secluded area on the south bank of the Boise River, in the middle of the Ada County urban area. The Boise River Greenbelt runs next to the campground, and it extends next to the river for miles west and east of the city.

3 Shafer Butte

Location: North of Boise
Sites: 7 (5 reservable, 2 first come, first served)
Facilities: Drinking water, vault toilets, fire rings, pull-through sites
Fee per night: $$
Elevation: 7,000 feet
Road conditions: Paved up to Bogus Basin, generally good gravel road from there to the campground
Management: Forest Service, Mountain Home Ranger District, (208) 587–7961
Reservations: Call (877) 444–6777 or visit Web site www.reserveamerica.com.
Activities: Hiking, picnicking
Season: June–October (depending on weather)
Finding the campground: From Boise drive 16 miles northeast on Bogus Basin Road, then 3 miles north on Forest Road 374, and then 1.5 miles east on Shafer Butte Road.
The campground: This is the federal campground closest to Idaho's largest metropolitan area, and it gets plenty of use. At 7,000 feet Boiseans can rise above the atmosphere of the city and see clear blue sky on days when inversion strikes below; many Boiseans already accustomed to skiing at Bogus Basin Ski Area (which is not far away, and en route here) have trekked the few extra miles to Shafer Butte to the attractive camping area.

[FACING PAGE] *Fishing on the Owyhee River in the southwest corner of the state (Photo by Linda Watkins)*

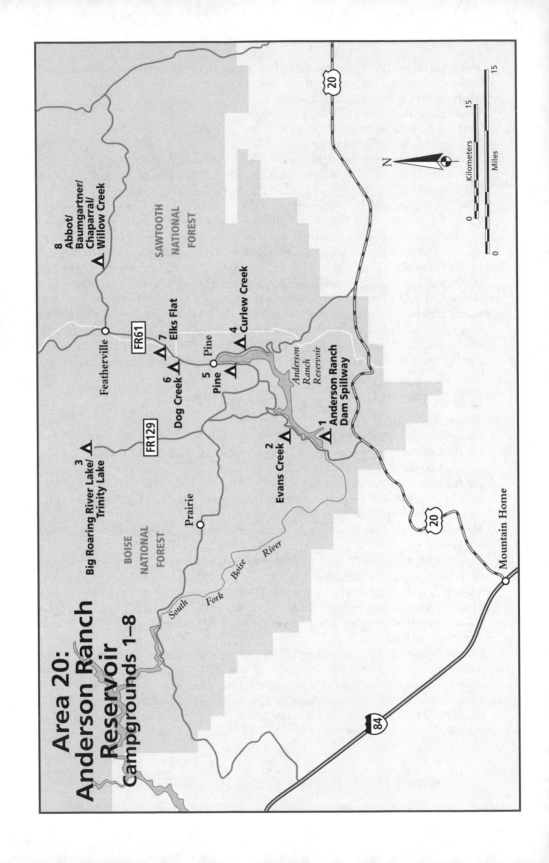

Area 20:
Anderson Ranch Reservoir

Among the regions containing the source water of the Boise River, some are very remote, but the Anderson Ranch Dam area is relatively easy to reach, and a sizable portion of the people in the Mountain Home area go there, to the communities of Pine and Featherville, regularly for weekend or longer recreation.

The area is easy to reach on relatively good roads. From Mountain Home drive north into the mountains on U.S. Highway 20; there are two cutoffs to the left, one on paved road and one on gravel, leading to the reservoir. The paved Pine-Featherville Road (the second choice) is an easy and fast run north, all the way to Featherville.

Although desert country leads up to the reservoir area, the camping regions are pleasantly forested, and hiking, fishing, and boating all are popular here. High up in the mountains, the temperature tends to be considerably lower in the summer than down in the hot Treasure Valley at Mountain Home.

For more information:

Boise National Forest
1249 South Vinnell Way
Boise, ID 83709
(208) 373–4100
www.fs.fed.us/r4/boise

Area 20

		Town	Sites	Max. RV length	Electric	Picnic	Fire rings	Toilets	Showers	Water	Dump station	Disability access	Recreation	Can reserve	Fees ($)	Season	Stay limit (days)
1	Anderson Ranch Dam Spillway	Mountain Home	3	32		•	•	V		•			BFHS			May–Oct.	14
2	Evans Creek	Featherville	8	32		•	•	V					FH			May–Oct.	14
3	Big Roaring River Lake/ Trinity Lake	Pine	16	22		•	•	V				•	FH		$$	June–Sept.	14
4	Curlew Creek	Pine	10	32		•	•	V		•			BF		$	May–Sept.	14
5	Pine	Pine	7	32		•	•	V					BF		$$–$$$	May–Sept.	14
6	Dog Creek	Pine	12	22		•	•	V		•			F	•	$	May–Oct.	14
7	Elks Flat	Pine	35	55		•	•	V		•			FH	•	$$	May–Oct.	14
8	Abbot/ Baumgartner/ Chaparral/ Willow Creek	Featherville	36	38		•	•	V		•		•	FHS	•		May–Sept.	14

1 Anderson Ranch Dam Spillway

Location: East of Pine
Sites: 3
Facilities: Drinking water, vault toilets, fire rings, pull-through sites, pets allowed
Fee per night: None
Elevation: 4,750 feet
Road conditions: Paved to within a couple of miles of Anderson Ranch Dam; the dirt and gravel road to the dam (where the campground is located) is somewhat steep but wide and an easy drive, even with an RV.
Management: Forest Service, Mountain Home Ranger District, (208) 587–7961
Reservations: No
Activities: Boating, fishing, hiking, picnicking, swimming
Season: May 1–October 30 (depending on weather)
Finding the campground: From Mountain Home drive 22 miles on US 20 northeast, take the first road north that points to Anderson Ranch Dam (the Anderson Ranch Dam Road, also designated Forest Road 61), and then go about 12 miles north. The campground can also be reached from Pine, but that narrow gravel road is a relatively exhausting journey.
The campground: This is an unusual site, a recreation area located just next to a large dam. Most of this area is just day use, for picnicking and hiking, but camping is permitted in a few designated spots. The landscape has only occasional trees (shade can be had, though this isn't a forested mountainside), and the ground is rocky. But the view of the reservoir can't be beat. Just pull up a chair, stare at the water reaching off into the distance, and bliss out.

2 Evans Creek

Location: Near Featherville
Sites: 8
Facilities: Vault toilets, fire grills, pull-through sites, pets allowed
Fee per night: None
Elevation: 4,850 feet
Road conditions: Moderately rugged. RVs and trailers are manageable for experienced backcountry drivers, but be aware that the path here is on sometimes narrow and often twisting gravel roads of variable quality (sometimes washboard-laden) and hugging the sides of mountains; the reservoir is a steep drop in some places. Plan to take your time getting here in the few miles from Anderson Ranch Dam (the road that far from US 20 is very good).
Management: Forest Service, Mountain Home Ranger District, (208) 587–7961
Reservations: No

[FACING PAGE] *Anderson Ranch Dam northeast of Mountain Home. Campgrounds are sprinkled along the banks of the reservoir in the background; the only access to some of them is the narrow lakeside road visible to the left.*

Activities: Fishing, hiking, picnicking
Season: May 15–October 1
Finding the campground: From Mountain Home drive 20 miles northeast on US 20; turn left on the first road to Anderson Ranch Dam (the Anderson Ranch Dam Road), and then continue 16 miles north and east along the reservoir.
The campground: A basic campground in a small crook of an inlet of the Anderson Ranch Reservoir. There's a good view (but not one of the best) of the reservoir from here; boat launching is available in the area. Campsites are mostly shady.

3 Big Roaring River Lake/Trinity Lake

Location: West of Pine
Sites: 16
Facilities: Drinking water, vault toilets, fire rings, barrier-free access
Fee per night: $$ at Big Roaring River Lake, no fee at Trinity
Elevation: 5,500 feet
Road conditions: Sometimes rough gravel. This is an OK drive for a pickup or SUV, a little more challenging for anyone hauling a trailer (but passable and not hard for experienced backcountry drivers). North of Anderson Ranch Dam, there are some narrow and twisting sections, so drive carefully.
Management: Forest Service, Fairfield Ranger District, (208) 764–2202
Reservations: No
Activities: Fishing, hiking, picnicking
Season: Variable, often from June through September (but call ahead)
Finding the campgrounds: From Mountain Home drive 27 miles on US 20 northeast, then 29 miles northeast on FR 61, then 15 miles northwest on Forest Road 172, and finally 3 miles south on Forest Road 129.
The campgrounds: These campgrounds are deep in the Boise Mountains, a truly remote area even for veteran Idaho campers. The Trinity Mountain peaks, visible from this area, are among the most spectacular in the state. Expect slow travel once you cross the Anderson Ranch Dam, and expect some sharp climbs. The scenery, as pristine as anything in Idaho, will make up for it. The campground is pretty, but be sure to bring what you need (and remember that the pack it in–pack it out ethic is especially important in hard-to-get-to places like this).

4 Curlew Creek

Location: South of Pine
Sites: 10
Facilities: Drinking water, vault toilets, fire rings, dump station, pets allowed
Fee per night: $
Elevation: 4,850 feet
Road conditions: Paved up to and partially within the campground
Management: Forest Service, Mountain Home Ranger District, (208) 587–7961

Reservations: No
Activities: Boating, fishing, picnicking
Season: May 1–September 30
Finding the campground: From Mountain Home drive 32 miles on US 20 northeast and then turn left (north) onto FR 61 (the Pine-Featherville Road, the second road to Pine) and continue 22 miles north.
The campground: On the sloping banks of the Anderson Ranch Dam Reservoir is a campground made for boaters. There are occasional trees (though much of the campground can bake in the summer sun), but the draw here is the lakefront. It's a popular spot with boaters from Mountain Home, so get here early if you're planning a weekend.

5 Pine

Location: Southeast of Pine
Sites: 7
Facilities: Tables with shade covers, vault toilets, fire rings
Fee per night: $$
Elevation: 4,850 feet
Road conditions: Via the Pine-Featherville Road from US 20, it's paved all the way, with near-highway speeds possible; the road southwest of Pine is nearly as good.
Management: Forest Service, Mountain Home Ranger District, (208) 587-7961
Reservations: No
Activities: Boating, fishing, picnicking
Season: May 20–September 30
Finding the campground: From Pine drive 3.1 miles southwest on the Prairie Road.
The campground: The operative word here is *boating*—that is the reason to camp here. The campground has shaded tables, but the campground site is out in the sun, beach-style. However, there are fine boat launches here (when the reservoir water levels are high enough); this recreation area is comanaged (with the Forest Service) by the Elmore County Waterways Commission. There's also an airplane landing strip about a quarter mile away. The road is paved up to the campground, which lies between the road and the reservoir. (On the other side of the road is a new housing development, which may help explain the paving up to this point.) Bring your own drinking water; this campground has none.

6 Dog Creek

Location: Between Pine and Featherville
Sites: 12
Facilities: Drinking water, vault toilets, fire rings
Fee per night: $$–$$$
Elevation: 4,950 feet
Road conditions: Excellent, paved all the way

Management: Forest Service, Fairfield Ranger District, (208) 764–2202
Reservations: Call (877) 444–6777 or visit Web site www.reserveamerica.com.
Activities: Fishing, picnicking
Season: May 15–October 1
Finding the campground: From Mountain Home drive 34 miles on US 20 northeast and then 24 miles north on FR 61 (the Pine-Featherville Road). The campground is about 3 miles north of Pine.
The campground: Years ago the Pine-Featherville Road was a slow, dusty, and washboarded misery for the hundreds (sometimes thousands) of people who roared up to the reservoir every Friday to come to their weekend homes in the summer. That road is a whole new world now, paved all the way from US 20 to Featherville, a fast drive and a pretty one, too. Dog Creek is located north of the reservoir but just a quarter mile from the South Fork of the Boise River, under cover of big ponderosa pines. All of these sites are well designated for tent camping (though RVs are OK as well), and drinking water is available.

7 Elks Flat

Location: Between Pine and Featherville
Sites: 35
Facilities: Drinking water, vault toilets, fire rings, pull-through sites, pets allowed
Fee per night: $$–$$$
Elevation: 4,850 feet
Road conditions: Excellent paved road all the way from US 20
Management: Forest Service, Mountain Home Ranger District, (208) 587–7961
Reservations: Call (877) 444–6777 or visit Web site www.reserveamerica.com; group sites available.
Activities: Fishing, hiking, picnicking
Season: May 15–October 1
Finding the campground: From Mountain Home drive 29 miles on US 20 northeast and then 22 miles northeast on FR 61 (the Pine-Featherville Road); the campground is 4.5 miles north of Pine.
The campground: One of the larger campgrounds in the Anderson Ranch area, this is a mostly flat grounds in a grass meadows, with trees (Douglas fir, ponderosa pine, cottonwoods) all around, at streamside on the South Fork of the Boise River. It's a standard Forest Service campground but with more facilities than most. A public telephone is available (most cellular phone reception is out of the question in this country). Elks Flat is designed for comfortable camping at both ends of the spectrum, from small-scale tenters (some sites are designed as tent pads) to groups (reservations for large groups are advised).

8 Abbot/Baumgartner/Chaparral/Willow Creek

Location: East of Featherville
Sites: 36 (split about evenly among the four campgrounds)
Facilities: Drinking water, vault toilets, fire rings, pets allowed, limited access
Fee per night: None
Elevation: 4,900 feet
Road conditions: Rough, in the final miles east of Featherville. The Forest Service suggests that RVs not be brought onto the Middle Fork Road; check to see that your vehicle has high clearance and is in good condition before setting out east from Featherville.
Management: Forest Service, Fairfield Ranger District, (208) 764–2202
Reservations: Available at Baumgartner only. Call (877) 444–6777 or visit Web site www.reserveamerica.com.
Activities: Fishing, hiking, picnicking, swimming
Season: May 20–September 28
Finding the campgrounds: From Featherville drive 12 miles east on Forest Road 227 (the Middle Fork Road).
The campgrounds: Abbot is east of Featherville on the South Fork of the Boise River. Baumgartner, Chaparral, and Willow Creek are separate campgrounds but located near one another, all on the Middle Fork of the Boise River. These campgrounds do have drinking water but few other commercial amenities; tenting (rather than RVing) is recommended here. The natural amenities compensate: This is one of Idaho's best fly-fishing areas (though not one of its best known). The landscape in this region is lushly forested, and the atmosphere high mountain. Many visitors find it one of Idaho's premier getaways.

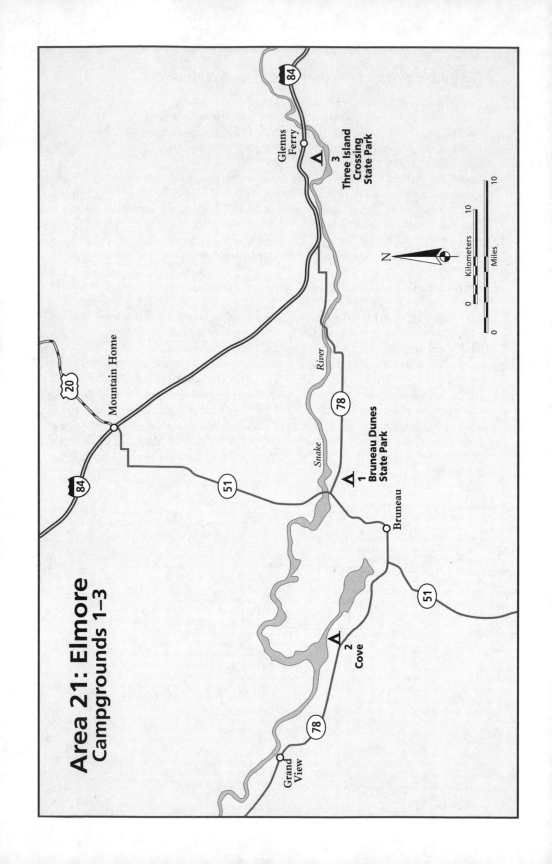

Area 21: Elmore
Campgrounds 1–3

84

20 Mountain Home

84

51

Snake

River

78

Glenns
Ferry

84

Three Island
Crossing
State Park
3

Bruneau Dunes
State Park
1

Bruneau

Cove
2

78

Grand
View

51

51

N

Kilometers 0   10

Miles 0   10

Area 21: Elmore

The valley area between Mountain Home and the Owyhee Mountains to the south is true western desert—sagebrush and all. Much of it looks unchanged since the Oregon Trail pioneers crossed it more than 150 years ago, though there are signs of the newer West as well, such as the Mountain Home Air Force Base (Idaho's major military installation) and the massive livestock feedlots near Bruneau.

There's plenty to see here, though you do have to know where to look.

The most popular destination is the Bruneau Sand Dunes, the most spectacular dunes in Idaho (there are a few other smaller ones). Partly because of the distance from city lights, this also is a popular hangout for those interested in astronomy.

The most popular event, however, is the Three Island Crossing reenacted each summer at Three Island State Park at Glenns Ferry. This is where Oregon Trail pioneers crossed—or tried to cross—the Snake River, sometimes with disastrous results.

For more information:

Mountain Home Chamber of Commerce
205 North Third East
Mountain Home, ID 83647
(208) 587-4334
www.mtnhome.org

Area 21

		Town	Sites	Max. RV length	Electric	Picnic	Fire rings	Toilets	Showers	Water	Dump station	Disability access	Recreation	Can reserve	Fees ($)	Season	Stay limit (days)
1	**Bruneau Dunes State Park**	Bruneau	73	70	•	•	•	F	•	•		•	FHS	•	$$–$$$	Year-round	
2	**Cove**	Bruneau	26	25		•	•	V		•			BFHS	•	$	April–Oct.	14
3	**Three Island Crossing State Park**	Glenns Ferry	101	60	•	•	•	F	•	•	•		FH		$	Year-round	

1 Bruneau Dunes State Park

Location: East of Bruneau
Sites: 73
Facilities: Drinking water, electric and water hookups, flush toilets, showers, fire rings, barrier-free access
Fee per night: $$–$$$
Elevation: 2,500 feet
Road conditions: Paved into the park
Management: Idaho Department of Parks and Recreation, (208) 366–7919
Reservations: Available via Web site www.idahoparks.org
Activities: Fishing, hiking, picnicking, swimming
Season: All year, technically; as a practical matter, May 1 through October 31 (depending on weather)
Finding the campground: From Mountain Home drive 18 miles south on Idaho Highway 51 into Bruneau and then 2 miles east on Idaho Highway 78.
The campground: This is a grassy area out in the desert. You didn't expect forests in a park renowned for its sand dunes, did you? The campground, which is relatively modern and has both electric and water hookups, is about a half mile from the nearest of the sand dunes and an easy walk to the rest. Boating and swimming are available at Dunes Lake in the park.

2 Cove

Location: West of Bruneau
Sites: 26
Facilities: Drinking water, vault toilets, fire rings, pull-through sites
Fee per night: $
Elevation: 2,900 feet
Road conditions: Paved up to the campground
Management: Bureau of Land Management, Boise Office, (208) 384–3300
Reservations: Call (208) 384–3300.
Activities: Boating, fishing, hiking, picnicking, swimming
Season: Year-round
Finding the campground: From Bruneau drive 7 miles west on ID 78.
The campground: This campground puts you well within the Birds of Prey National Conservation Area—but don't worry, it's safe. You're just off the highway (and not far from supplies), but the great canyon vistas give you the definite feeling of being way out there. Birds of prey certainly can be seen here; fishing, boating, and hiking also are popular. This is a newly renovated campground with extensive facilities and easy pull-throughs for RVs. Swimming and Jet Skiing are allowed, as are pets.

3 Three Island Crossing State Park

Location: West of Glenns Ferry
Sites: 101
Facilities: Drinking water, dump station, electric hookups, flush toilets, showers, fire rings
Fee per night: $
Elevation: 2,560 feet
Road conditions: Paved to the campground
Management: Idaho Department of Parks and Recreation, (208) 366–2394
Reservations: Available via Web site www.idahoparks.org
Activities: Fishing, hiking, picnicking
Season: All year, technically; as a practical matter, May 1 through October 31 (depending on weather)
Finding the campground: From Mountain Home go east on Interstate 84 for 23 miles to Glenns Ferry. From downtown Glenns Ferry follow Madison Street 2 miles west along the river.
The campground: One of just a handful of public campgrounds along the Snake River, and one of the largest state campgrounds in Idaho, this is a full-service campground with modern conveniences and a historic location. At this point on the Snake River, Oregon Trail travelers would cross—or try to cross—the river with their covered wagons, this being deemed the best point on the Snake River to do so. Most made it, some didn't. Summer celebrations of those efforts are scheduled nowadays, and convenience is the order of the day. The campground is mildly shaded but mostly open-air with a good view of the river.

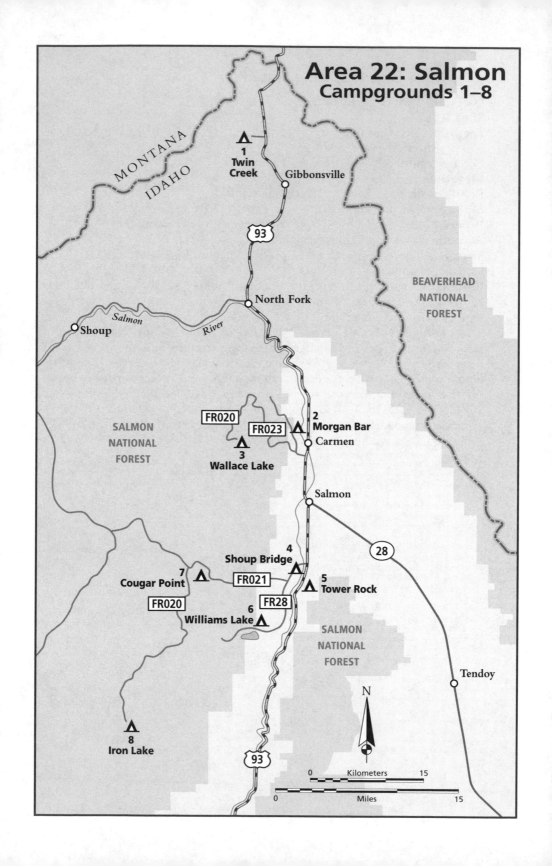

Area 22: Salmon
Campgrounds 1–8

MONTANA
IDAHO

△
1
Twin
Creek

Gibbonsville

93

BEAVERHEAD
NATIONAL
FOREST

North Fork

Salmon River

Shoup

SALMON
NATIONAL
FOREST

FR020
FR023

2 △ Morgan Bar
Carmen

△
3
Wallace Lake

Salmon

4
Shoup Bridge

FR021

7 △
Cougar Point

△
5
Tower Rock

FR020

FR28

6
Williams Lake △

SALMON
NATIONAL
FOREST

Tendoy

28

△
8
Iron Lake

93

N

0   Kilometers   15

0   Miles   15

Central Idaho

Area 22: Salmon

At the point where the Salmon River—the "River of No Return"—ends its flow to the northeast and turns west, toward its eventual merger with the Snake River, the city of Salmon was founded as a depot for people working in the mining, timber, and ranching industries. Salmon remains such a place, but increasingly it is also a recreation center, with outfitters and guides among the leading businesses in this small town.

From Salmon and North Fork the adventurous can put in on the long, lively river ride down the Salmon River to Vinegar Creek just east of Riggins, where most of these trips—often lasting five days—"take out" of the river.

Even without setting out on such an extensive trip, the Salmon area is full of recreation opportunity. Hunting and fishing are big activities throughout the region and a primary purpose for many people who visit the many public campgrounds in the area.

For more information:

Salmon Valley Chamber of Commerce
200 Main Street
Salmon, ID 83467
(208) 756–2100
www.salmoninternet.com

Salmon-Challis National Forest
Route 2, Box 600
Salmon, ID 83467
(208) 756–5100
www.fs.fed.us/r4/sc

---

1 Twin Creek

Location: Northwest of Gibbonsville
Sites: 46
Facilities: Drinking water, vault toilets, fire rings
Fee per night: $
Elevation: 6,600 feet
Road conditions: Paved to the last half mile, good gravel within
Management: Forest Service, Salmon/Cobalt Ranger Districts, (208) 756–5100
Reservations: No
Activities: Fishing, hiking, picnicking

Area 22

Town	Sites	Max. RV length	Electric	Picnic	Fire rings	Toilets	Showers	Water	Dump station	Disability access	Recreation	Can reserve	Fees ($)	Season	Stay limit (days)
1 Twin Creek	Gibbons- ville	46	32		•	•	V		•			FH		$	June–Sept.	14
2 Morgan Bar	Salmon	8	28		•	•	V		•			BFHS		$	April–Oct.	14
3 Wallace Lake	Salmon	12	16		•	•	V		•			BF		$	June–Sept.	14
4 Shoup Bridge	Salmon	5	28		•	•	V		•			BF	•	$	Year-round	14
5 Tower Rock	Salmon	6	28		•	•	V		•			BFS		$	April–Oct.	14
6 Williams Lake	Salmon	11	28		•	•	V		•			BFHS		$	May–Oct.	14
7 Cougar Point	Salmon	12	20		•	•	V		•			FH		$	June–Sept.	14
8 Iron Lake	Salmon	8	20		•	•	V		•			BF		$	July–Sept.	14

Season: June 1–September 15
Finding the campground: From Salmon drive 39 miles north on U.S. Highway 93 (past the Gibbonsville exit) and then half a mile northwest on Forest Road 449.
The campground: Twin Creek is close to the Lost Trail Pass, high in the Bitterroots among the subalpine firs and located along the like-named creek. This Forest Service site is a relatively flat woodsy area with well-spaced camping pads.

2 Morgan Bar

Location: North of Salmon
Sites: 8
Facilities: Drinking water, vault toilets, fire rings
Fee per night: $
Elevation: 4,050 feet
Road conditions: Excellent, paved almost to the campground
Management: Bureau of Land Management, Salmon Field Office, (208) 756-5400
Reservations: Campsites cannot be reserved, but the pavilion can be. Call the local BLM office at (208) 756-5400.
Activities: Boating, fishing, hiking, picnicking, swimming
Season: April 1–October 31
Finding the campground: From Salmon drive about 3 miles north on US 93 to the Lemhi County Fairgrounds, then turn left onto Diamond Creek Road and continue for 1.5 miles to the Snake River; the campground is on the right.
The campground: A prime site on the main Salmon River, near the city of Salmon, this is one of those campgrounds with a history, being the longtime homestead of the Morgan family. The family grew orchards, and some of the

descendant trees still are visible around the campground. Boating and swimming are easy here, and there's a wonderful view of the Beaverhead Mountains to the east. A couple of good hiking trails also are available.

3 Wallace Lake

Location: Northwest of Salmon
Sites: 12
Facilities: Drinking water, vault toilets, fire rings
Fee per night: $
Elevation: 8,800 feet
Road conditions: Generally good gravel travel and suitable for high-clearance cars and pickups. Tight switchbacks in some places could make this a rough ride for RVs and trailers; passable for experienced backcountry drivers but otherwise not recommended for larger vehicles.
Management: Forest Service, Salmon/Cobalt Ranger Districts, (208) 756–5100
Reservations: No
Activities: Boating, fishing, picnicking
Season: June 15–September 20
Finding the campground: From Salmon drive 3.2 miles north on US 93 to just south of Carmen, then 14 miles northwest on Forest Road 023 (Stormy Peak Road), then 4 miles south on Forest Road 020 (Ridge Road).
The campground: This is another high-mountain creekside location, remote enough to discourage all but the most determined hunters and anglers but a rewarding location for those campers.

4 Shoup Bridge

Location: South of Salmon
Sites: 5
Facilities: Drinking water, vault toilets, fire rings, boat launch
Fee per night: $
Elevation: 4,050 feet
Road conditions: Paved to the campground
Management: Bureau of Land Management, Salmon Field Office, (208) 756–5400
Reservations: Call (208) 756–5400.
Activities: Boating, fishing, picnicking
Season: All year, though practical use runs generally from late April through October
Finding the campground: From Salmon drive 5 miles south on US 93; enter the campground to the west from the highway.
The campground: Located on a narrow strip of ground between US 93 and the Salmon River, this is a small campground but a pretty one, well shaded beneath the trees and right on the riverbank. A boat launch is available. Shoup Bridge is one of the prettier BLM campgrounds and is kept with a relatively natural look.

5 Tower Rock

Location: South of Salmon
Sites: 6
Facilities: Drinking water, vault toilets, fire rings
Fee per night: $
Elevation: 4,000 feet
Road conditions: Good, paved nearly to the campground
Management: Bureau of Land Management, Salmon Field Office, (208) 756–5400
Reservations: No
Activities: Boating, fishing, picnicking, swimming
Season: April 1–October 31
Finding the campground: From Salmon drive 5 miles south on US 93 and then, as the BLM says, "look for the site on the left along the river and below the bluffs." Or just look for all the boaters.
The campground: Tower Rock is an aptly named site, with high rock cliffs all around. Meriwether Lewis and William Clark camped either on this campground or near it in 1805. Today, this is a major river put-in site and also a major Lewis and Clark Expedition bicentennial celebration location. The site was worked on and upgraded extensively in 2001; the campground is much more developed than previously. It is open-air, located in a meadow rather than a woods, but good for river recreation.

6 Williams Lake

Location: South of Salmon
Sites: 11
Facilities: Drinking water, vault toilets, fire rings, boat launch (nearby)
Fee per night: $
Elevation: 4,250 feet
Road conditions: There are some switchbacks over Williams Creek Summit, and the road is prone to washboards, but the 7-mile forest road here is wide and mostly easy to travel. All kinds of vehicles should have little difficulty with it.
Management: Forest Service, Salmon/Cobalt Ranger Districts, (208) 756–5100
Reservations: No
Activities: Boating, fishing, hiking, picnicking, swimming
Season: May 1–October 31
Finding the campground: From Salmon drive south 4 miles on US 93, then cross the Shoup Bridge, and drive 7 miles on Forest Road 28.
The campground: Here is an easy-access lakefront site on an easy-driving forest road—what more could you ask for? You'll not be surprised to learn this is a popular site, especially with boaters. The partly shaded campground, with well-spaced pads, is located on the northwest shore of the lake; a resort is located on the opposite side of the lake.

7 Cougar Point

Location: South of Salmon
Sites: 12
Facilities: Drinking water, vault toilets, fire rings
Fee per night: $
Elevation: 6,600 feet
Road conditions: Generally good, though pickups and RVs are preferred here
Management: Forest Service, Salmon/Cobalt Ranger Districts, (208) 756-5100
Reservations: No
Activities: Fishing, hunting, picnicking
Season: June 1–September 20
Finding the campground: From Salmon drive 5 miles south on US 93 and then 12 miles west on the Williams Creek Road (Forest Road 021) up into the mountains.
The campground: This is one of the more accessible campgrounds coming from Salmon; the forest road to the campground doesn't yet hit its most rugged spots. Good forest cover shades the sites, and this is a fine jumping-off point for hunting.

8 Iron Lake

Location: South of Salmon
Sites: 8
Facilities: Drinking water, vault toilets, fire rings
Fee per night: $
Elevation: 8,800 feet
Road conditions: Very rough in spots—rocky and pitted, narrow and steep. Take your pickup or other high-clearance vehicle, and take it slow.
Management: Forest Service, Salmon/Cobalt Ranger Districts, (208) 756-5100
Reservations: No
Activities: Boating, fishing, picnicking
Season: July 15–September 20
Finding the campground: From Salmon drive 5 miles south on US 93, then 12 miles west on the Williams Creek Road (FR 021), and then at Williams Summit turn left and go 21 miles south on FR 020.
The campground: Both tents and trailers are allowed here, but this is a very primitive site that takes quite a bit of work to get to. It is a well-forested location at the center of several trails, and the fishing location high up on Iron Creek (this campground is near its headwaters) as well as in Iron Lake (which is close by) is pristine. Plan to take a little while getting here, and be fully stocked before you come.

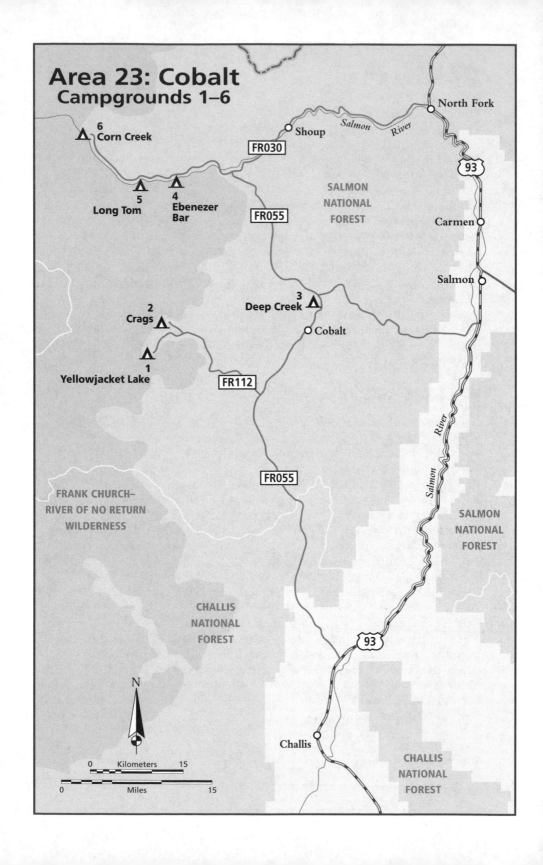

Area 23: Cobalt
Campgrounds 1–6

6
Corn Creek

Shoup

Salmon River

North Fork

FR030

US 93

SALMON
NATIONAL
FOREST

5
Long Tom

4
Ebenezer
Bar

FR055

Carmen

Salmon

2
Crags

3
Deep Creek

Cobalt

1
Yellowjacket Lake

FR112

FR055

FRANK CHURCH–
RIVER OF NO RETURN
WILDERNESS

Salmon River

SALMON
NATIONAL
FOREST

CHALLIS
NATIONAL
FOREST

US 93

N

0   Kilometers   15

0   Miles   15

Challis

CHALLIS
NATIONAL
FOREST

Area 23: Cobalt

The mountains west of Salmon were popular territory in the mining days when precious metals were routinely extracted at places such as Leesburg and Cobalt. Little of these communities remain now; several qualify as ghost towns. Hardly any people live in this region year-round—and not many more live here seasonally.

The backcountry gravel road through Cobalt and Shoup (the latter community named after Idaho's first governor) winds over and between spectacular mountains. It is one of the lesser-known and less-traveled recreation areas in Idaho, but that's because of its remoteness, not because of the quality of the area. If you have some time and want get seriously away from modern civilization, this may be just the place for you.

Almost all of the country in this area is in the Salmon-Challis National Forest, and a check with the ranger there about road and fire conditions is strongly advised before heading very deep into these backwoods.

A quick note about road travel through this country. There are no paved roads in it, excepting the road from North Fork to Shoup in the north and U.S. Highway 93 on the southern edge of the area. In between, the best route is Forest Road 055, the Morgan Creek Road (often called the Panther Creek Road in its northern reach), which runs from just west of Shoup southward to US 93 about 10 miles northeast of Challis. It is generally a passable road for most vehicles, tracking along with Panther Creek for the northern two-thirds of its run. The tiny community of Cobalt is located about midway along it. However, the roads spiking off from it are much more rugged; don't expect the same road conditions to pertain.

For more information:

Salmon-Challis National Forest
Route 2, Box 600
Salmon, ID 83467
(208) 756–5100
www.fs.fed.us/r4/sc

1 Yellowjacket Lake

Location: West of Cobalt
Sites: 7
Facilities: Drinking water, vault toilets, fire rings
Fee per night: $
Elevation: 8,200 feet
Road conditions: Good through the Morgan Creek Road but often bad on Forest Road 112 as it follows the South Fork Creek, becoming still more rugged—narrow, rock-strewn, generally bumpy, and slow—thereafter.
Management: Forest Service, Salmon/Cobalt Ranger Districts, (208) 756–5100
Reservations: No

Area 23

		Town	Sites	Max. RV length	Electric	Picnic	Fire rings	Toilets	Showers	Water	Dump station	Disability access	Recreation	Can reserve	Fees ($)	Season	Stay limit (days)
1	Yellowjacket Lake	Cobalt	7	22		•	•	V		•			FH		$	July–Oct.	14
2	Crags	Cobalt	24	16		•	•	V		•			FH		$	July–Oct.	14
3	Deep Creek	Cobalt	U	22			•	V					BFHS		$	March–Oct.	14
4	Ebenezer Bar	North Fork/ Shoup	14	32		•	•	V		•			BFH		$	June–Oct.	14
5	Long Tom	North Fork/ Shoup	5	32		•	•	V		•			BFHS		$	June–Oct.	14
6	Corn Creek	North Fork/ Shoup	12	22		•	•	V		•			BFHS		$	March–Oct.	14

Activities: Fishing, hiking, picnicking
Season: July 1–October 1
Finding the campground: From Cobalt drive 9 miles south on FR 055 (Morgan Creek Road), then 7 miles west on FR 112, and then 16 miles north on Forest Road 113.
The campground: This campground is located near Crags and shouldn't be confused with the Yellowjacket area that lies about 6 miles (as the crow flies) to the south. (That Yellowjacket area is an old mining district, with a small amount of ranching also active.) Like Crags, this is a very remote area, and also like Crags, this is a good point for jumping off into the Frank Church–River of No Return Wilderness Area from the east side. The campground is in a pretty wooded mountain area, with several small water bodies nearby.

2 Crags

Location: West of Cobalt
Sites: 24
Facilities: Drinking water, vault toilets, fire rings
Fee per night: $
Elevation: 8,400 feet
Road conditions: Good through the gravel Morgan Creek Road/Panther Creek Road, turning rough on FR 112 as it follows the South Fork Creek, and then turning much more rugged—narrow, rock-strewn, generally bumpy and slow—thereafter.
Management: Forest Service, Salmon/Cobalt Ranger Districts, (208) 756–5100
Reservations: No
Activities: Fishing, hiking, picnicking

Season: July 1–October 15

Finding the campground: From Cobalt drive 9 miles southwest on FR 055 (Morgan Creek Road/Panther Creek Road), then 7 miles northwest on FR 112, then 13 miles north on Forest Road 113, and then 2 miles north on Forest Road 114.

The campground: Located on the western border of the Frank Church–River of No Return Wilderness, this is a good place to take off into the wilderness country for a week of backpacking. But you'll have to work to get here. This is a good destination campground for a couple of weeks in the wilderness.

3 Deep Creek

Location: Southwest of North Fork and Shoup, northwest of Cobalt
Sites: Number undetermined
Facilities: Vault toilets, fire rings
Fee per night: $
Elevation: 5,000 feet
Road conditions: Paved from North Fork to Shoup, good gravel road (sometimes washboarded) along the river thereafter and on the Morgan Creek Road
Management: Forest Service, Salmon/Cobalt Ranger Districts, (208) 756–5100
Reservations: No
Activities: Boating, fishing, hiking, swimming
Season: March 1–October 31
Finding the campground: From North Fork drive 25 miles west on Forest Road 030 (Salmon River Road), about 6 miles west of Shoup. Turn south and drive 20 miles on FR 055 (Morgan Creek Road). From Cobalt drive 2 miles north on FR 055.

The campground: Deep back in the woods but along pretty good gravel roads, Deep Creek is located where the like-named creek dumps into Panther Creek. This is a mostly undeveloped campground, so bring your own amenities—including drinking water—and be sure to pack it out if you pack it in.

4 Ebenezer Bar

Location: West of North Fork and Shoup
Sites: 14
Facilities: Drinking water, vault toilets, fire rings, pull-through sites, pets allowed
Fee per night: $
Elevation: 3,100 feet
Road conditions: Paved from North Fork to Shoup, good gravel road (sometimes washboarded) along the river thereafter
Management: Forest Service, Salmon/Cobalt Ranger Districts, (208) 756–5100
Reservations: No
Activities: Boating, fishing, hiking, picnicking
Season: June 1–October 15
Finding the campground: From North Fork drive 34.4 miles west on FR 030 (Salmon River Road), about 13 miles west of Shoup.

The campground: This is a fine riverside locale not far from Shoup but deep into the wilds. (The Frank Church–River of No Return Wilderness boundary is less than a mile to the south.) A cable crossing of the river is available here.

5 Long Tom

Location: West of North Fork and Shoup
Sites: 5
Facilities: Drinking water, vault toilets, fire rings, pets allowed
Fee per night: $
Elevation: 3,000 feet
Road conditions: Paved from North Fork to Shoup, good gravel road (sometimes washboarded) along the river thereafter
Management: Forest Service, Salmon/Cobalt Ranger Districts, (208) 756-5100
Reservations: No
Activities: Boating, fishing, hiking, picnicking, swimming
Season: June–October
Finding the campground: From North Fork drive 38 miles west on FR 030 (Salmon River Road), about 16 miles west of Shoup.
The campground: Long Tom is a fine riverside site, where the Middle Fork of the Salmon River pours into the main stem. That makes it a relatively busy location, because the Middle Fork is a very popular floating route for adventurous white-water enthusiasts. (You may be put in mind of a backcountry Grand Central Station.)

6 Corn Creek

Location: West of North Fork and Shoup
Sites: 12
Facilities: Drinking water, vault toilets, fire rings, river access
Fee per night: $
Elevation: 2,800 feet
Road conditions: Paved from North Fork to Shoup, good gravel road (sometimes washboarded) along the river thereafter
Management: Forest Service, Salmon/Cobalt Ranger Districts, (208) 756-5100
Reservations: No
Activities: Boating, fishing, hiking, picnicking, swimming
Season: March 1–October 31
Finding the campground: From North Fork drive 44 miles west on FR 030 (Salmon River Road), about 25 miles west of Shoup.
The campground: The road ends here—literally. Corn Creek is as far as you go along the Salmon River before bumping into the Frank Church–River of No Return Wilderness Area, where no motor vehicles are allowed. (The road from North Fork to here was built by the Civilian Conservation Corps in the 1930s; the plan then was to extend the road west all the way down the river to Riggins. Budget and environmental considerations eventually put a stop to that

would-have-been highway. The downstream section ends at Vinegar Creek, a few miles east of Riggins in western Idaho.) This is the main designated put-in point for rafters headed down the main Salmon River, and it is also a take-out point for people who have ridden the Salmon from Stanley or the city of Salmon. Boat ramps and facilities are, obviously, available. It's a pretty site, with plenty of pine cover and hiking trailheads available, but be prepared for plenty of activity (rafters coming in and out, jet boaters arriving, outfitters using it as a launching site)—this isn't the quietest spot on the river.

Area 24: Stanley Basin

Close to the very center of Idaho, the Stanley Basin is renowned as one of the prettiest places in the state. Here is the Salmon River as a high mountain stream, running fast and with great purity; here are the majestic Sawtooth Mountains, shooting up in the sky so high they're visible from scores of miles around. Here are legendary high mountain lakes, such as Redfish Lake, some of the finest hiking trails in Idaho, and several excellent guest ranches.

Locally, debate has vigorously evolved about how much development, how many more houses and commercial developments, should be allowed. So far, the human incursion here remains relatively small; Stanley recently proclaimed its population as sixty-nine. Much of this area is in any event barred from development. The Sawtooth National Recreation Area (SNRA), set up specifically by Congress in 1972 as a recreation area (as well as for some wildlands protection) lies to its southeast, reaching south (and accessible along Idaho Highway 75) almost to the Ketchum area. And due east of Stanley sit the magnificent White Cloud Mountains.

The Sawtooth Wilderness Area is east of the Stanley Basin. This is remote and spectacular country, the heart of the jagged Sawtooths, dotted with small mountain lakes. There are no formally designated campgrounds here, however, and you have to hike in—no motor vehicles are allowed inside the wilderness area. Those who do make the effort will find ample reward.

The many campgrounds elsewhere in this area (there are more public campground spaces in this region than in any other in Idaho) are widely varied, not least in their popularity. The most popular single public campground area in Idaho may be nationally known Redfish Lake, located on several shores of the largest lake in the region. The Redfish Lake listings in this section are divided among the campgrounds located there (Sunny Gulch, Chinook Bay, Glacier View, Outlet, Sockeye, Mount Heyburn, Point) as well as a separate Redfish listing.

Nearly all of the developed campgrounds in the SNRA are fee-based, and most have local campground managers (called concessionaires). Be aware, too, that in general hiking on established trails is a for-fee matter. Parking at a trailhead (and there are forty-three major trailheads in the SNRA and the Ketchum Ranger District) generally will carry a charge. You'll find plenty to choose from; the SNRA office estimates 750 miles of designated hiking trails in the area.

This is not especially good country for ATV enthusiasts, however. ATVs generally are not allowed in SNRA camping areas except on specific Forest Service roads.

Spaces in some of these campgrounds can be reserved, but others cannot. All spaces that are not (or cannot be) reserved are first come, first served.

For more information:

Stanley-Sawtooth Chamber of Commerce
Community Building, Highway 21
Stanley, ID 83278
(208) 774–3411
www.stanleycc.org

Sawtooth National Recreation Area
Sawtooth Wilderness Area
HC 64 Box 8291
Ketchum, ID 83340
(208) 727–5013
www.northrim.net/sawtoothnf

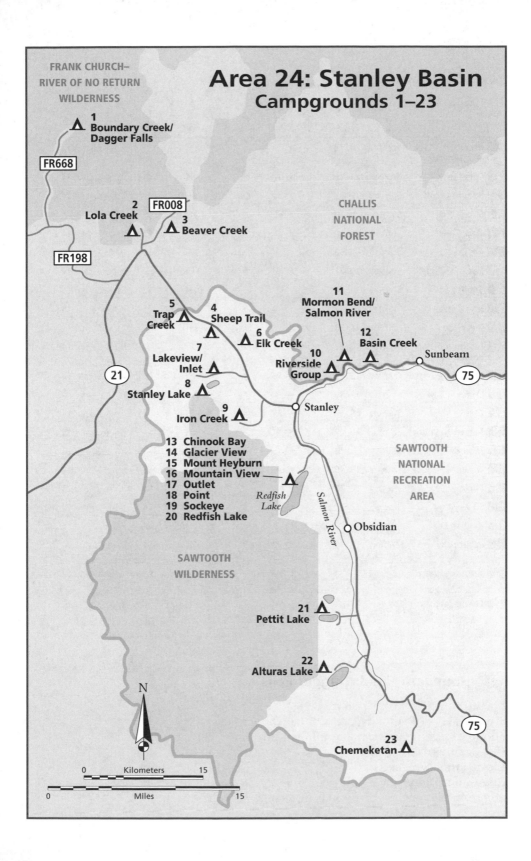

Area 24: Stanley Basin
Campgrounds 1–23

FRANK CHURCH–
RIVER OF NO RETURN
WILDERNESS

1 Boundary Creek/
Dagger Falls

FR668

2 Lola Creek

FR008

3 Beaver Creek

CHALLIS
NATIONAL
FOREST

FR198

5 Trap Creek

4 Sheep Trail

11 Mormon Bend/
Salmon River

6 Elk Creek

12 Basin Creek

7 Lakeview/
Inlet

10 Riverside Group

Sunbeam

75

21

8 Stanley Lake

Stanley

9 Iron Creek

13 Chinook Bay
14 Glacier View
15 Mount Heyburn
16 Mountain View
17 Outlet
18 Point
19 Sockeye
20 Redfish Lake

Redfish Lake

Salmon River

SAWTOOTH
NATIONAL
RECREATION
AREA

Obsidian

SAWTOOTH
WILDERNESS

21 Pettit Lake

22 Alturas Lake

75

N

23 Chemeketan

0   Kilometers   15

0   Miles   15

Area 24

	Town	Sites	Max. RV length	Electric	Picnic	Fire rings	Toilets	Showers	Water	Dump station	Disability access	Recreation	Can reserve	Fees ($)	Season	Stay limit (days)
1 Boundary Creek/ Dagger Falls	Stanley	24	22		•	•	V		•			FH	•	$	June–Sept.	14
2 Lola Creek	Stanley	21	16		•	•	V		•			FH		$	June–Sept.	14
3 Beaver Creek	Stanley	8	32		•	•	V		•		•	FH		$	June–Sept.	14
4 Sheep Trail	Stanley	4	30		•	•	V		•			FH	•	$$	June–Sept.	14
5 Trap Creek	Stanley	3	30		•	•	V		•			F	•	$$	June–Sept.	14
6 Elk Creek	Stanley	1	30		•	•	V		•			FH	•	$$	June–Sept.	14
7 Lakeview/Inlet	Stanley	20	22		•	•	V		•			FHS		$	June–Sept.	14
8 Stanley Lake	Stanley	19	22		•	•	V		•			BFHS	•	$$	June–Sept.	14
9 Iron Creek	Stanley	9	22		•	•	V		•		•	F	•	$$	June–Sept.	14
10 Riverside Group	Stanley	18	22		•	•	V		•			FH	•	$	June–Sept.	14
11 Mormon Bend/ Salmon River	Stanley	15	22		•	•	V		•			F		$	June–Sept.	14
12 Basin Creek	Stanley	15	22		•	•	V		•			F		$	May–Sept.	14
13 Chinook Bay	Stanley	13	30		•	•	F		•	•		BFS		$-$$	June–Sept.	14
14 Glacier View	Stanley	65	32		•	•	F,V		•	•		BFHS	•	$-$$	June–Sept.	14
15 Mount Heyburn	Stanley	20	22		•	•	V		•			BFS	•	$$	June–Sept.	14
16 Mountain View	Stanley	7	22		•	•	F		•			BFS		$-$$	June–Sept.	14
17 Outlet	Stanley	19	40		•	•	V		•	•		BFS	•	$$	June–Sept.	14
18 Point	Stanley	16	20		•	•	F		•			FH	•	$$	June–Sept.	14
19 Sockeye	Stanley	23	22		•	•	V		•	•		BFS	•	$$	June–Sept.	14
20 Redfish Lake	Stanley	14	22		•	•	V		•	•		BFHS	•	$$$	May–Oct.	14
21 Pettit Lake	Stanley/ Obsidian	12	30		•	•	V		•			BFHS		$$	May–Oct.	14
22 Alturas Lake	Stanley/ Obsidian	12	30		•	•	V		•			FHS	•	$$	May–Oct.	14
23 Chemeketan	Stanley/ Obsidian	19	30		•	•	V					FH	•	$	May–Oct.	14

1 Boundary Creek/Dagger Falls

Location: Northwest of Stanley
Sites: 24 (14 at Boundary Creek, 10 at Dagger Falls)
Facilities: Drinking water, vault toilets, fire rings, pets allowed
Fee per night: $
Elevation: 5,800 feet
Road conditions: Generally good gravel road for the first 6 or 7 miles, then progressively rougher as it winds into the mountains

Management: Forest Service, Stanley Zone Office, (208) 774–3000
Reservations: Call (877) 444–6777 or visit Web site www.reserveamerica.com.
Activities: Fishing, hiking, picnicking
Season: June 15–September 10
Finding the campgrounds: From Stanley drive 20 miles northwest on Idaho Highway 21, then 11 miles west on Forest Road 198 (Fir Creek Road), and then 13 miles north on Forest Road 668 (Boundary Creek Road).
The campgrounds: These two campgrounds are next door to each other at the end of Boundary Creek Road and right on the southern border of the Frank Church–River of No Return Wilderness. (The road punches an incursion into the wilderness area boundary.) During high water, this is the main put-in point for rafting trips on the legendary Middle Fork of the Salmon River.

2 Lola Creek

Location: Northwest of Stanley
Sites: 21
Facilities: Drinking water, cooking grills, vault toilets
Fee per night: $
Elevation: 6,600 feet
Road conditions: Paved nearly to the campground
Management: Forest Service, Stanley Zone Office, (208) 774–3000
Reservations: No
Activities: Fishing, hiking, picnicking
Season: June 15–September 15
Finding the campground: From Stanley drive 17 miles northwest on ID 21 and then 1 mile northwest on Forest Road 083.
The campground: Forget the campground name; the relevant creek here is Marsh Creek, a fine fishing spot, and the location of the Marsh Creek trailhead for good hiking. The campground is forested and well appointed.

3 Beaver Creek

Location: Northwest of Stanley
Sites: 8
Facilities: Drinking water, vault toilets, fire rings, pull-through sites, barrier-free access
Fee per night: $
Elevation: 6,700 feet
Road conditions: Very good; easy driving on the gravel roads
Management: Forest Service, Stanley Zone Office, (208) 774–3000
Reservations: No
Activities: Fishing, hiking, horseback riding, picnicking
Season: June 15–September 10
Finding the campground: From Stanley drive 17 miles northwest on ID 21 and then 3 miles north on Forest Road 008 (Beaver Creek Road).
The campground: Beaver Creek is good for general camping but set up especially for people with horses; corrals and horse trailheads are located here.

Motor homes and trailers up to 32 feet are easily accommodated. This is one of the two or three best campgrounds in central Idaho for horse enthusiasts. The forested setting on Beaver Creek is the equal of most of those in the area; there are some spectacular Sawtooth mountain views in the area.

4 Sheep Trail

Location: West of Stanley
Sites: 4 group sites (40 people max)
Facilities: Drinking water, vault toilets, fire rings
Fee per night: $$
Elevation: 6,600 feet
Road conditions: Excellent; paved ID 21 up to the campground, good gravel and dirt within
Management: Forest Service, Stanley Zone Office, (208) 774-3000
Reservations: Call (877) 444-6777 or visit Web site www.reserveamerica.com.
Activities: Fishing, hiking, picnicking
Season: June 15–September 15 (depending on weather)
Finding the campground: From Stanley drive 12.2 miles west on ID 21 to the Sheep Trail entrance; it is well signed.
The campground: Sheep Trail is a small, flat, shady outpost on the west side of the Stanley Basin, with what you might take as rustic charm (wooden fence posts and the like). This campground seems relatively oriented to groups. Fishing is a main draw; there's close access to Trap and Valley Creeks.

5 Trap Creek

Location: West of Stanley
Sites: 3 group sites (40 people max)
Facilities: Drinking water, vault toilets, fire rings
Fee per night: $$
Elevation: 6,670 feet
Road conditions: Paved nearly to the campground, easily accessible for all vehicles
Management: Forest Service, Stanley Zone Office, (208) 774-3000
Reservations: Call (877) 444-6777 or visit Web site www.reserveamerica.com.
Activities: Fishing, picnicking
Season: June 15–September 15
Finding the campground: From Stanley drive 12 miles west on ID 21, then turn left (east) onto Forest Road 540; the campground is very close to the highway.
The campground: Trap Creek is a small, wooded, mountain campground on the northwest edge of the Sawtooth National Recreation Area. Close to Banner Summit (which often snows in solidly for part of the winter), this is one of the highest-elevation campgrounds in the Stanley area and may have one of the shorter camping seasons. Because it is relatively distant from Stanley and not located on a lake, however, it may be relatively easy to snag a site here, as opposed to some of the other closer-in and lake-fronted campgrounds.

6 Elk Creek

Location: West of Stanley
Sites: 1 group site
Facilities: Drinking water, vault toilets, fire rings
Fee per night: $$
Elevation: 6,540 feet
Road conditions: Paved up to the campground
Management: Forest Service, Stanley Zone Office, (208) 774-3000
Reservations: Call (877) 444-6777 or visit Web site www.reserveamerica.com.
Activities: Fishing, hiking, picnicking
Season: June 15-September 15
Finding the campground: From Stanley drive 10.5 miles west on ID 21 to the ELK CREEK CAMPGROUND sign.
The campground: This woodsy mountain campground is near and similar to Sheep Trail. Both are oriented toward group activities (though they allow individual campers as well) and have access to several good hiking trails.

7 Lakeview/Inlet

Location: West of Stanley
Sites: 20 (6 at Lakeview, 14 at Inlet)
Facilities: Drinking water, vault toilets, fire rings
Fee per night: $
Elevation: 6,540 feet
Road conditions: From ID 21, paved the several miles into the campgrounds; gravel and dirt in the campgrounds. Access is easy for almost all vehicles.
Management: Forest Service, Stanley Zone Office, (208) 774-3000
Reservations: No
Activities: Fishing, hiking, picnicking, swimming
Season: June 15-September 15
Finding the campgrounds: From Stanley drive 5 miles northwest on ID 21 and then 5.5 miles west on Forest Road 455.
The campgrounds: These are the two westernmost campgrounds on popular Stanley Lake (a much sought-after camping location but usually less crowded than the Redfish Lake area). The campgrounds themselves are on forested country sloping down toward the lake. There isn't the spectacle of high Sawtooth Mountains in the immediate background as at Redfish (though there are good views of McGowan Peak), but the scene is absolutely pristine—the image of a clear blue mountain lake set against a dark green forest. The campgrounds have close access to several fine trails (Bridal Veil and Alpine Way are both well known and highly regarded by many campers), and Inlet has a fine swimming beach.

8 Stanley Lake

Location: West of Stanley
Sites: 19
Facilities: Drinking water, vault toilets, fire rings
Fee per night: $$
Elevation: 6,540 feet
Road conditions: From ID 21, paved the several miles into the campgrounds; gravel and dirt in the campgrounds. Access is easy for almost all vehicles.
Management: Forest Service, Sawtooth National Recreation Area, (208) 727-5000
Reservations: Call (877) 444-6777 or visit Web site www.reserveamerica.com.
Activities: Boating, fishing, picnicking, swimming
Season: June 15–September 15 (depending on weather)
Finding the campground: From Stanley drive 5 miles west on ID 21 and then 2.5 miles west on FR 455.
The campground: Of the three campgrounds at Stanley Lake (Lakeview and Inlet are the others), this one is closest to ID 21—but you don't give up the wonderful lake scenery for that. Stanley Lake is the best of the three campgrounds for boating, but it shares with the others excellent access to trails and other recreational opportunities. This is a forested, hilly country (hilly in the immediate area, that is—after all, the Sawtooths aren't far away).

9 Iron Creek

Location: Southwest of Stanley
Sites: 9
Facilities: Drinking water, vault toilets, fire rings, barrier-free access
Fee per night: $$
Elevation: 6,700 feet
Road conditions: Good; mostly paved close to the campgrounds, gravel and dirt within; friendly for most vehicles
Management: Forest Service, Sawtooth National Recreation Area, (208) 727-5000
Reservations: Advised
Activities: Fishing, picnicking
Season: June 15–September 15 (depending on weather)
Finding the campground: From Stanley drive 3.2 miles west on ID 21 and then drive 4 miles south on Forest Road 619.
The campground: Reservations should be made far in advance. The area is forested; some of the RV sites are pull-throughs. There is developed access in this area for people with disabilities.

10 Riverside Group

Location: East of Stanley
Sites: 18
Facilities: Drinking water, vault toilets, fire rings

Fee per night: $
Elevation: 6,000 feet
Road conditions: Paved to the campground
Management: Forest Service, Sawtooth National Recreation Area, (208) 727-5000
Reservations: Call (877) 444-6777 or visit Web site www.reserveamerica.com.
Activities: Fishing, hiking, picnicking
Season: June 15–September 15 (depending on weather)
Finding the campground: From Stanley drive 6.8 miles east on ID 75; campground entrance is on the highway.
The campground: This is a pleasant group campground (as noted) on the north shore of the Salmon River, east of Stanley; it is similar to the Mormon Bend and Salmon River campgrounds but more oriented to group activities. Access is easy.

11 Mormon Bend/Salmon River

Location: East of Stanley
Sites: 15
Facilities: Drinking water, vault toilets, fire rings
Fee per night: $
Elevation: 6,120 feet
Road conditions: Paved to the campground
Management: Forest Service, Stanley Zone Office, (208) 774-3000
Reservations: No
Activities: Fishing, picnicking
Season: June 15–September 15
Finding the campgrounds: From Stanley drive 7 miles east on ID 75; enter the campgrounds from the highway.
The campgrounds: Both of these campgrounds are located around bends in the Salmon River between Stanley and Sunbeam; the countryside is mostly desert in appearance, but there's plenty of shade at the campgrounds. Both are relatively flat, with good river access.

12 Basin Creek

Location: East of Stanley
Sites: 15
Facilities: Drinking water, vault toilets, fire rings
Fee per night: $
Elevation: 6,025 feet
Road conditions: Paved to the campground
Management: Forest Service, Stanley Zone Office, (208) 774-3000
Reservations: No
Activities: Fishing, picnicking
Season: May 15–September 15
Finding the campground: From Stanley drive 8.9 miles east on ID 75.
The campground: Basin Creek has a pretty riverside location, deep in the

Salmon River canyon, with scattered trees. The spaces are packed in a little more than in some campgrounds in this area, and there's not a lot of shade.

13 Chinook Bay

Location: South of Stanley
Sites: 13
Facilities: Drinking water, flush toilets, fire rings, barrier-free access
Fee per night: $-$$
Elevation: 6,500 feet
Road conditions: Good; mostly paved close to the campgrounds, gravel and dirt within; friendly for most vehicles
Management: Forest Service, Sawtooth National Recreation Area, (208) 727-5000
Reservations: No
Activities: Boating, fishing, picnicking, swimming
Season: June 15-September 15
Finding the campground: From Stanley drive 5 miles south on ID 75 and then half a mile southwest on Forest Road 214.
The campground: Located close to ID 75 on Little Redfish Lake, this is a relatively flat and convenient campground. Little Redfish is not quite so swamped with traffic as the central Redfish Lake area, but the traffic going by is considerable, and the two Little Redfish campgrounds (this one and Mountain View) tend to fill up early in overflow fashion. (By the way, on the other side of ID 75—away from the lakes—at the Redfish entrance, there's also an overflow campground, which gets plenty of use in the summer.) There is developed access in this area for people with disabilities. The fishing access is excellent and boating is allowed—but only nonmotorized boats.

14 Glacier View

Location: South of Stanley
Sites: 65
Facilities: Drinking water, flush and vault toilets, fire rings, barrier-free access, playground
Fee per night: $-$$
Elevation: 6,550 feet
Road conditions: Good; mostly paved close to the campgrounds, gravel and dirt within; friendly for most vehicles
Management: Forest Service, Sawtooth National Recreation Area, (208) 727-5000
Reservations: Call (877) 444-6777 or visit Web site www.reserveamerica.com.
Activities: Boating, fishing, hiking, picnicking, swimming
Season: June 15-September 15
Finding the campground: From Stanley drive 5 miles south on ID 75 and then 2.4 miles southwest on FR 214.
The campground: This is another of the superpopular Redfish Lake camping spots, with terrific lake views (as the name of the campground suggests). Best

advice is to make your reservations well in advance; if you time your arrival just right, you may find a spot (but don't count on it). If you're determined to stay at this well-known and wonderfully scenic area, those in the know say that the area is relatively quiet, and access to it relatively easy, during the brief periods before Memorial Day and after Labor Day. The area is forested; some of the RV sites are pull-throughs. There is developed access in this area for people with disabilities.

15 Mount Heyburn

Location: South of Stanley
Sites: 20
Facilities: Drinking water, vault toilets, fire rings
Fee per night: $$
Elevation: 6,600 feet
Road conditions: Good; mostly paved close to the campgrounds, gravel and dirt within; friendly for most vehicles
Management: Forest Service, Sawtooth National Recreation Area, (208) 727–5000
Reservations: Call Sawtooth National Recreation Area, (208) 727–5000.
Activities: Boating, fishing, picnicking, swimming
Season: June 15–September 15 (depending on weather)
Finding the campground: From Stanley drive 5 miles south on ID 75, and then turn right (west) at the Redfish Lake sign and drive 3.1 miles southwest on FR 214.
The campground: This is one of the superbusy campgrounds in the Redfish Lake complex. Consider making your reservations even months in advance; if you time your arrival just right, you may be able to get a spot on a first-come-first-served basis (but don't count on it). If you're determined to stay at this well-known and wonderfully scenic area, those in the know say that the area is relatively quiet, and access to it relatively easy, during the brief periods before Memorial Day and after Labor Day. The area is forested; some of the RV sites are pull-throughs. There is some access for boat launching here.

16 Mountain View

Location: South of Stanley
Sites: 7
Facilities: Drinking water, flush toilets, fire rings, barrier-free access
Fee per night: $–$$
Elevation: 6,500 feet
Road conditions: Good; mostly paved close to the campgrounds, gravel and dirt within; friendly for most vehicles
Management: Forest Service, Sawtooth National Recreation Area, (208) 727–5000
Reservations: No
Activities: Boating, fishing, picnicking, swimming
Season: June 15–September 15 (depending on weather)

Finding the campground: From Stanley drive 5 miles south on ID 75, and then turn right (west) at the Redfish Lake sign and continue about half a mile southwest on FR 214.

The campground: Located close to ID 75 on the banks of Little Redfish Lake, this is a relatively flat and convenient campground. Little Redfish is not quite so swamped with traffic as the central Redfish Lake area, but the traffic going by is considerable, and the two Little Redfish campgrounds (this one and Chinook Bay) tend to fill up early in overflow fashion. (By the way, on the other side of ID 75—away from the lakes—at the Redfish entrance, there's also an overflow campground, which gets plenty of use in the summer.) There is developed access in this area for people with disabilities. The fishing access is excellent and boating is allowed—but only nonmotorized boats.

17 Outlet

Location: South of Stanley
Sites: 19
Facilities: Drinking water, vault toilets, fire rings, barrier-free access
Fee per night: $$
Elevation: 6,550 feet
Road conditions: Good; mostly paved close to the campgrounds, gravel and dirt within; friendly for most vehicles
Management: Forest Service, Sawtooth National Recreation Area, (208) 727-5000
Reservations: Call (877) 444-6777 or visit Web site www.reserveamerica.com.
Activities: Boating, fishing, picnicking, swimming
Season: June 15–September 30 (depending on weather)
Finding the campground: From Stanley drive 5 miles south on ID 75 and then 2.4 miles southwest on FR 214.
The campground: Outlet is located within close walking distance of the "town"—visitor center, restaurant, and cabins—and adjacent beach. As such, it is another of the superbusy campgrounds in the Redfish Lake complex, so plan accordingly. Those in the know say that the area is relatively quiet, and access to it relatively easy, during the brief periods before Memorial Day and after Labor Day. There is developed access in this area for people with disabilities. The area is forested; some of the RV sites are pull-throughs. The campground area at Outlet is watered by irrigation on Sundays, and the campground is closed during that time.

18 Point

Location: South of Stanley
Sites: 16
Facilities: Drinking water, flush toilets, fire rings
Fee per night: $$
Elevation: 6,550 feet
Road conditions: Good; mostly paved close to the campgrounds, gravel and dirt within; friendly for most vehicles

Management: Forest Service, Sawtooth National Recreation Area, (208) 727–5000
Reservations: Call (877) 444–6777 or visit Web site www.reserveamerica.com.
Activities: Fishing, hiking, picnicking
Season: June 15–September 15 (depending on weather)
Finding the campground: From Stanley drive 5 miles south on ID 75 and then 2.6 miles southwest on FR 214.
The campground: Point is the only developed campground on the western side of Redfish Lake, which separates you a bit from the crowds but also makes it one of the most in-demand locations in the Redfish Lake complex. The Redfish Lake area is relatively quiet, and access to it relatively easy, just before Memorial Day and after Labor Day. The area is forested; some of the RV sites are pull-throughs. The Point site is closed on Mondays for irrigation. Note: This is the only campground in the Redfish Lake area that does not have developed access for people with disabilities.

19 Sockeye

Location: South of Stanley
Sites: 23
Facilities: Drinking water, vault toilets, fire rings, barrier-free access
Fee per night: $$
Elevation: 6,600 feet
Road conditions: Good; mostly paved close to the campgrounds, gravel and dirt within; friendly for most vehicles
Management: Forest Service, Sawtooth National Recreation Area, (208) 727–5000
Reservations: Advised
Activities: Boating, fishing, picnicking, swimming
Season: June 15–September 15 (depending on weather)
Finding the campground: From Stanley drive 5 miles south on ID 75 and then 3.2 miles southwest on FR 214.
The campground: Sockeye is the campground farthest south on Redfish Lake, some distance from the cabin and visitor center area. Remember: This is one of the most in-demand campgrounds in Idaho, and reservations should be made far in advance. The easiest times to find spots here are in the brief periods before Memorial Day and after Labor Day. The area is forested; some of the RV sites are pull-throughs. There is developed access in this area for people with disabilities. Sockeye also has access to boat ramps; this is probably the best campground on Redfish Lake for boaters.

20 Redfish Lake

Location: South of Stanley
Sites: 14
Facilities: Drinking water, vault toilets, fire rings, barrier-free access
Fee per night: $$$
Elevation: 6,600 feet

Road conditions: Good; mostly paved close to the campgrounds, gravel and dirt within; friendly for most vehicles
Management: Forest Service, Sawtooth National Recreation Area, (208) 727–5000
Reservations: Call SNRA office, (208) 727–5000.
Activities: Boating, fishing, hiking, picnicking, swimming
Season: June 15–September 15 (depending on weather)
Finding the campground: From Stanley drive 5 miles south on ID 75 and then 3.5 miles west on FR 214.
The campground: Yes, Redfish Lake deserves its reputation as one of America's premier camping locations, for the scenery alone. The lake—the largest in central Idaho—is as pretty as any in Idaho, and the sight of one of the most majestic of the Sawtooth Mountains (Mount Heyburn) towering over it really does inspire awe. It is also one of the best-provisioned camping areas in Idaho. There's a good restaurant, plus laundry, a couple of convenience stores, a gas station, and much more. The Redfish Lodge is also much in demand; information about it can be found at the Web site www.redfishlake.com or by calling (208) 774–3536. The beachfront area alone is a prize (though it tends to be packed with sun worshippers). If you're determined to stay here, try the brief periods before Memorial Day and after Labor Day. The area is forested; some of the RV sites are pull-throughs. There is developed access in this area for people with disabilities.

21 Pettit Lake

Location: South of Obsidian
Sites: 12
Facilities: Drinking water, vault toilets, fire rings
Fee per night: $$
Elevation: 7,000 feet
Road conditions: Paved nearly to the campground
Management: Forest Service, Sawtooth National Recreation Area, (208) 727–5000
Reservations: No
Activities: Boating, fishing, hiking, picnicking, swimming
Season: May 20–October 15
Finding the campground: From Obsidian drive 9.8 miles south on ID 75 and then 3.4 miles southwest on Forest Road 205.
The campground: Fittingly for its name, Pettit Lake is the smallest and probably least known of the string of Stanley Basin lakes, but it is also plenty busy at times. Since this campground is first come, first served, be sure to get here early—well in advance of the weekend. What you get is a richly wooded and mildly hilly landscape on the north side of the lake, only about 4 miles from the east side of the Sawtooth Wilderness Area. That means that some of the best (if sometimes exhausting) hiking opportunities in the state open up here.

22 Alturas Lake

Location: South of Obsidian
Sites: 12
Facilities: Drinking water, vault toilets, fire rings
Fee per night: $$$
Elevation: 7,000 feet
Road conditions: Paved nearly to the campground
Management: Forest Service, Sawtooth National Recreation Area, (208) 727–5000
Reservations: Advised; call (877) 444–6777 or visit www.reserveamerica.com.
Activities: Boating, fishing, hiking, picnicking, swimming
Season: May 20–October 15
Finding the campground: From Obsidian drive 9.8 miles south on ID 75 and then 5.5 miles southwest on FR 205.
The campground: This is one of those very busy lakeside campgrounds in the Stanley Basin, with the usual pluses and minuses. The bright side is a spectacular lakeside location high in the Sawtooth Mountains (so you get those wonderful views of the high, jagged mountains rising over the namesake Alturas Lake). The downside is the crowds, meaning that you often have to plan far in advance to find a good site here. You can make reservations, and they're advised; a quick call to the SRNA office to check on current conditions probably would also be a good idea.

23 Chemeketan

Location: South of Obsidian
Sites: 19
Facilities: Vault toilets, fire rings, group sites
Fee per night: $
Elevation: 7,500 feet
Road conditions: Rugged, narrow, and bumpy in its last couple of miles
Management: Forest Service, Stanley Zone Office, (208) 774–3000
Reservations: Call (877) 444–6777 or visit Web site www.reserveamerica.com.
Activities: Fishing, hiking, picnicking
Season: May–October (depending on weather)
Finding the campground: From Obsidian drive 19 miles south on ID 75 and then 4.5 miles southwest on Forest Road 215.
The campground: Chemeketan is not one of the busier sites in this region; it is not close to one of the larger lakes. It is also not one of the more developed—it has no drinking water—but an attractive wooded streamside campground. It offers merely a fine and simple camping experience in the woods, as compared with the traffic-jammed grounds of national renown (such as Redfish) located nearby. Obsidian is 11 miles south of Stanley.

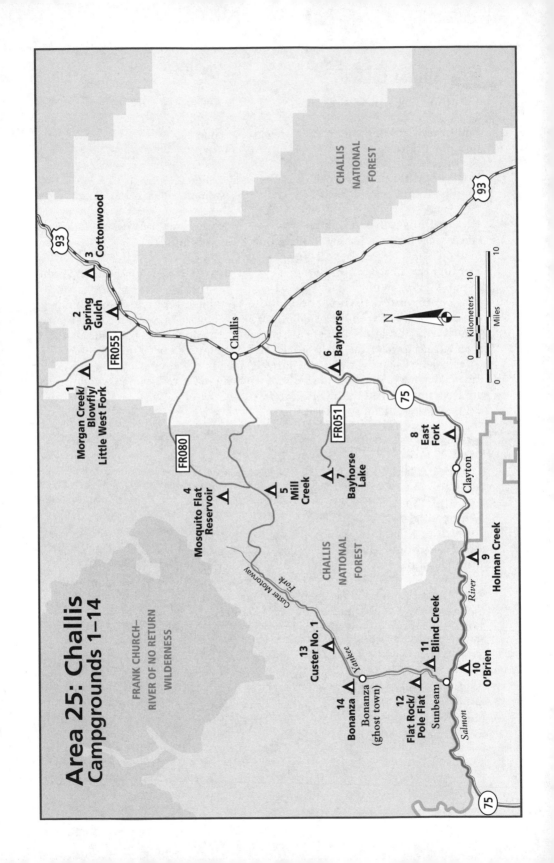

Area 25: Challis
Campgrounds 1–14

FRANK CHURCH—
RIVER OF NO RETURN
WILDERNESS

93

Cottonwood

3

2
Spring
Gulch

FR055

1
Morgan Creek/
Blowfly/
Little West Fork

Challis

93

CHALLIS
NATIONAL
FOREST

6 Bayhorse

75

FR080

FR051

4
Mosquito Flat
Reservoir

5
Mill
Creek

7
Bayhorse
Lake

8
East
Fork

Clayton

9
Holman Creek

CHALLIS
NATIONAL
FOREST

Custer Motorway

East Fork

13
Custer No. 1

Yankee Fork

14
Bonanza

Bonanza
(ghost town)

12
Flat Rock/
Pole Flat

Sunbeam

11
Blind Creek

10
O'Brien

Salmon River

75

N

Kilometers   10

0   10

Miles

0

Area 25: Challis

To the people who live there, the Challis region is a ranching and mining area; to visitors it is one of the popular hunting regions in Idaho. (Make your plans to stay in this area well ahead of time if you're arriving in hunting season.) But the mining—historical mining—actually provides some of the best sightseeing in the area, in century-old mining areas like Yankee Fork west of Challis.

Yankee Fork is worth a special mention. It was a gold mining district in the 1870s and for some decades later. In 1879 a road was built from Challis west to the mining towns of Custer and Bonanza, and it was soon continued south to Sunbeam (which is on Idaho Highway 75). The impact of the mining is still easily visible, since this was dredge mining, and the "dredge piles" of excavated rock still exist in huge piles around the valley. The Challis-to-Sunbeam road now is called the Custer Motorway, but give pause before you give in to the vision of an easy, fast traipse over a paved highway. Only the first few miles in each direction are paved; the center area, which tops Mill Creek Summit, can be very rugged and almost impassable for anything other than a sturdy pickup or four-wheel drive.

Most of the area around Challis is managed either by the Salmon-Challis National Forest or by the Bureau of Land Management.

For more information:

Challis Area Chamber of Commerce
P.O. Box 1130
Challis, ID 83226
(208) 879–2771

Salmon-Challis National Forest
Route 2, Box 600
Salmon, ID 83467
(208) 756–5100
www.fs.fed.us/r4/sc

Bureau of Land Management
HC 63, Box 1670
Challis, ID 83226
(208) 879–4181

1 Morgan Creek/Blowfly/Little West Fork

Location: North of Challis
Sites: Unmarked
Facilities: Vault toilets, fire rings
Fee per night: None
Elevation: 6,400 feet
Road conditions: Gravel after leaving U.S. Highway 93 and narrow but passable

Area 25

		Town	Sites	Max. RV length	Electric	Picnic	Fire rings	Toilets	Showers	Water	Dump station	Disability access	Recreation	Can reserve	Fees ($)	Season	Stay limit (days)
1	Morgan Creek/Blowfly/Little West Fork	Challis	U			•	•	V					F			June–Sept.	14
2	Spring Gulch	Challis	10	30		•	•	V		•			FS		$	May–Oct.	14
3	Cottonwood	Challis	14	30		•	•	V		•	•	•	BFHS		$	Year-round	14
4	Mosquito Flat Reservoir	Challis	9	32		•	•	V					FS			June–Oct.	14
5	Mill Creek	Challis	8	35		•	•	V		•			F		$	June–Sept.	14
6	Bayhorse	Challis	11	28		•	•	V		•			BFH		$	Year-round	14
7	Bayhorse Lake	Challis	6	21		•	•	V					FH		$	July–Sept.	14
8	East Fork	Challis/Clayton	10	25		•	•	V		•			BFS		$	Year-round	14
9	Holman Creek	Clayton	13	22		•	•	V		•			F		$$–$$$	June–Sept.	14
10	O'Brien	Stanley	24	22		•	•	V		•			F		$$	June–Sept.	14
11	Blind Creek	Stanley	5	22		•	•	V		•			FH		$	June–Sept.	16
12	Flat Rock/Pole Flat	Stanley	21	32		•	•	V		•			F		$	June–Sept.	14
13	Custer No. 1	Stanley	6	32		•	•	V					FH		$	June–Sept.	14
14	Bonanza	Stanley	12	35		•	•	V		•			FH	•	$	June–Sept.	14

Management: Forest Service, Challis Ranger District, (208) 879–4100
Reservations: No
Activities: Fishing, picnicking
Season: June 15–September 15 (depending on weather)
Finding the campgrounds: From Challis drive north on US 93 about 8 miles to Forest Road 055 (Morgan Creek Road, which leads to Cobalt). From there, continue about 5 miles northwest to the Morgan Creek Campground, and another 4 miles north from there up Forest Road 176 (the Little West Road) to Little West Fork.
The campgrounds: These are relatively primitive sites—neither drinking water nor camping fees—but they are pretty backwoods mountain locations. They are close to dispersed camping; you can set up pretty much where you like here. All of these campgrounds are remote mountain locations, with intermittent forest landscapes.

2 Spring Gulch

Location: North of Challis
Sites: 10
Facilities: Drinking water, vault toilets, fire rings
Fee per night: $

Elevation: 6,200 feet
Road conditions: Paved to the campground
Management: Forest Service, Challis Ranger District, (208) 879–4100
Reservations: No
Activities: Fishing, picnicking, swimming
Season: May 1–October 31
Finding the campground: From Challis drive 10 miles northeast on US 93. The campground is just west of the highway.
The campground: A mildly shaded location among the cotton trees, Spring Gulch is located right on the Salmon River. The location is excellent; the campground amenities are normal Forest Service sparse.

3 Cottonwood

Location: North of Challis
Sites: 14
Facilities: Drinking water, vault toilets, fire rings, dump station, barrier-free access, pull-through sites, river access, pets allowed
Fee per night: $
Elevation: 5,700 feet
Road conditions: Paved to and through the campground
Management: Bureau of Land Management, Challis Field Office, (208) 879–4181
Reservations: Call (208) 756–5400 for current status.
Activities: Boating, fishing, hiking, picnicking, swimming
Season: All year (though effectively open from midspring through midfall)
Finding the campground: From Challis drive 15 miles north on US 93; enter the campground from the highway on the northwest side.
The campground: Campgrounds are not a major activity of the BLM, and most of their sites in Idaho are relatively plain, but Cottonwood is a sharp exception. A thorough renovation in 1998 created sites that are paved throughout, RV-friendly, and fully accessible, with a thoughtful mix of shade and sun. Individual campers are welcome, but Cottonwood is especially well set up for groups. Added facilities include barbecue racks and a dump station. This is a rare BLM site with resident campground hosts (in the summer and early fall). And—oh, yes—this area is right on the Salmon River, with all the fishing opportunities that implies (especially for steelhead), and close by the highway for easy supply runs.

4 Mosquito Flat Reservoir

Location: West of Challis
Sites: 9
Facilities: Drinking water, vault toilets, fire rings, pull-through sites, pets allowed
Fee per night: None
Elevation: 7,000 feet

The Cottonwood Campground on the Salmon River, managed by the Bureau of Land Management, north of Challis, is one of the most modern and best-appointed public campgrounds in central Idaho.

Road conditions: Paved for the first 3 miles, then increasingly rugged gravel road; passable for most vehicles
Management: Forest Service, Challis Ranger District, (208) 879–4100
Reservations: No
Activities: Fishing, picnicking, swimming
Season: June–October
Finding the campground: From central Challis drive 15 miles west on Forest Road 080 (Challis Creek Road/Custer Motorway), then turn right (north) at the campground sign.
The campground: This is a high mountain lakeside campground. Mosquito Flat is a small body of water, but a concrete boat ramp is easily available, and the views over the basin are excellent. The campground is set up for a variety of uses: day use, single overnight use, and longer stays. There is limited access for people with disabilities.

5 Mill Creek

Location: West of Challis
Sites: 8
Facilities: Drinking water, vault toilets, fire rings, pull-through sites
Fee per night: $
Elevation: 7,500 feet
Road conditions: The Garden Creek Road is good and easy, but this stretch of the Custer Motorway is rugged. Some of the people in the area have recommended against driving it at all, partly because of the nature of some road reconstruction work, partly because the pass that precedes this campground (coming from Challis) is challenging anyway. If you go, go prepared.
Management: Forest Service, Challis Ranger District, (208) 879-4100
Reservations: For group area, call (877) 444-6777 or visit Web site www. reserveamerica.com.
Activities: Fishing, picnicking
Season: June-September
Finding the campground: From downtown Challis drive 4.5 miles west on Garden Creek Road and then 11 miles west on Custer Motorway (which sounds more developed than it is).
The campground: This is a forested, remote area. There is some access for people with disabilities. Mill Creek has a group reservation area, the only area on this campground that can be reserved.

6 Bayhorse

Location: South of Challis
Sites: 11
Facilities: Drinking water, vault toilets, fire rings, river access
Fee per night: $
Elevation: 5,250 feet
Road conditions: Good, paved highway up to the campground
Management: Bureau of Land Management, Challis Field Office, (208) 879-4181
Reservations: No
Activities: Boating, fishing, hiking, picnicking
Season: All year (though available as a practical matter roughly from May to October)
Finding the campground: From Challis drive 2 miles south on US 93 and then 6 miles southwest on ID 75 to the campground sign; the campground is between the highway and the Salmon River.
The campground: You do have a highway on one side of you (which does have some convenience benefit), but then there's the glorious Salmon River on the other side. The southern part of the campground is well designed for RV stays. Fishing the river is easy from here. Much of the camp underwent a major remodeling in 2001, so most of the facilities are new. Camping sites are

clearly defined here (not always the case at BLM sites). This is also a good place to start horse trips—trails are located not far away—but the BLM notes that horses are not allowed inside the campground itself. Boating may be possible, depending on river level, but there are no facilities for launches.

7 Bayhorse Lake

Location: South of Challis
Sites: 6
Facilities: Vault toilets, fire rings, pets allowed
Fee per night: $
Elevation: 8,550 feet
Road conditions: The forest road passage is best undertaken with a high-clearance RV. The Forest Service remarks, "This dirt road is narrow and steep and while trailers are allowed, caution is advised." No argument here.
Management: Forest Service, Challis Ranger District, (208) 879–4100
Reservations: No
Activities: Boating, fishing, hiking, picnicking
Season: July 1–September 10
Finding the campground: From Challis drive 2 miles south on US 93, then 7 miles south on ID 75, and then 8 miles west on Forest Road 051.
The campground: Bayhorse Lake is not to be confused with the other Bayhorse; among other things, this one is much more remarkable. It is one of the highest-elevation campgrounds in Idaho (take note of the late-starting season), with one of the most dramatic locations of any campground in Idaho. There are actually two lakes here, Big and Little Bayhorse, and a number of other streams as well; all are superb fishing areas. For the pure, high—very high—mountain country experience, this campground will do very well. If you're planning a weekend here, though, get in early: This is a popular location, for obvious reasons, and it's not on the reservation system. Also be advised to bring your own drinking water; the campground has none.

8 East Fork

Location: Southwest of Challis, just east of Clayton
Sites: 10
Facilities: Drinking water, vault toilets, fire rings
Fee per night: $
Elevation: 5,200 feet
Road conditions: Paved to the campground
Management: Bureau of Land Management, Challis Field Office, (208) 879–4181
Reservations: No
Activities: Boating, fishing, picnicking, swimming
Season: Year-round, but as a practical matter from late spring to midfall
Finding the campground: From Challis drive 18 miles southwest, first on US 93 and then on ID 75; enter the campground from the highway on the north side. From Clayton drive 3 miles east on ID 75.

The campground: Here is another one of those good BLM Salmon River sites, with excellent fishing access. This is an open-air—relatively unshaded, though trees planted in the mid-1990s will eventually provide some canopy—facility on the riverbank. There's water all around. The site is named for the confluence of the East Fork of the Salmon River and the main stem; the campground is a short hike to the riverside, and fishing is available there.

9 Holman Creek

Location: West of Clayton
Sites: 13
Facilities: Drinking water, vault toilets, fire rings
Fee per night: $$-$$$
Elevation: 5,200 feet
Road conditions: Paved nearly up to the campground
Management: Forest Service, Challis Ranger District, (208) 879-4100
Reservations: No
Activities: Fishing, picnicking
Season: June 15–September 15
Finding the campground: From Clayton drive 7 miles west on ID 75 and exit at the Holman Creek campground sign; the campground is a half mile from the highway.
The campground: This is one of the few camping areas in the far northeast reach of the Sawtooth National Recreation Area. Most of the countryside is desert sagebrush in character, but Holman Creek is tucked back in a piney draw. It's a mile or so from the Salmon River but in an attractive spot in its own right.

10 O'Brien

Location: East of Stanley
Sites: 24 (9 at Upper O'Brien and 15 and Lower O'Brien)
Facilities: Drinking water, vault toilets, fire rings
Fee per night: $$
Elevation: 5,730 feet
Road conditions: Gravel after leaving ID 75 and fairly narrow but passable for most vehicles
Management: Forest Service, Stanley Zone Office, (208) 774-3000
Reservations: No
Activities: Fishing, picnicking
Season: June 15–September 15
Finding the campground: From Stanley drive 16.9 miles east on ID 75 and then south on Forest Road 454 for 2 miles to Upper O'Brien and 4 miles to Lower O'Brien.
The campground: Backed up against the Sawtooth National Recreation Area—on its northeast side—this is a great spot for hiking and fishing. It's more secluded from the highway than most of the other campgrounds in the area, and it's also quite popular in the summer.

11 Blind Creek

Location: Northeast of Stanley
Sites: 5 (1 disabled-accessible)
Facilities: Drinking water, vault toilets, fire rings, pets allowed
Fee per night: $
Elevation: 6,100 feet
Road conditions: Paved to the campground
Management: Forest Service, Yankee Fork Office, (208) 838-2201
Reservations: No
Activities: Fishing, hiking, picnicking
Season: June 15–September 10 (depending on weather)
Finding the campground: From Stanley drive 14.9 miles northeast on ID 75 to Sunbeam and then 1 mile north on Yankee Fork Road (Forest Road 013).
The campground: Blind Creek is the first campground you come to when turning off at Sunbeam to ride up into the Yankee Fork country on FR 013, a segment of the Custer Motorway also known as Yankee Fork Road. The Yankee Fork area was the scene of active dredging for gold, and vast piles of dredged-up rock are stacked along the Yankee Fork valley. At the wooded Blind Creek area, relatively little of the mining district is evident. More of it is visible at the next two campgrounds, Flat Rock and Pole Flat. Blind Creek does have a nice overlook of the Yankee Fork River and a small supply center at Sunbeam Village about a mile away, but it is not secluded from the road. Be aware that bears are active in the area, so take precautions. There's a sixteen-day limit on stays.

12 Flat Rock/Pole Flat

Location: Northeast of Stanley
Sites: 21 (9 at Flat Rock, 12 at Pole Flat)
Facilities: Drinking water, vault toilets, fire rings
Fee per night: $
Elevation: 6,250 feet
Road conditions: Paved to the campgrounds (pavement ends just after reaching the campgrounds)
Management: Forest Service, Yankee Fork Office, (208) 838-2201
Reservations: No
Activities: Fishing, picnicking
Season: June 15–September 15
Finding the campgrounds: From Stanley drive 14.5 miles northeast on ID 75 to Sunbeam and then 2 miles north on the Yankee Fork Road/FR 013.
The campgrounds: These two cozy, forested campgrounds are close neighbors on the paved portion of the Yankee Fork Road; the Yankee Fork River is across the road from the campgrounds. They are nicely developed campgrounds backed up against a mountainside, with some small dredge pilings along its side, just to remind you that you're in an old dredge mining district. The Forest Service notes that bears are highly active in the area, so be careful to stow away your food when you're not fixing or eating it.

13 Custer No. 1

Location: Northeast of Stanley
Sites: 6
Facilities: Vault toilets, fire rings, pets allowed
Fee per night: $
Elevation: 6,600 feet
Road conditions: Generally good; the gravel road along the Yankee Fork usually is well maintained.
Management: Forest Service, Yankee Fork Office, (208) 838-2201
Reservations: No
Activities: Fishing, hiking, picnicking
Season: June 15–September 10
Finding the campground: From Stanley drive 14.5 miles northeast on ID 75 to Sunbeam, then north past Blind Creek Campground another 7 miles on FR 013 (the Yankee Fork Road and Custer Motorway), and then 3 miles northeast on Forest Road 070.
The campground: This is a relatively primitive site, with no water and only vault toilets for facilities. However, the Forest Service calls it a "Little used campground that sits in timber along the road. Ideal for large groups. Interesting rock formations along the river side." The forested location along the Yankee Fork River is pretty.

14 Bonanza

Location: Northeast of Stanley
Sites: 12 (family and group sites)
Facilities: Drinking water, vault toilets, fire rings, pets allowed
Fee per night: $
Elevation: 6,200 feet
Road conditions: From Sunbeam the Yankee Road Motorway is paved for 3 miles and then becomes a wide gravel road (prone to washboarding) for the next 6 miles.
Management: Forest Service, Yankee Fork Office, (208) 838-2201
Reservations: Call (877) 444-6777 or visit Web site www.reserveamerica.com.
Activities: Fishing, hiking, picnicking
Season: June 15–September 10
Finding the campground: From Stanley drive 14.9 miles northeast on ID 75, then 8 miles north on Yankee Fork Road/FR 013, and then a quarter mile west on Forest Road 074.
The campground: This is a family- and group-oriented campground, located close to the old Bonanza ghost town—which is definitely worth a visit. Between the old buildings in town and the dredge equipment (and dredge piles) nearby, you can get a real feeling for the old mining community. This is the only campground in the Yankee Fork area that does accept reservations.

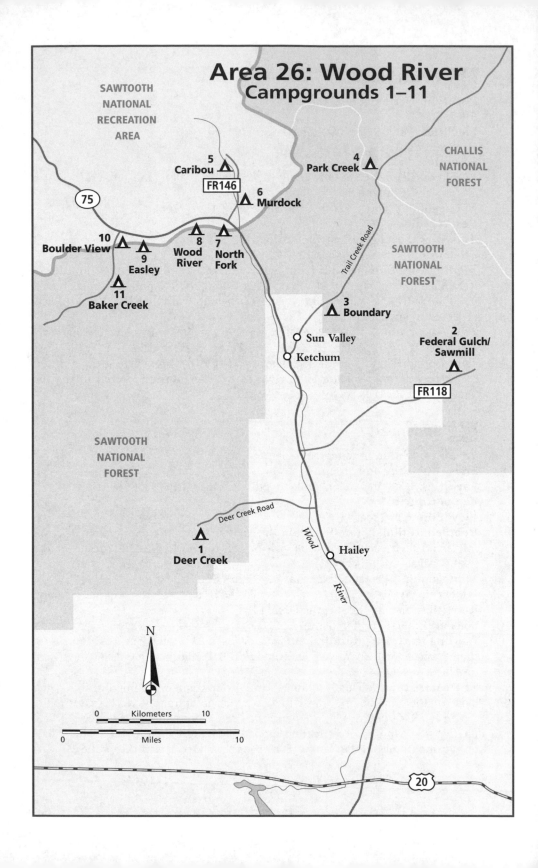

Area 26: Wood River
Campgrounds 1–11

SAWTOOTH
NATIONAL
RECREATION
AREA

CHALLIS
NATIONAL
FOREST

5
Caribou △

4
Park Creek △

FR146

6
△ Murdock

75

10
Boulder View △

△
8
Wood
River

△
7
North
Fork

SAWTOOTH
NATIONAL
FOREST

△
9
Easley

Trail Creek Road

11
Baker Creek △

3
△ Boundary

○ Sun Valley
○ Ketchum

2
Federal Gulch/
Sawmill
△

FR118

SAWTOOTH
NATIONAL
FOREST

Deer Creek Road

△
1
Deer Creek

Wood

○ Hailey

River

N

0   Kilometers   10

0   Miles   10

20

Area 26: Wood River

The Sun Valley area is the best-known recreation spot in Idaho, renowned mainly for its ski areas but also for its summer recreation and resort facilities. Its international fame is such that the Sun Valley–Ketchum–Hailey area has become home to movie stars and corporate CEOs, and the visitor traffic is such that traffic jams are not uncommon on the streets of Ketchum.

The campgrounds in this area, however, are well outside the heavily populated area, in the folds of the mountains overlooking the Wood River, which slows through the Sun Valley area. Elk and mule deer are often seen in these areas; mountain goats and moose are spotted on occasion. This is high mountain country, relatively cool even in the summer, early to receive snow in the fall.

The federal jurisdictions here have some significance for campers. The public lands near Ketchum, Hailey, and Sun Valley are operated by the Ketchum Ranger District in the Sawtooth National Forest. Because of the population center nearby, the district has placed a number of restrictions on use of the lands, including no camping outside designated spots.

About 8 miles north of Ketchum is the southern boundary of the Sawtooth National Recreation Area (which is, confusingly, also national forest land—but never mind that). The SNRA was created in 1976 as a recreation area. Here restrictions are a little looser. The SNRA, for example, encourages a policy of "dispersal," of camping outside designated campgrounds but preferably in areas that have also been used by other campers. If you're interested in doing that, check in with the SNRA headquarters on Idaho Highway 75, and the staff there can direct you to places with fire rings and established trails. The "dispersal" policy is expected to remain in place as long as dispersal campers exercise forest etiquette—packing out garbage, fully dousing fires, leaving behind little trace they were there.

The SNRA also manages its campgrounds differently. It contracts with concessionaires, who are campground managers; campground fees are divided between concessionaires and the SNRA. This approach tends to raise slightly the cost of staying at the campgrounds, but it does mean a manager is on hand. Also note that there are trailhead fees for parking at the head of certain established trails.

This is not especially good country for ATV enthusiasts, however. ATVs generally are not allowed in SNRA camping areas except on specific Forest Service roads.

The following listings will note whether the campground is in the Ketchum Ranger District or the SNRA.

Note that spaces in some of these campgrounds can be reserved, but others cannot. All spaces which are not (or cannot be) reserved are first come, first served.

For more information:

Sun Valley–Ketchum Chamber of Commerce
P.O. Box 2420
Sun Valley, ID 83353
(208) 774–3411
www.visitsunvalley.com

Sawtooth National Recreation Area Visitor Center
Star Route [8 miles north of Ketchum on ID 75]
(208) 727–5000

Salmon-Challis National Forest
Route 2, Box 600
Salmon, ID 83467
(208) 756–5100
www.fs.fed.us/r4/sc

Sawtooth National Forest
2647 Kimberly Road E
Twin Falls, ID 83301
(208) 737–3200
www.northrim.net.sawtoothnf

---

1 Deer Creek

Location: West of Hailey
Sites: 3
Facilities: Drinking water, vault toilets, fire rings
Fee per night: $
Elevation: 6,700 feet
Road conditions: Relatively easy-driving gravel roads into the mountains
Management: Forest Service, Ketchum Ranger District, (208) 622–5371
Reservations: No
Activities: Fishing, picnicking
Season: May 15–October 15
Finding the campground: From Hailey drive about 3 miles north on ID 75, and then turn west onto Deer Creek Road and continue about 8 miles into the mountains west of the Wood River Valley.
The campground: There are several small camping areas well up in the hills along Deer Creek, a pretty area outside the Wood River Valley bustle.

---

2 Federal Gulch/Sawmill

Location: East of Sun Valley
Sites: 6
Facilities: Drinking water (Federal Gulch only), vault toilets, picnic tables, fire rings
Fee per night: $
Elevation: 6,800 feet
Road conditions: From busy ID 75, the road is gravel and dusty, but an easy drive, up into the mountains east of the Wood River Valley.

Area 26

		Town	Sites	Max. RV length	Electric	Picnic	Fire rings	Toilets	Showers	Water	Dump station	Disability access	Recreation	Can reserve	Fees ($)	Season	Stay limit (days)
1	Deer Creek	Hailey	3	25		•	•	V		•			FHS		$	May–Oct.	14
2	Federal Gulch/ Sawmill	Hailey/ Ketchum	6	22		•	•	V		•			F		$	May–Oct.	3
3	Boundary	Ketchum	5	32		•	•	V		•			F		$	June–Oct.	14
4	Park Creek	Ketchum	15	16		•	•	V		•			FH		$	July–Sept.	14
5	Caribou	Ketchum	7	22		•	•	V		•			FH		$$	June–Oct.	14
6	Murdock	Ketchum	11	22		•	•	V					FH		$$	June–Oct.	14
7	North Fork	Ketchum	29	22		•	•	V		•			FH		$	June–Oct.	14
8	Wood River	Ketchum	30			•	•	V		•			FH	•	$	June–Oct.	14
9	Easley	Ketchum	10	22		•	•	V		•			FS	•	$$	June–Oct.	14
10	Boulder View	Ketchum	10	22		•	•	V		•			FH	•	$$	June–Oct.	14
11	Baker Creek	Ketchum	10	32		•	•	V		•			S		$	June–Oct.	14

Management: Forest Service, Ketchum Ranger District, (208) 622–5371
Reservations: No
Activities: Fishing, picnicking
Season: May 15–October 15 (depending on weather)
Finding the campgrounds: From Hailey drive 6 miles north (or, from Ketchum drive about 6 miles south) on ID 75 and then 11.5 miles east on Forest Road 118.
The campgrounds: These campgrounds are located on the east creek well east of the Wood River Valley. The landscape is borderline between desert and forest, but shade is available. The unusually short three-day stay limit is an indicator of how busy this area can become. Small trailers are allowed.

3 Boundary

Location: Northeast of Ketchum
Sites: 5
Facilities: Vault toilets, picnic tables, fire rings
Fee per night: $
Elevation: 5,700 feet
Road conditions: Good and paved until close to the campground
Management: Forest Service, Ketchum Ranger District, (208) 622–5371
Reservations: No
Activities: Fishing, picnicking
Season: June 15–October 15

Finding the campground: From ID 75 in downtown Ketchum, take the Sun Valley Road east to Sun Valley, continue on it up into the mountains; this becomes Trail Creek Road. The campground is located about 3 miles up that road.

The campground: This is a popular Ketchum-area camp for picnicking and other day use, but limited camping is available as well. The countryside is high desert, with some mountain forests in the area.

4 Park Creek

Location: Northeast of Sun Valley
Sites: 15
Facilities: Drinking water, vault toilets, picnic tables, fire rings
Fee per night: $
Elevation: 7,700 feet
Road conditions: Good and paved at the lower levels, but as Trail Creek Road moves up into the mountains, it becomes a narrow, rough (and worn) gravel road. The Forest Service has noted for this area, and for good reason, "Make sure you bring a spare tire!"
Management: Forest Service, Challis Ranger District, (208) 879–4321
Reservations: No
Activities: Fishing, hiking, picnicking
Season: July–September
Finding the campground: From busy ID 75 in downtown Ketchum, take Sun Valley Road east to Sun Valley, continue on it up into the mountains; this becomes Trail Creek Road. The campground is located about 12 miles up that road.

The campground: More remote and primitive than you'd expect, Park Creek Campground is only a few miles away from Sun Valley.

5 Caribou

Location: North of Ketchum
Sites: 7
Facilities: Drinking water, vault toilets, fire rings
Fee per night: $$
Elevation: 6,300 feet
Road conditions: The dirt road from the SNRA headquarters into the campground is good but prone to washboarding.
Management: Forest Service, Sawtooth National Recreation Area, (208) 727–5000
Reservations: No
Activities: Fishing, hiking, picnicking
Season: June 1–October 15
Finding the campground: From Ketchum drive almost 8 miles north on ID 75 to the Sawtooth National Recreation Area headquarters and then 3 miles north on Forest Road 146 (North Fork Road).

The campground: Caribou is an attractive site, though well away from the main Wood River activities. The chief attraction of this site is the close-by access to the Boulder Mountain area trails.

6 Murdock

Location: North of Ketchum
Sites: 11
Facilities: Vault toilets, fire rings
Fee per night: $$
Elevation: 6,300 feet
Road conditions: Good and easily passable flat gravel road, with some washboarding and dust to be expected
Management: Forest Service, Sawtooth National Recreation Area, (208) 727-5000
Reservations: No
Activities: Fishing, hiking, picnicking
Season: June 1–October 15
Finding the campground: From Ketchum drive almost 8 miles north on ID 75 to the SNRA headquarters and then 2 miles north on North Fork Road (FR 146).
The campground: Popular with Idaho campers, this smallish campground is close to the SNRA headquarters (just a couple of miles down the road) and even closer to an RV dump station, where water is available also. It's a restful place but also a good place to use as a base for hiking. A stream of the Wood River runs adjacent.

7 North Fork

Location: North of Ketchum
Sites: 29
Facilities: Drinking water, vault toilets, fire rings
Fee per night: $
Elevation: 6,280 feet
Road conditions: The gravel road can be washboarded but is easy access for most camping vehicles.
Management: Forest Service, Sawtooth National Recreation Area, (208) 727-5000
Reservations: No
Activities: Fishing, hiking, picnicking
Season: June 1–October 15
Finding the campground: From Ketchum drive almost 8 miles north on ID 75 to the SNRA headquarters, and then continue east on gravel road for about 3 miles to the campgrounds, following the signs.
The campground: Much like the Murdock site, North Fork is a quiet, shady area along the Wood River—a good spot for fishing. Like most other public campgrounds in this area, it is located in the river valley, not high up in the mountains (the substantial elevation here notwithstanding).

8 Wood River

Location: North of Ketchum
Sites: 30
Facilities: Drinking water, vault toilets, fire rings
Fee per night: $
Elevation: 6,350 feet
Road conditions: The campground is adjacent to paved ID 75; the gravel roads within the site are easy access (but sometimes pitted, so watch your speed and the road in front of you).
Management: Forest Service, Sawtooth National Recreation Area, (208) 727-5000
Reservations: Call (877) 444-6777 or visit Web site www.reserveamerica.com.
Activities: Fishing, hiking, picnicking
Season: June 1–October 15
Finding the campground: From Ketchum drive about 9 miles north on ID 75 (past the SNRA headquarters) to the camp entrance.
The campground: This campground gets heavy use, partly because of the fine location on the Wood River (many of the campsites are both shaded and river-adjacent) and because of the varied activities possible here. Besides fishing and hiking (there are some excellent hiking trails close by), there's a campground amphitheater. Also next door is a large day-use picnic area, which also gets plenty of traffic.

9 Easley

Location: North of Ketchum
Sites: 10
Facilities: Drinking water, vault toilets, fire rings
Fee per night: $$
Elevation: 6,800 feet
Road conditions: Close by ID 75; the pockmarked gravel road is barely a mile long.
Management: Forest Service, Sawtooth National Recreation Area, (208) 727-5000
Reservations: Call (877) 444-6777 or visit Web site www.reserveamerica.com.
Activities: Fishing, picnicking, swimming
Season: June 15–September 15
Finding the campground: From Ketchum drive 14 miles north on ID 75, and then turn off to the west at the campground sign.
The campground: This is one of the more developed public campgrounds in the state, owing partly to the private groups involved with it. (The campground store—an unusual thing in public campgrounds—is owned and operated by the Idaho Baptist Convention.) This campground has a swimming pool and hot springs as well as camping sites along the Wood River. The location is pretty, if a little busy. Easley is a favorite location for church and school groups in the region. There's available parking for extra vehicles.

10 Boulder View

Location: North of Ketchum
Sites: 10
Facilities: Drinking water, vault toilets, fire rings, pets allowed
Fee per night: $$
Elevation: 6,800 feet
Road conditions: Very good; gravel on the short distance from ID 75 into the campground.
Management: Forest Service, Sawtooth National Recreation Area, (208) 727-5000
Reservations: Call (877) 444-6777 or visit Web site www.reserveamerica.com.
Activities: Fishing, hiking, picnicking
Season: June 1-October 15
Finding the campground: From Ketchum drive 14.5 miles north on ID 75 and then turn left just beyond Easley Road.
The campground: This campground almost is an extension of the Easley complex, which is within walking distance to the south. Like most of the other campgrounds in this region, Boulder View is directly on the Wood River in an attractive shaded area.

11 Baker Creek

Location: North of Ketchum
Sites: 10
Facilities: Drinking water, vault toilets, fire rings
Fee per night: $
Elevation: 6,880 feet
Road conditions: Generally good gravel up to the campground
Management: Forest Service, Ketchum Ranger District, (208) 622-5371
Reservations: No
Activities: Picnicking, swimming
Season: June 1-October 15
Finding the campground: From Ketchum drive 15 miles north on ID 75 and then 1 mile west on Baker Creek Road.
The campground: This campground has been undeveloped, so check with the Ketchum Ranger District on its status when you consider this one. The area does allow for snowmobiling and a wide range of summer uses.

Area 27: Blaine Valley

One of the highest valleys in Idaho runs east-west south of the Sun Valley area, from the lava fields of Craters of the Moon in the east to the mountains near Anderson Ranch Reservoir in the west. It is flat country, but it has a short growing season, so it has never attracted large numbers of farmers.

It is attracting large numbers of recreation visitors, though, because various places in it are excellent for fishing, hunting, hiking, and other purposes. The Magic Reservoir is a popular gathering spot for boaters (beware the steep grades headed into the basin). About a half hour due east is the Silver Creek area, made famous for its terrific fly-fishing by Ernest Hemingway.

For more information:

Sawtooth National Forest
2647 Kimberly Road E
Twin Falls, ID 83301
(208) 737–3200
www.northrim.net.sawtoothnf

Bureau of Land Management
400 West F Street
P.O. Box 2-B
Shoshone, ID 83352
(208) 732–7200

Bureau of Reclamation
1359 Hansen Avenue
Burley, ID 83318
(208) 678–0461

Area 27

	Town	Sites	Max. RV length	Electric	Picnic	Fire rings	Toilets	Showers	Water	Dump station	Disability access	Recreation	Can reserve	Fees ($)	Season	Stay limit (days)
1 Bounds/Canyon Transfer Camp	Fairfield	16			•	•	V		•			FH		$	May–Sept.	14
2 Myrtle Point/ Lava Point/Lava Cove	Shoshone	U	22		•	•	V					BF			Year-round	14
3 Little Wood Reservoir	Carey	U				•	V		•			BFS		$	May–Sept.	14
4 High-Five	Carey	4				•						F		$	May–Sept.	14

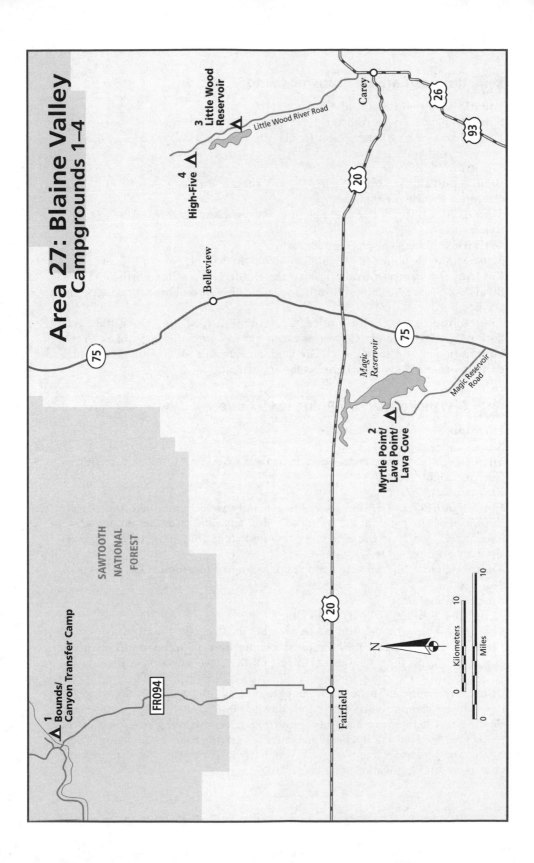

Area 27: Blaine Valley
Campgrounds 1–4

1 Bounds/
Canyon Transfer Camp

FR094

SAWTOOTH
NATIONAL
FOREST

75

Belleview

High-Five
4

3
Little Wood
Reservoir

Little Wood River Road

Carey

26

20

93

Magic
Reservoir

75

Magic Reservoir
Road

Myrtle Point/
Lava Point/
Lava Cove
2

20

Fairfield

N

Kilometers   10

0

Miles   10

0

1 Bounds/Canyon Transfer Camp

Location: North of Fairfield
Sites: 16 (6 at Canyon Transfer, 10 at Bounds)
Facilities: Drinking water, vault toilets, fire rings, pets allowed
Fee per night: $
Elevation: 5,585 feet
Road conditions: Gravel, narrow, and rugged; bring a sturdy and high-clearance vehicle for this one.
Management: Forest Service, Ketchum Ranger District, (208) 622–5371
Reservations: No
Activities: Fishing, hiking, picnicking
Season: May–September (depending on weather)
Finding the campgrounds: From Fairfield drive 19 miles north on Forest Road 094 (Soldier Mountain Road), 3 miles northwest on Forest Road 093, and 5 miles northwest on FR 094.
The campgrounds: Bounds offers more prime fishing area along the South Fork of the Boise River. (Canyon is about a mile away on Big Smokey Creek, but the fishing is just as good.) The landscape around Bounds is more wooded than around Canyon, where it's more open-air.

2 Myrtle Point/Lava Point/Lava Cove

Location: North of Shoshone
Sites: Undesignated number
Facilities: Boat launch access (except at Lava Cove), vault toilets, fire rings
Fee per night: None
Elevation: 4,900 feet
Road conditions: The desert road is generally well maintained, but beware the washboarding and (in the spring and after any rain) potential muddy areas. Part of the road near the lake is narrow and steep, but most motor vehicles should find it passable.
Management: Bureau of Land Management, Shoshone District, (208) 732–7200
Reservations: No
Activities: Boating, fishing, picnicking
Season: All year (though limited by weather as a practical matter)
Finding the campgrounds: From Shoshone drive 18 miles north on Idaho Highway 75 and then 4 miles northwest on the Magic Reservoir Road to the cutoffs to the three campgrounds.
The campgrounds: These three campgrounds all are barely developed (primitive) desert campgrounds that perch on the west banks of Magic Reservoir. Boating and fishing are good here, but take it easy coming in—some of the roads near the lake are steep and make trailer driving more challenging. There is no garbage service here, so pack it out if you pack it in. Be sure to bring your own drinking water; none is available on-site.

3 Little Wood Reservoir

Location: Northwest of Carey
Sites: Undesignated number (about 20)
Facilities: Drinking water, vault toilets, fire rings, river access, pull-through sites, pets allowed
Fee per night: $
Elevation: 5,500 feet
Road conditions: Paved nearly to the Little Wood Reservoir, but the pavement is often broken.
Management: Bureau of Reclamation, Burley office, (208) 678-0461
Reservations: Generally none, but for information call (208) 436-4187.
Activities: Boating, fishing, swimming
Season: May 15-September 30
Finding the campground: From Carey drive 1 mile north on U.S. Highway 93 and then about 10 miles northwest on the Little Wood River Road.
The campground: A remote but easily accessed lakefront campground, Little Wood is larger than High-Five and has a campground host during the season. This is a desert area, with plenty of sagebrush and a modest crop of juniper trees. This campground is well set up for fishing, with shoreline angling possibilities as well as boating; a boat ramp is available. The reservoir is not large, however, and you'll rarely see Jet Skiers or other boating enthusiasts. The grounds have what amounts to about twenty camping spaces, but they aren't on pads or otherwise designated; this is a "find your own spot" primitive campground.

4 High-Five

Location: Northwest of Carey
Sites: 4 (approximately)
Facilities: Pull-through sites, fire rings, pets allowed
Fee per night: $
Elevation: 5,500 feet
Road conditions: Paved (though the pavement is sometimes badly worn) two-thirds of the way from Carey, then good gravel road along the river. However, a sharp turn at a crossing of the river makes this road problematic for vehicles more than about 25 feet in length (though some do make it).
Management: Bureau of Reclamation, (208) 678-0461
Reservations: Generally none, but for information call (208) 678-0461.
Activities: Fishing
Season: May 15-September 30
Finding the campground: From Carey drive 1 mile north on US 93, then about 10 miles northwest on the Little Wood River Road, and then continue north on it about 15 miles.
The campground: High-Five is a generally primitive campground—it has no water and no toilets—though it was refurbished and upgraded a bit by the Bureau of Reclamation in the late 1990s. This is not a forested area; at High-Five

you can expect a desert atmosphere with some shade from juniper trees. In contrast to the Little Wood Reservoir campground area, this is a riverside campground (along the Little Wood, which runs parallel and to the east of the much more famous Big Wood where Ketchum and Hailey sit) rather than a lakeside campground. This campground, like the Little Wood, is a whole world away from the better-known recreational sites to the west, and it is also usually less crowded. The exceptions: during hunting season and at certain key points during fishing seasons.

Area 28: Magic Valley

The part of south-central Idaho near the Snake River is called the Magic Valley for the way the landscape turned green when it was plied with irrigation water from the Snake. (Farther away from the Snake, the landscape once more looks like its natural self: sagebrush-littered desert.) Along the many miles of the Snake River, the major human settlement is the gambling outpost of Jackpot, Nevada, on the Idaho border.

But as with most desert lands, there's much more that is visible to those who are watchful. Scattered streams and lakes show off fine distant-horizon landscapes and plentiful fishing and hiking.

The campgrounds here come in two main areas. One is the Rock Creek area southeast of Twin Falls (directly south of the small city of Hansen), which features mountain sites managed by the Forest Service. The other, to the north of the city of Shoshone, is a vast area managed by the Bureau of Land Management, including several remote and relatively primitive camping sites.

For more information:

Bureau of Land Management
400 West F Street
P.O. Box 2-B
Shoshone, ID 83352
(208) 732–7200

Area 28

		Town	Sites	Max. RV length	Electric	Picnic	Fire rings	Toilets	Showers	Water	Dump station	Disability access	Recreation	Can reserve	Fees ($)	Season	Stay limit (days)
1	Schipper/Birch Glen	Hansen	8			•	•	V		•			H			June–Sept.	14
2	Penstemon	Hansen	12	22		•	•	V		•			H		$	June–Sept.	14
3	Pettit	Hansen	9	22		•	•	V		•			H		$	June–Sept.	14
4	Diamondfield Jack	Hansen	7	35		•	•	V		•			FH		$	Year-round	14
5	Porcupine Springs	Hansen	15	32		•	•	V		•		•	H		$$–$$$	June–Sept.	14
6	Lud Drexler Park	Rogerson	20	25		•	•	V		•			BFH		$	Year-round	14
7	Gray's Landing/ Norton Bay	Rogerson	U			•	•	V					BF			Year-round	14
8	Thorn Creek	Gooding	U			•	•	V					BF			Year-round	14

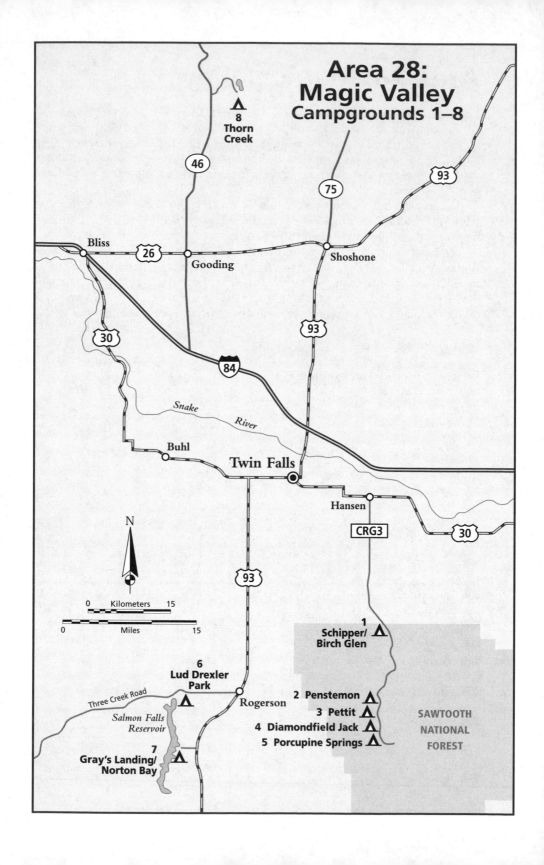

Area 28:
Magic Valley
Campgrounds 1–8

8
Thorn Creek

46

75

93

Bliss   26   Gooding   Shoshone

30

84

Snake   *River*

Buhl

Twin Falls

Hansen

CRG3

30

N

0   Kilometers   15

0   Miles   15

93

1
Schipper/ Birch Glen

6
Lud Drexler Park

Three Creek Road

Salmon Falls Reservoir

Rogerson

2 **Penstemon**

3 **Pettit**

4 **Diamondfield Jack**

5 **Porcupine Springs**

SAWTOOTH

NATIONAL

FOREST

7
Gray's Landing/ Norton Bay

▮**1**▮ Schipper/Birch Glen

Location: South of Hansen
Sites: 8 (6 at Schipper, 2 at Birch Glen)
Facilities: Drinking water (Birch Glen only), vault toilets, fire rings
Fee per night: None
Elevation: 4,600 feet
Road conditions: Paved to the campground
Management: Forest Service, Burley/Twin Falls Ranger District, (208) 678–0430
Reservations: No
Activities: Hiking, picnicking
Season: June–September
Finding the campgrounds: From Hansen drive 18 miles south on Twin Falls County Road G3.
The campgrounds: Schipper is a little more primitive (no water) than some of the other sites in the Rock Creek area. Be aware that only limited space is available for motor homes; if you have any question about whether yours might fit, call the ranger district. Birch Glen (with just two sites), which is next door, has a few more facilities, including water.

▮**2**▮ Penstemon

Location: South of Hansen
Sites: 12
Facilities: Drinking water, vault toilets, fire rings
Fee per night: $
Elevation: 6,650 feet
Road conditions: Paved to the campgrounds
Management: Forest Service, Burley/Twin Falls Ranger District, (208) 678–0430
Reservations: No
Activities: Hiking, picnicking
Season: June 1–September 30
Finding the campground: From Hansen drive 24.1 miles south on Twin Falls CR G3.
The campground: This is actually two campgrounds, Upper and Lower Penstemon, which are close by but different in appeal. Lower Penstemon has a few large group sites, frequented mainly by family groups, while Upper Penstemon is geared toward single-RV users. Like the other three in this area, the location is wooded.

▮**3**▮ Pettit

Location: South of Hansen
Sites: 9
Facilities: Drinking water, vault toilets, fire rings
Fee per night: $

Elevation: 6,800 feet
Road conditions: Paved to the campground
Management: Forest Service, Burley/Twin Falls Ranger District, (208) 678–0430
Reservations: No
Activities: Hiking, picnicking
Season: June 1–September 30
Finding the campground: From Hansen drive 27 miles south on Twin Falls CR G3.
The campground: A prettier Rock Creek site than Diamondfield Jack, Pettit sits among the pine trees just below a desert springs. Of the campgrounds in this area, this one has the easiest road access.

4 Diamondfield Jack

Location: South of Hansen
Sites: 7
Facilities: Drinking water (hand pump), vault toilets, fire rings
Fee per night: $
Elevation: 7,000 feet
Road conditions: Paved to the campground
Management: Forest Service, Burley/Twin Falls Ranger District, (208) 678–0430
Reservations: Call (877) 444–6777 or visit Web site www.reserveamerica.com (for group site).
Activities: Fishing, hiking, picnicking
Season: All year, though in practice limited by weather
Finding the campground: From Hansen drive 28 miles south on Twin Falls CR G3.
The campground: This Rock Creek–area campground is up and above the Snake River Valley, mildly shaded but still in generally desert country. Diamondfield Jack (named for a colorful Old West figure who was convicted and later cleared of murder in Idaho) is most popular in the winter, when Magic Valley people pile up here for snowmobiling and cross-country skiing. The restrooms are heated in the winter. You can reserve the one group site, but the individual sites are first come, first served.

5 Porcupine Springs

Location: South of Hansen
Sites: 15
Facilities: Drinking water, vault toilets, fire rings, barrier-free access
Fee per night: $$–$$$
Elevation: 6,950 feet
Road conditions: Paved almost to the campground, with well-maintained lane-and-a-half gravel road the last couple of miles
Management: Forest Service, Burley/Twin Falls Ranger District, (208) 678–0430

Reservations: No
Activities: Hiking, horseback riding, picnicking
Season: June 1–September 30
Finding the campground: From Hansen drive 31 miles south on Twin Falls CR G3.
The campground: The largest and most popular of the Rock Creek sites, Porcupine is also the best appointed for people with disabilities and well designed for horseback riding. (The site designers even set up a device that helps disabled riders to mount a horse.) The wooded setting along the spring is the most attractive of the campgrounds in this area. Porcupine has been recently refurbished and has a relatively modern feel to it.

6 Lud Drexler Park

Location: West of Rogerson
Sites: 20
Facilities: Drinking water (faucet), picnic tables, vault toilets, fire rings, dump station
Fee per night: $
Elevation: 4,500 feet
Road conditions: The 7 miles of desert gravel road is (depending on when the grading crew was last in the area) either a wide, flat, pleasant road or pothole hell.
Management: Bureau of Land Management, Burley District, (208) 678-5514
Reservations: Call the local BLM office at (208) 678-5514.
Activities: Boating, fishing, hiking, picnicking
Season: All year, though in practice limited by weather
Finding the campground: From U.S. Highway 93 at Rogerson, drive 8 miles south and then take the Three Creek Road west 7 miles to Salmon Falls Dam.
The campground: Lud Drexler is more developed than most BLM campgrounds, with actual designated camping sites and even a dump station. This is an open desert site where the predominant vegetation is sagebrush; some trees have been planted, but they are small and provide minimal shade. However, the fishing (for trout, walleye, kokanee) is said to be good at Salmon Falls Reservoir, and that is what draws many of the campers here. There is no garbage service here, so pack it out if you pack it in.

7 Gray's Landing/Norton Bay

Location: Southwest of Rogerson
Sites: Undesignated number
Facilities: Picnic tables, vault toilets, fire rings
Fee per night: None
Elevation: 4,500 feet
Road conditions: The 2 miles of gravel desert road are mostly flat and wide but generally roughly graded: Drive slow and prepare to bounce a lot.
Management: Bureau of Land Management, Burley District, (208) 678-5514
Reservations: No

Activities: Boating, fishing, picnicking
Season: All year, though in practice limited by weather
Finding the campgrounds: From Rogerson drive 8 miles south on US 93 and then 2 miles west on Salmon Falls Reservoir Road to the campgrounds.
The campgrounds: Smaller and less developed than Lud Drexler, these two campground areas near each other on the reservoir shoreline also offer good access for boating and fishing on Salmon Falls Reservoir. They are open-air desert sites; don't expect a lot of shade. (In the summer be sure to bring your own.) Don't expect any water, either. (Bring your own of that, too.) There is no garbage service here, so pack it out if you pack it in.

8 Thorn Creek

Location: North of Gooding
Sites: Undesignated number
Facilities: Vault toilets, fire rings
Fee per night: None
Elevation: 4,500 feet
Road conditions: The desert road is generally well maintained, wide and easy to travel in the summer; beware of sticky muddy spots in the spring.
Management: Bureau of Land Management, Shoshone District, (208) 886–2206
Reservations: No
Activities: Boating, fishing, picnicking
Season: All year, though in practice limited by weather
Finding the campground: From Gooding drive 21 miles north on Idaho Highway 46 and then east for 4 miles on desert road (follow the signs to the campground).
The campground: Located out in the desert (no woods in the area) on Thorn Creek Reservoir, this is a favored fishing hole for many Magic Valley residents; the BLM figures that most of the visitors here come from within a two-hour radius. If you like desert camping—which can have a deeply calming and cool appeal especially at night—this is a good bet. But be aware: This is a typical BLM site, which means few facilities (no local drinking water) and not even any designated camping sites. There is no garbage service here, so pack it out if you pack it in.

Area 29: Cassia

The Burley and Rupert area along the Snake River has its attractions. Lake Walcott, one of the first bodies of water created by the Bureau of Reclamation in this region, is one of them. And there are events, such as boat racing on the Snake River near Burley in the spring.

The most spectacular landscapes, however, can be found in the mountains to the south, over in the valleys of Albion and the City of Rocks (a national monument). These are places that remind the visitor of the canyonlands of southern Utah, but in some ways eerier. To drive through the City of Rocks is to pass through something that in an odd way almost feels like a ghost town that never was.

For more information:

Mini-Cassia Chamber of Commerce
324 Scott Avenue
Rupert, ID 83350
(208) 679-4793

Sawtooth National Forest
2647 Kimberly Road E
Twin Falls, ID 83301
(208) 737-3200
www.northrim.net.sawtoothnf

Bureau of Land Management
15 East 200 South
Burley, ID 83318
(208) 677-6641

City of Rocks National Reserve
P.O. Box 169
Almo, ID 83312
(208) 824-5519

---

1 Brackenbury

Location: South of Albion
Sites: 14
Facilities: Drinking water, vault toilets, fire rings
Fee per night: $
Elevation: 8,350 feet
Road conditions: Good, paved road (albeit sometimes steep) up to the campground, gravel road within
Management: Forest Service, Burley/Twin Falls Ranger District, (208) 678-0430

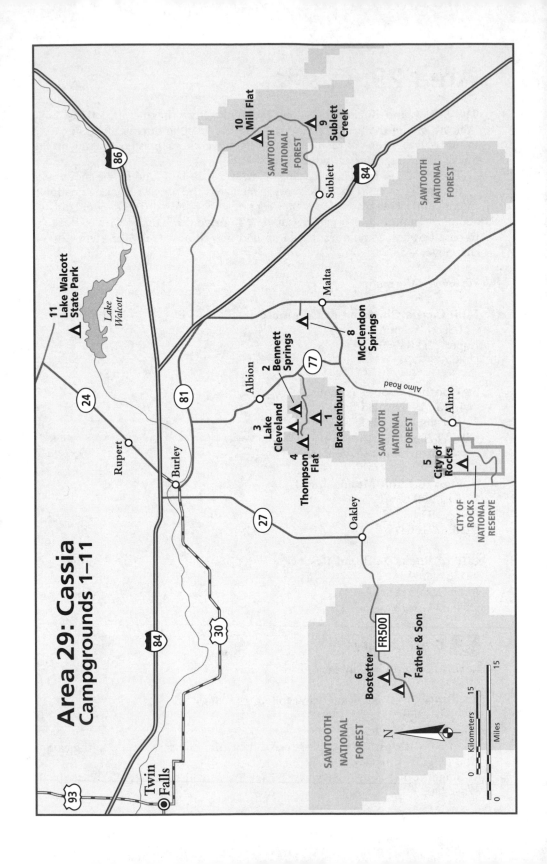

Area 29: Cassia Campgrounds 1–11

Area 29

	Town	Sites	Max. RV length	Electric	Picnic	Fire rings	Toilets	Showers	Water	Dump station	Disability access	Recreation	Can reserve	Fees ($)	Season	Stay limit (days)
1 Brackenbury	Albion	14	30		•	•	V		•			F	•	$	July–Sept.	14
2 Bennett Springs	Albion	7	30		•	•	V					H	•	$	May–Oct.	14
3 Lake Cleveland	Albion	7	20		•	•	V					F	•	$	July–Sept.	14
4 Thompson Flat	Albion	16	22		•	•	V					H	•	$	May–Oct.	14
5 City of Rocks	Almo	78			•	•	V		•			H	•	$	March–Nov.	
6 Bostetter	Oakley	18	16		•	•	V		•			FH	•	$	June–Oct.	14
7 Father & Son	Oakley	19	12		•	•	V		•			FH	•	$	June–Oct.	14
8 McClendon Springs	Malta	U			•	•	V					H			May–Nov.	14
9 Sublett Creek	Sublett	7	22		•	•	V		•			H	•	$	June–Nov.	14
10 Mill Flat	Sublett						V		•				•		June–Nov.	
11 Lake Walcott State Park	Rupert	22	35		•	•	F		•	•	•	BFH	•	$$	Year-round	

Reservations: Call (877) 444–6777 or visit Web site www.reserveamerica.com.
Activities: Fishing, picnicking
Season: July 10–September 30 (depending on weather)
Finding the campground: Follow Idaho Highway 77 southeast of Albion 5.5 miles, and then go 9.6 miles west on Forest Road 549 (the road to the Pomerelle Ski Area).
The campground: Brackenbury is the lowest in elevation of the Pomerelle-area campgrounds and the most difficult to spot (there's a turnoff at 9.6 miles off Forest Road 549). This is a richly forested campground tucked away on a mountainside, but with limited view.

2 Bennett Springs

Location: South of Albion
Sites: 7
Facilities: Vault toilets, fire rings
Fee per night: $
Elevation: 7,400 feet
Road conditions: Good, paved road (albeit sometimes steep) up to the campground, gravel road within; watch the steep descent into the campground off the Pomerelle Road.
Management: Forest Service, Burley/Twin Falls Ranger District, (208) 678–0430
Reservations: Call (877) 444–6777 or visit Web site www.reserveamerica.com.
Activities: Hiking, picnicking

Season: May 15–October 31 (depending on weather)
Finding the campground: Follow ID 77 southeast of Albion 5.5 miles, and then continue 7 miles southwest on FR 549 (the road to the Pomerelle Ski Area).
The campground: Bennett Springs is a small but popular campground, especially because those higher up the mountain (Lake Cleveland, Thompson Flat), while more spectacular, have shorter seasons. The campground is located in a pretty wooded draw with an energetic stream flowing through the middle; a picture-perfect campground, though with limited services—no drinking water, no dump station. You're roughing it here in gorgeous landscape. Be aware too of the high elevation; the air turns quite brisk in the nighttime.

3 Lake Cleveland

Location: South of Albion
Sites: 7
Facilities: Vault toilets, fire rings
Fee per night: $
Elevation: 8,300 feet
Road conditions: Good, paved road (albeit sometimes steep) up to the campground, gravel road within
Management: Forest Service, Burley/Twin Falls Ranger District, (208) 678-0430
Reservations: Call (877) 444–6777 or visit Web site www.reserveamerica.com.
Activities: Fishing, picnicking
Season: July 10–September 30 (depending on weather)
Finding the campground: Follow ID 77 southeast of Albion 5.5 miles, and then go 10 miles west on FR 549 (the road to the Pomerelle Ski Area).
The campground: This one's on the very short list of most spectacular settings of any campground in Idaho. Picture this: You climb for 10 miles up the road toward Pomerelle Ski Area, which lets you look down not only over the city of Albion but over the Snake River Plain beyond, and beyond that all the way—more than 100 miles—to the Sawtooth Mountains. Look up, and you'll see, atop Harrison Mountain, a lookout station so well situated it can see over a huge swath of Idaho. On the side of this mountain, in a shallow pocket, is round (and perfectly blue) little Lake Cleveland and next to it a string of camping spots. Facilities are modest, but the location can't be beat. A couple of seasonal notes: Because of the high elevation, the site usually doesn't open until sometime in July (a call ahead would be advisable); and, while fishing is allowed in the lake, fish populations aren't sustained there naturally, so fresh stocks of fish are planted there every summer. That means, of course, fishing will be unproductive until the state fisheries people arrive. A further note: Local legend has it that Lake Cleveland is an extinct volcano. (From above, it certainly looks like one.) The Forest Service says that no, it isn't; it was gouged out by a glacier.

4 Thompson Flat

Location: South of Albion
Sites: 16
Facilities: Vault toilets, fire rings
Fee per night: $
Elevation: 9,500 feet
Road conditions: Good, paved road (albeit sometimes steep) near to the campground, an often rugged gravel road (perhaps best traversed by a pickup, SUV, or like vehicle) within
Management: Forest Service, Burley/Twin Falls Ranger District, (208) 678-0430
Reservations: Call (877) 444-6777 or visit Web site www.reserveamerica.com.
Activities: Hiking, picnicking
Season: May 15–October 31 (depending on weather)
Finding the campground: Follow ID 77 southeast of Albion 5.5 miles, and then continue 10 miles west on FR 549 (the road to the Pomerelle Ski Area).
The campground: Thompson Flat has one of the highest elevations of any campground in Idaho. It has views and local scenery less spectacular than some of the other campgrounds in these mountains and is preferred more by hunters and serious high-altitude hikers.

5 City of Rocks

Location: South of Albion and southwest of Almo
Sites: 78
Facilities: Drinking water, vault toilets
Fee per night: $
Elevation: 5,390 feet
Road conditions: Gravel, but easily passable in season
Management: Idaho Department of Parks and Recreation, National Park Service, (208) 824-5519
Reservations: Call (877) 444-6777 or visit Web site www.reserveamerica.com.
Activities: Hiking, picknicking
Season: March 1–November 30
Finding the campground: From Albion take ID 77 south about 14 miles, then turn right (west) on the Almo Road to Almo; the pavement ends at the small town of Almo. The campground is 3 miles southwest of Almo on City of Rocks Road.
The campground: The rock sculptures—sculpted over hundreds of thousands of years by wind and water—tower overhead, almost wherever you go in this park area. Camping is relatively primitive for a Park Service location. The gravel and dirt road connecting Almo to the east and Oakley to the west (on opposite sides of the City of Rocks) is generally good in the summer but subject to deep mud during other seasons; check ahead with Idaho Parks and Recreation.

6 Bostetter

Location: West of Oakley
Sites: 18
Facilities: Drinking water, vault toilets, fire rings
Fee per night: $
Elevation: 7,100 feet
Road conditions: Gravel road but generally well maintained (rougher as you climb into the mountains) and usually fine for trailers
Management: Forest Service, Burley/Twin Falls Ranger District, (208) 678-0430
Reservations: Call (877) 444-6777 or visit Web site www.reserveamerica.com.
Activities: Fishing, hiking, picnicking
Season: June 1-October 15 (depending on weather)
Finding the campground: From Oakley drive 19.7 miles west on Forest Road 500.
The campground: This campground and nearby Father & Son are not as heavily used as the Rock Creek campgrounds (such as Porcupine) to the west, but that may be your ticket if you look to escape the crowds. Not that smaller crowds are Bostetter's only assets. The location among the pine trees is pretty, families from the Twin Falls and Burley areas do like to spend the weekend up here, and in the fall hunters do crowd the site—this is a top-of-the-line hunting jumping-off point.

7 Father & Son

Location: West of Oakley
Sites: 19
Facilities: Drinking water, vault toilets, fire rings
Fee per night: $
Elevation: 7,200 feet
Road conditions: Gravel road but generally well maintained (rougher as you climb into the mountains) and usually fine for trailers
Management: Forest Service, Burley/Twin Falls Ranger District, (208) 678-0430
Reservations: Call (877) 444-6777 or visit Web site www.reserveamerica.com.
Activities: Fishing, hiking, picnicking
Season: June 1-October 15 (depending on weather)
Finding the campground: From Oakley drive 21 miles west on FR 500.
The campground: Father & Son is a lot like Bostetter, even woodsier and somewhat higher in elevation, which often makes it pleasantly cool in the summer. And like Bostetter, it is a hunters' favorite in the fall.

8 McClendon Springs

Location: Northwest of Malta
Sites: No designated sites (room for about 5 RVs or tents)
Facilities: Picnic tables, fire rings, vault toilets
Fee per night: None
Elevation: 4,900 feet
Road conditions: An easy, lane-and-a-half gravel road
Management: Bureau of Land Management, Burley District, (208) 678–5514
Reservations: Ordinarily none, but call (208) 678–5514 for availability.
Activities: Hiking, picnicking
Season: May 15–November 15
Finding the campground: From Malta drive 1.5 miles west on South Burrow Pit Road, and 2 miles north.
The campground: Think "oasis"—this is a spot of green on a high desert floor, in a large valley. The green comes from a spring (after which the campground was named) located nearby and a pond next to the camping area. The campground is located next to the Old California Trail (which split off from the Oregon Trail east of here); a good hike can be had walking along the old ruts. This campground has no drinking water.

9 Sublett Creek

Location: Southeast of Sublett
Sites: 7
Facilities: Drinking water, vault toilets, fire rings
Fee per night: $
Elevation: 5,400 feet
Road conditions: Semirugged; after the first few miles traveling farm country on wide and easy gravel roads, the roads turn narrow and winding, closely hugging foothills and overlooking water bodies. Passable in most vehicles, but most comfortably in a pickup or sturdy SUV.
Management: Forest Service, Burley/Twin Falls Ranger District, (208) 678–0430
Reservations: Call (877) 444–6777 or visit Web site www.reserveamerica.com.
Activities: Hiking, ATVs, picnicking
Season: June 1–November 15 (depending on weather)
Finding the campground: From Sublett drive east on the Sublett Road (bearing gently south) about 11 miles to the campground, almost entirely over gravel roads.
The campground: This campground, along with Mill Flat to the north, is one of Idaho's premier "ATV heaven" locations—camping areas where ATVers are actually welcome and where trails are set up for them. You get to the campground passing by the pretty Sublett Reservoir; the campground straddles the active Sublett Creek, which feeds it. The landscape is mostly desert, but there are plenty of trees and other vegetation near the creek. This is a relatively re-

mote area, far from population centers, and only the determined camp here—most of the time. But Forest Service personnel report that in some seasons, notably Memorial Day weekend, this campground (and Mill Flat) often are packed with hundreds of campers there to run ATVs. One other point: The Oregon Trail ran near here, and a Seventh-Day Adventist youth group placed a memorial to the trail and to its Hudspeth Cutoff (also near here, where settlers had to choose between heading to Oregon or to California). The road you take here is rough enough, in fact, to put you in mind of the Oregon Trail.

10 Mill Flat

Location: Northeast of Sublett
Sites: Variable
Facilities: Vault toilets
Fee per night: None
Elevation: 6,200 feet
Road conditions: Semirugged; after the first few miles of farm country on wide and easy gravel roads, the roads turn narrow and winding and become challenging near the campground. Passable in most vehicles, but most comfortably in a pickup or sturdy SUV.
Management: Forest Service, Burley/Twin Falls Ranger District, (208) 678–0430
Reservations: Call (877) 444–6777 or visit Web site www.reserveamerica.com.
Activities: ATVs
Season: June 1–November 15 (depending on weather)
Finding the campground: From Sublett drive east (bearing gently south) on Sublett Road up to Sublett Reservoir. On the far side of it, watch for the sign that directs you straight ahead into the mountains for another 10 miles or so.
The campground: Like Sublette to the southeast, this campground is a favorite with the ATV crowd because of the trails. There aren't a lot of services, but the countryside is attractive and satisfyingly remote.

11 Lake Walcott State Park

Location: Northeast of Rupert
Sites: 22
Facilities: Drinking water, flush toilets, fire rings, dump stations, playground, pull-through sites, barrier-free access, lake access, pets allowed
Fee per night: $$
Elevation: 3,800 feet
Road conditions: Paved up to the campground and most of the way throughout
Management: Idaho Department of Parks and Recreation, (208) 436–1258
Reservations: Available via Web site www.idahoparks.org
Activities: Boating, fishing, hiking, picnicking
Season: All year, technically; as a practical matter, about May 1 through October 31 (depending on weather)

Finding the campground: From Rupert drive northeast on Idaho Highway 24 to Minidoka Dam Road (north of Acequia), then about 3 miles east to the lake.

The campground: The campground is located next to the Minidoka National Wildlife Refuge, which includes all of Lake Walcott and considerable land on its eastern side, so there are loads of animals to see. The location on the shore of Lake Walcott (an artificial lake created by a Bureau of Reclamation dam) is like an oasis in the desert (and in fact sagebrush country predominates outside the bounds of the shady and almost forested park). Walcott is a favorite with Boy Scout and other groups. It is a well-maintained and manicured park, with facilities for both RVs and tents. It also is a general-purpose recreation area that includes an eighteen-hole disk golf course and other sports facilities. It also is a nature preserve area, and a wide range of plants and animals (about 150 species of birds) can be seen. One is of special note: Idaho's largest cottonwood tree.

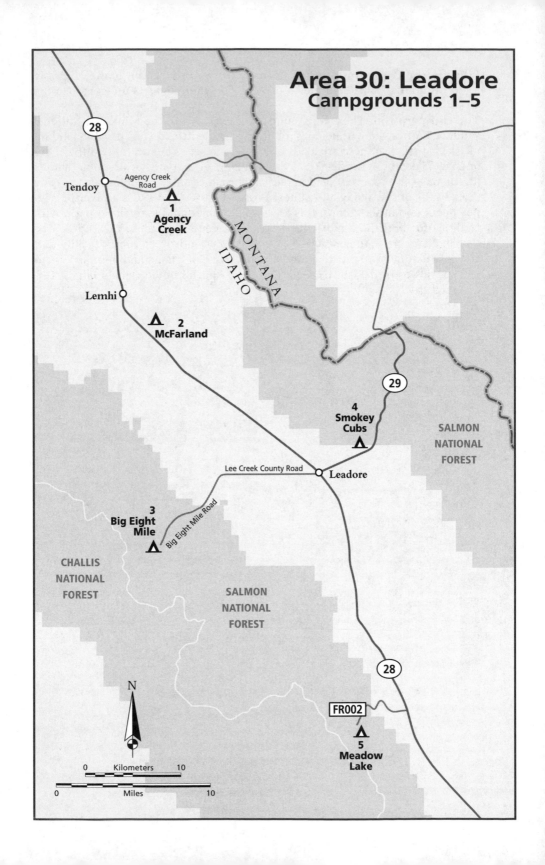

Area 30: Leadore

If you want to leave the crowd behind, this is one of the best places Idaho has to offer—a vast region where nearly all of the few people live in two small communities, and the third most substantial is a ghost town. The largest community, Leadore (pronounced "lead-ore," as in the mining term), is home to about seventy-five people.

As in so much of eastern Idaho, much of this country is desert and plains in the valleys but forested in the mountains—and away from the highway, there are a lot of mountains. The public lands (and most of the land here is public) are almost all managed by either the Forest Service or the Bureau of Land Management.

There may be few people here, but animals are everywhere. Birders can watch more than a hundred species that have been recorded, and deer and coyotes often are seen in this area.

For more information:

Salmon-Challis National Forest
Route 2, Box 600
Salmon, ID 83467
(208) 756–5100
www.fs.fed.us/r4/sc

Area 30

		Town	Sites	Max. RV length	Electric	Picnic	Fire rings	Toilets	Showers	Water	Dump station	Disability access	Recreation	Can reserve	Fees ($)	Season	Stay limit (days)
1	Agency Creek	Tendoy	U			•	•	V					FH			May–Oct.	14
2	McFarland	Leadore	10	28		•	•	V		•			FH		$	May–Oct.	14
3	Big Eight Mile	Leadore	U	24		•	•	V		•			FH			May–Oct.	16
4	Smokey Cubs	Leadore	8	28		•	•	V		•			FH			May–Oct.	14
5	Meadow Lake	Leadore	15	16		•	•	V		•			BFH	•	$	July–Sept.	16

1 Agency Creek

Location: East of Tendoy
Sites: Undetermined number
Facilities: Vault toilets, fire rings, pets allowed
Fee per night: None
Elevation: 7,200 feet
Road conditions: Narrow but passable gravel road
Management: Bureau of Land Management, Challis Field Office, (208) 879-4181
Reservations: No
Activities: Fishing, hiking, picnicking
Season: June–October (depending on weather)
Finding the campground: From Tendoy drive east 5 miles on Agency Creek Road.
The campground: Quiet and barely used except during hunting season—when hunters do pack in—this barely developed location is notable as the campground closest to the Lemhi Pass, which is on the Continental Divide (which also separates Idaho and Montana here). This is where, in 1805, Meriwether Lewis and William Clark crossed into Idaho on their trek to the Pacific. (A memorial to Sacajawea, the Indian guide who helped Lewis and Clark, has been placed at the top of the pass.) Outside of hunting season the campground is (usually) almost perfectly peaceful.

2 McFarland

Location: Northwest of Leadore
Sites: 10
Facilities: Drinking water (hand pump), vault toilets, fire rings
Fee per night: $
Elevation: 6,200 feet
Road conditions: Paved to the campground, good gravel within; all flat
Management: Bureau of Land Management, Challis Field Office, (208) 879-4181
Reservations: Ordinarily none, but for information call (208) 879-4181.
Activities: Fishing, hiking, picnicking
Season: May 15–October 30 (depends on weather)
Finding the campground: From Leadore drive northwest on Idaho Highway 28 about 10 miles; campground is on the right.
The campground: McFarland is in an open meadow in the ranching country, and there's privately owned land in most directions here (as campground signs duly note). As at several BLM campgrounds in this area, camping is organized around a circle, with the few campground services (toilets) in the middle of the circle. The whole area is ringed with trees and shrubs, providing some seclusion from neighboring properties, though little from the highway. Some fishing opportunities are available but are limited; check the signs in the campground to determine where you can and can't go. (Some nearby fishing spots are on private property.) This is a good campground for overnighting en route on a journey, but it's not much of a recreation spot.

3 Big Eight Mile

Location: West of Leadore
Sites: 4 tent sites, unspecified trailer sites
Facilities: Drinking water, vault toilets, fire rings
Fee per night: None
Elevation: 7,500 feet
Road conditions: Occasionally rough, narrow gravel road (after the highway)
Management: Forest Service, Leadore Ranger District, (208) 768-2500
Reservations: No
Activities: Fishing, hiking, picnicking
Season: May 15-October 30 (depending on weather)
Finding the campground: From Leadore drive 6.7 miles west on Lee Creek County Road, then 1.5 miles southwest on Big Eight Mile County Road, and then 5 miles southwest on Forest Road 096.
The campground: Hiking and fishing are the main draws at this remote, mountainous campground. The area has a nice overlook of the Lemhi Valley. The trailheads of two major trails are here. One is the Big Eight Mile Trail, where ATVs and motorbikes are allowed access; the trail uphill leads to an alpine meadow and a terrific view of the Pahsimeroi Valley. The other is the Patterson Trail, which is an old wagon road that also allows for motorbike and ATV use.

4 Smokey Cubs

Location: East of Leadore
Sites: 8
Facilities: Drinking water, vault toilets, fire rings, pets allowed
Fee per night: None
Elevation: 4,200 feet
Road conditions: Paved to the campground
Management: Bureau of Land Management, Challis Field Office, (208) 879-4181
Reservations: No
Activities: Fishing, hiking, picnicking
Season: May 15-October 30 (depending on weather)
Finding the campground: From Leadore drive 3 miles east on Idaho Highway 29.
The campground: Similar to McFarland, this is more picnic area and rest stop than campground, though camping is allowed. As at McFarland, camping is arranged mostly around a circle (though here, there is an additional camping area behind the trees that line the circle). It's a well-maintained site and of special interest to hikers: It is on the Nez Perce National Historic Trail. The campground is located on ID 29, which runs from Leadore into Montana; the pavement covers the first 5 miles out of Leadore (about a mile beyond the campground) but turns to gravel as it winds through the mountains.

5 Meadow Lake

Location: South of Leadore
Sites: 15
Facilities: Drinking water, vault toilets, fire rings
Fee per night: $
Elevation: 9,160 feet
Road conditions: Crank up the four-wheel drive if you have one. The Forest Service remarks on this route: "a gravel road that climbs 2,080 feet in less than 7 miles to the campground." You're heading up high into the mountains in a very remote area, under often steep conditions. Still, the road is well maintained.
Management: Forest Service, Leadore Ranger District, (208) 768-2500
Reservations: Call (877) 444-6777 or visit Web site www.reserveamerica.com.
Activities: Boating, fishing, hiking, picnicking
Season: July 4–Labor Day (usually)
Finding the campground: From Leadore drive 17 miles southeast on ID 28 and then 4 miles southwest on Forest Road 002 (Gilmore Road).
The campground: Meadow Lake is one of this guide's top camping recommendations for those who want a great view with relatively small crowds. It is a contender for highest elevation of any Idaho campground—and one of the most stunning views for those hardy souls who get there. Meadows Lake is relatively shallow but pristine; if its mountains (Meadow Lake Peak, at 10,720 feet, presides over the waterfront) and lake are smaller than, say, Redfish Lake farther west, they are no less attractive, and far fewer people come here. Fishing is popular in the summer once 3,000 rainbow trout are stocked in the lake. This is the only public fee campground in the Leadore area. Note the relatively short season, which reflects the high altitude. The lake's water comes from snowmelt; the area was formed by glacier activity. The short (1.3 miles) Meadow Lake Trail starts here and peaks at the Lemhi Divide, which has a broad view of the Lost River area. Much of this area was burned in a massive fire in 1988.

Area 31: Lost River

They call it the Lost River for a specific reason: It does not flow into a larger stream but down into the ground. (It is presumed to flow underground through the Snake River Aquifer and eventually into the Snake River, near Hagerman.) But the area around Arco and Mackay could be called the "lost river" area as well because water is so scarce in this region.

This area may look plain, but it's remarkable for several reasons.

On the west side lies the Craters of the Moon National Reserve (formerly Monument). This vast lava-strewn area has been thought to be so much like the lunar surface that astronauts have trained there.

On the east and north side are the mountains—high mountains. Of the twenty-five highest mountains in Idaho, twenty-four of them are located here, including Idaho's highest peak, Mount Borah, at 12,662 feet. The U.S. Forest Service, which manages the Mount Borah area, does allow for some informal camping at the base of the mountain (three sites for tents, several others a little farther away for trailers and motor homes). Camping at this location is mainly for climbers of the mountain. Toilet facilities are provided but no drinking water, and there is no fee for camping here. It can be accessed from U.S. Highway 93 north of Mackay, and just north of the Trail Creek Road turnoff. The campground is informal enough to lack a formal name or designation, hence its presence here rather than in the list below.

For more information:

Arco Chamber of Commerce
213 West Grand Avenue
Arco, ID 83213
(208) 527–8977

Craters of the Moon National Reserve
P.O. Box 29
Arco, ID 83213
(208) 527–3257

1 Craters of the Moon National Reserve

Location: Southwest of Arco
Sites: 52
Facilities: Drinking water, barrier-free access, flush and vault toilets, fire rings, pull-through sites
Fee per night: $$
Elevation: 5,900 feet
Road conditions: Paved in nearly all of the few places you can drive. A general transportation warning: Don't try walking (or otherwise traveling) directly on the lava flows; the lava spikes can be surprisingly sharp and even cut through shoes (much less feet).

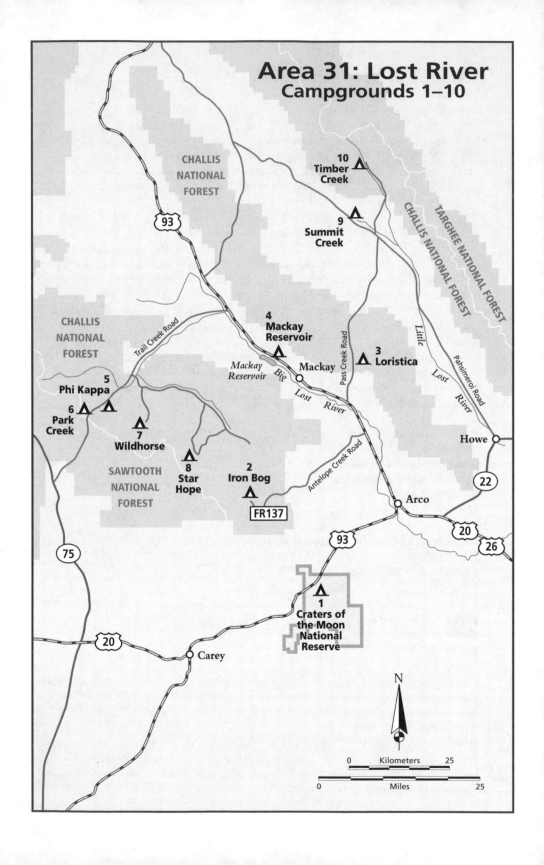

Area 31

		Town	Sites	Max. RV length	Electric	Picnic	Fire rings	Toilets	Showers	Water	Dump station	Disability access	Recreation	Can reserve	Fees ($)	Season	Stay limit (days)
1	Craters of the Moon National Reserve	Arco	52	35		•	•	F,V		•		•	H		$$	May–Oct.	
2	Iron Bog	Mackay	21	32		•	•	V		•			FH		$	May–Oct.	16
3	Loristica	Mackay	8			•	•	V		•			FH	•	$$$	July–Sept.	16
4	Mackay Reservoir	Mackay	57	28		•	•	V		•	•		BFHS		$$	May–Nov.	14
5	Phi Kappa	Mackay	21			•	•	V		•			FH		$	May–Oct.	16
6	Park Creek	Mackay	13	32		•	•	V		•			FH		$	June–Sept.	16
7	Wildhorse	Mackay	12			•	•	V		•			FH		$	June–Oct.	16
8	Star Hope	Mackay	21	32		•	•	V		•			FH	•		June–Sept.	14
9	Summit Creek	Howe	12	30		•	•	V		•			FH			May–Oct.	14
10	Timber Creek	Howe	7	32		•	•	V		•			BFH			May–Oct.	16

Management: National Park Service, Craters of the Moon National Reserve, (208) 527–3257
Reservations: No
Activities: Hiking, picnicking
Season: May 1–October 1
Finding the campground: From Arco drive 18 miles southwest on US 93 to the visitor center area at the national monument.
The campground: Your author has a special connection to this campground: It was the first Idaho camping spot he ever stayed in, in 1970. Visitor facilities have expanded and modernized since then, but the beautiful eerie nature of the place hasn't changed and possibly never will. The landscape genuinely looks like something from another planet; just staring at it has its own rewards. It is so stunning that this was one of the first places in the nation, back in 1924, to be declared a national monument. There are fine loop roads and trails, sufficient to give any visitor a good feel for this place. It is not a conventional park: You won't see any forests here, and the enormous lava fields of eastern Idaho can be spotted on maps as those areas where there are no communities and not even any roads. But desolate though this place may seem, observers have found hundreds of species of plants (most noticeable during a spectacular but brief wildflower display in the spring) and animals including marmots, bobcats, and chipmunks.

2 | Iron Bog

Location: South of Mackay
Sites: 21
Facilities: Drinking water, vault toilets, fire rings

Fee per night: $
Elevation: 7,200 feet
Road conditions: Pretty good to the Lost River area but rougher as you ascend steeply into the mountains for the last half dozen or so miles. Take it slow and careful.
Management: Forest Service, Lost River Ranger District, (208) 588-3400
Reservations: No
Activities: Fishing, hiking, picnicking
Season: May 30–October 15
Finding the campground: From Mackay drive 10 miles southeast on US 93, then 15 miles southwest on Antelope Creek Road (a county road), and then 7.2 miles southwest on Forest Road 137.
The campground: No forests here, only a few smallish trees and brush; a few sites are shaded, most are not. Don't write this one off, though. Nearby Iron Bog Lake and Brockie Lake are both good fishing sites, and the Smiley Mountain area offers some great mountain hiking. The drinking water is by hand pump.

3 Loristica

Location: Northeast of Mackay
Sites: 8 group sites
Facilities: Drinking water, vault toilets, fire rings, pets allowed
Fee per night: $$$
Elevation: 7,400 feet
Road conditions: Mostly good road but diminishing in quality as you climb the mountains. Recommendation: Call the USFS Lost River ranger office for current conditions.
Management: Forest Service, Lost River Ranger District, (208) 588-3400
Reservations: Reservations are required here; call (208) 588-3400.
Activities: Fishing, hiking, picnicking
Season: July–September (sometimes longer depending on weather)
Finding the campground: From Mackay drive 7 miles south on US 93, then turn left onto Pass Creek Road. Drive it for 12 miles to Pass Creek Summit, and then turn left onto the Loristica Road. Follow it 1.7 miles to a fork in the road; a right turn there takes you into the campground.
The campground: Loristica is aimed at groups, and it is the only campground in the Lost River area where reservations are required (the sites tend to fill up early). This is another of the lightly forested mountain meadow sites.

4 Mackay Reservoir

Location: Northwest of Mackay
Sites: 57
Facilities: Drinking water, vault toilets, fire rings, dump station, pets allowed
Fee per night: $$
Elevation: 5,500 feet
Road conditions: Paved nearly to the campground

Management: Bureau of Land Management, Challis Office, (208) 756–5400
Reservations: None, but for information on availability call (208) 756–5400.
Activities: Boating, fishing, hiking, picnicking, swimming
Season: May 1–November 30
Finding the campground: From Mackay drive 4 miles northwest on US 93 and turn left at the campground sign; campground is accessible along a road running downhill from the highway westward to the reservoir.
The campground: Mackay Reservoir tends to rise and fall dramatically depending on water conditions—the water here is used for farm irrigation. The park is located next to what is one of the reservoir's shorelines; when the reservoir is full, a boat ramp and docks are available for use. When the water's down, just leave your boat at home and enjoy the picnicking. This is a mostly open-air campground, which has scattered trees for shade.

5 Phi Kappa

Location: West of Mackay
Sites: 21
Facilities: Drinking water (hand pumps), vault toilets, fire rings, picnic tables
Fee per night: $
Elevation: 8,800 feet
Road conditions: Good and paved at the lower levels, but as Trail Creek Road moves up into the mountains, it becomes a narrow and rough (and worn) gravel road. The Forest Service has noted for this area, "Make sure you bring a spare tire!"
Management: Forest Service, Lost River Ranger District, (208) 588–3400
Reservations: No
Activities: Fishing, hiking, picnicking
Season: May 15–October 15
Finding the campground: From Mackay drive 16 miles northwest on US 93 and then 15 miles west on Trail Creek Road.
The campground: Considering that this campground is only about 16 miles south of posh Sun Valley (though don't expect that getting here will happen at highway speed), this is a remarkably remote and primitive area. Wildlife is abundant, and the high mountain forested areas are spectacular. This campground, located in what is basically desert country, is a mix of shaded and open areas.

6 Park Creek

Location: Southwest of Mackay
Sites: 13
Facilities: Drinking water, vault toilets, fire rings, pets allowed (on leash)
Fee per night: $
Elevation: 7,800 feet
Road conditions: Trail Creek Road is narrow gravel, a twisty single lane up into the mountains and in places—near the mountain passes and at certain times—so rough as to constitute a hazard to vehicles. Recommendation: Ask

for current advice from the USFS ranger district.

Management: Forest Service, Lost River Ranger District, (208) 588–3400
Reservations: No
Activities: Fishing, hiking, picnicking
Season: June 15–October 15 (depending on weather)
Finding the campground: From Mackay drive 16 miles northwest on US 93 and then turn left (west) onto Trail Creek Road and continue for 26 miles.
The campground: Wooded campgrounds are uncommon in this region, but this is one—it sits above the mountain timberline. There's a small pond nearby, and you'll find a couple of small lakes a little farther off. One group camping site is available here.

7 Wildhorse

Location: Southwest of Mackay
Sites: 12
Facilities: Drinking water, vault toilets, fire rings, pets allowed
Fee per night: $
Elevation: 7,400 feet
Road conditions: Mostly good road but diminishing in quality as you climb the mountains. Recommendation: Call the USFS Lost River ranger office for current conditions.
Management: Forest Service, Lost River Ranger District, (208) 588–3400
Reservations: No
Activities: Fishing, hiking, picnicking
Season: June 15–October 15
Finding the campground: From Mackay drive 16 miles northwest on US 93, then 17 miles southwest on Trail Creek Road, then 2 miles south on Forest Road 135, and then 4 miles on Forest Road 136.
The campground: Located near the meandering Wild Horse Creek, this campground has some terrific mountain peak views, a comfortable mountain meadow setting, and good shade for its campsites.

8 Star Hope

Location: Southwest of Mackay
Sites: 21 (one with barrier-free access)
Facilities: Drinking water, vault toilets, fire rings, pets allowed
Fee per night: None at press time, but expected to return to $
Elevation: 8,000 feet
Road conditions: Mostly good road but diminishing in quality as you climb the mountains. Recommendation: Call the USFS Lost River ranger office for current conditions.
Management: Forest Service, Lost River Ranger District, (208) 588–3400
Reservations: No
Activities: Fishing, hiking, picnicking
Season: June 30–September 15 (depending on weather)
Finding the campground: From Mackay drive 16 miles northwest on US 93,

and then turn left (west) onto the Trail Creek Road. Follow it 18 miles to the Copper Basin Road; turn left (south) and drive 13 miles to the Copper Basin Loop Road. Turn right (west) and follow it 9 miles to the campground.

The campground: High up in the Pioneer Mountains near the headwaters of the Star Hope Creek, this campground is located in a high mountain meadow—one of the highest elevations of any Idaho campground. It is also relatively advanced for a Forest Service campground in this area; at least one with barrier-free access site and toilet are available, and the water is available by faucet instead of hand pump.

9 Summit Creek

Location: North of Howe
Sites: 12
Facilities: Vault toilets, fire rings
Fee per night: None
Elevation: 6,300 feet
Road conditions: The Pahsimeroi Road is generally well maintained, as it is the only major route through this long valley.
Management: Bureau of Land Management, Challis Field Office, (208) 879–4181
Reservations: Call (208) 756–5400.
Activities: Fishing, hiking, picnicking
Season: May 1–October 31 (depending on weather)
Finding the campground: From Howe (a small community 23 miles northeast of Arco), drive 18 miles north on the Pahsimeroi Road (the only road that runs through Howe); or, from the north, turn off US 93 northeast of Challis at Ellis and follow the Pahsimeroi Road southeast for about 50 miles to Summit Creek.
The campground: A trout fishing mecca, Summit Creek is located on the banks of the like-named stream, which is shaded with birch trees. Barney Hot Springs, across the creek, is usually just cool enough for bathing and is a rest center for some campers. About Barney, the Bureau of Land Management notes in one of its publications: "Strangely, there is a population of tropical fish in the pool that are fun to watch and feed. They are the descendants of aquarium fish someone must have dumped in years ago." There is also, for fishing, Summit Reservoir a couple of walkable miles away. Yet for all this water, there's none to drink at the campground; be sure to bring your own.

10 Timber Creek

Location: Northeast of Howe
Sites: 7
Facilities: Drinking water, vault toilets, fire rings, pets allowed (on leash)
Fee per night: None
Elevation: 7,340 feet
Road conditions: Mostly good valley road (the Pahsimeroi Road is well maintained) but narrow and rough in some places (mainly on the Sawmill Canyon Road)

Management: Forest Service, Lost River Ranger District, (208) 588-3400
Reservations: No
Activities: Boating, fishing, hiking, picnicking
Season: May 30–October 15 (depending on weather)
Finding the campground: From Howe turn onto the Little Lost/Pahsimeroi Road, and drive it 37 miles to the Sawmill Canyon Road. Turn right and follow it to Timber Creek Road; turn left and follow it to the Timber Creek Campground Road, which leads into the campground.
The campground: This is a pleasant wooded area, quite shady, with less desert feel than you might expect; part of the reason is that it is well up in the mountains. The campground is divided into Upper and Lower areas; most of the campsites are in the Upper area, and this also is where some boating in the Timber Creek Reservoir is possible.

Eastern Idaho

Area 32: Dubois

The drive along the northernmost part of Interstate 15 in Idaho suggests nothing so much as a flat, dry, windswept, uninteresting landscape. Many travelers doubtless see no reason to stop or even slow down.

They'd see the reason if they pulled off the highways and hit the back roads. Eastern Idahoans know this country, around Medicine Creek west of I–15 and Kilgore east of it, as some of the state's best undiscovered camping territory. The landscapes, the fishing, the hunting—this is one of the premier places in Idaho not yet found by the crowds.

Just be aware of the relatively short warm season: This is high country. Even most of the locals have headed south by around Thanksgiving.

For more information:

Bureau of Land Management
1405 Hollipark Drive
Idaho Falls, ID 83401
(208) 524–7500

---

1 Birch Creek

Location: Northwest of Mud Lake
Sites: 16
Facilities: Vault toilets, fire rings
Fee per night: None
Elevation: 6,500 feet
Road conditions: Paved highway to the campground entrance, gravel within
Management: Bureau of Land Management, Idaho Falls office, (208) 524–7500
Reservations: No
Activities: Fishing, picnicking
Season: May–September
Finding the campground: From Mud Lake drive northwest on Idaho Highway 28 for 25 miles.
The campground: Many BLM sites are like this one, essentially semideveloped—though more development, including a well for potable water, is expected in the next few years (so a fee may be coming, too). You'll find a toilet, a picnic table, and a flat area where people can pitch a tent or pull up an RV, plus some nice shade trees—and not a lot else. (It's considered a step away

231

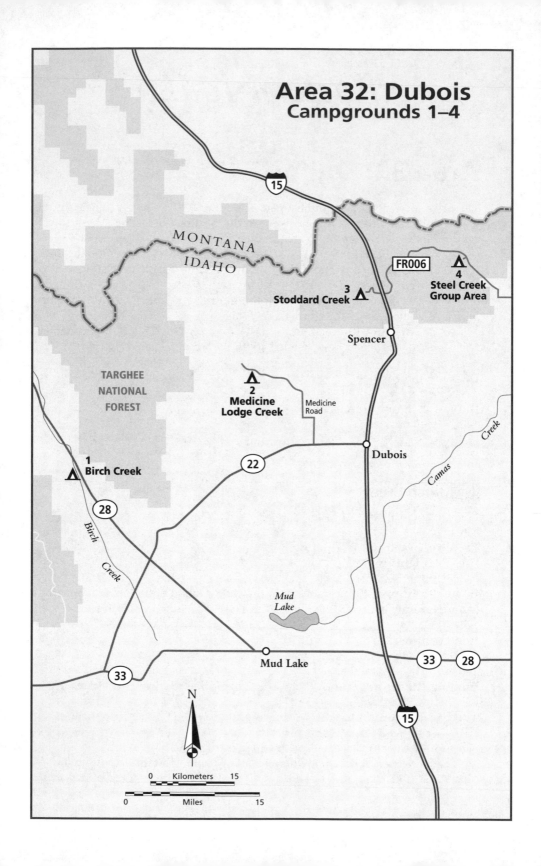

Area 32: Dubois
Campgrounds 1–4

15

MONTANA
IDAHO

FR006

Stoddard Creek 3 ▲

4 ▲
Steel Creek
Group Area

Spencer

TARGHEE
NATIONAL
FOREST

2 ▲
Medicine
Lodge Creek

Medicine
Road

Camas
Creek

1 ▲ Birch Creek

Dubois

22

28

Birch

Creek

Mud
Lake

Mud Lake

33

33

28

N

15

0   Kilometers   15

0   Miles   15

Area 32

	Town	Sites	Max. RV length	Electric	Picnic	Fire rings	Toilets	Showers	Water	Dump station	Disability access	Recreation	Can reserve	Fees ($)	Season	Stay limit (days)
1 Birch Creek	Mud Lake	16	25		•	•	V					F			May–Sept.	14
2 Medicine Lodge Creek	Dubois	U			•	•	V					FH			May–Oct.	1 4
3 Stoddard Creek	Spencer	24	32		•	•	V		•			FH		$–$$	May–Oct.	
4 Steel Creek	Spencer	1	22		•	•	V		•			FH	•	$	May–Oct.	14

from dispersed camping.) The creekside location, with some trees in the area, is appealing, though. This is a popular fishing spot, especially since fish are stocked in Birch Creek every year, and the fishing is easy. Some limited all-terrain vehicle use is allowed. A host does watch over the campground in the summer.

2 Medicine Lodge Creek

Location: Northwest of Dubois
Sites: Undesignated number
Facilities: Vault toilets, fire rings
Fee per night: None
Elevation: 6,800 feet
Road conditions: Dusty and washboarded but passable desert gravel roads to the campground
Management: Bureau of Land Management, Idaho Falls office, (208) 524–7500; Dubois, (208) 374–5422
Reservations: No
Activities: Fishing, hiking, picnicking
Season: May 15–October 15
Finding the campground: From Dubois drive west 7 miles on Idaho Highway 22 and then north on Medicine Road, and follow the signs to the campground.
The campground: A small, remote, and barely developed campground, Medicine Lodge Creek—also called Weber Creek Campground in some references—is just about large enough for one family group. It is located in a canyon between desert mountains, but the location next to Medicine Lodge Creek is shaded by trees. No drinking water is available, so bring your own.

3 Stoddard Creek

Location: Northwest of Spencer
Sites: 24
Facilities: Drinking water, vault toilets, fire rings, pull-through sites
Fee per night: $–$$

Elevation: 6,200 feet
Road conditions: Paved to the campground
Management: Forest Service, Dubois Ranger District, (208) 373-5422
Reservations: Call Dubois Ranger District, (208) 373-5422 (group sites only).
Activities: Fishing, hiking, picnicking
Season: May 15-October 15
Finding the campground: From Spencer drive 3.5 miles north on I-15, take the Stoddard Creek exit, and then continue 1 mile northwest on Forest Road 003.
The campground: This large forested campground has a mix of individual and group sites; reservations are made only for group sites, while individual sites are first come, first served. From the vantage point of I-15, you wouldn't think a forested campground could possibly be located nearby—this area of the freeway, through Clark County, looks as barren and windswept as anywhere in the upper Great Plains. Stoddard Creek will surprise you.

4 Steel Creek Group Area

Location: Northeast of Spencer
Sites: 1
Facilities: Drinking water, fire ring, vault toilet
Fee per night: $
Elevation: 6,600 feet
Road conditions: Gravel with some mountain travel and some steep sections, but relatively wide and well maintained
Management: Forest Service, Dubois Ranger District, (208) 373-5422
Reservations: Required; call the Dubois Ranger District, (208) 373-5422.
Activities: Fishing, hiking, picnicking
Season: May 15-October 15
Finding the campground: From Spencer drive 5 miles north on I-15, turn off at the Stoddard Creek exit, and then drive 17 miles southeast on Forest Road 006, then 1.2 miles west on Forest Road 478.
The campground: This remote forested campground is located near West Camas Creek, up in the Centennial Mountains. It's a good fishing site, and you definitely won't encounter any crowds back here—there's only one camping site! To stay here you must make a reservation through the Dubois Ranger District office.

Area 33: Fremont

The corner of Idaho that butts up against Yellowstone National Park may lack some of the specific attractions of the park—Old Faithful, for example, is in Wyoming—but the kind of land is much the same. This area of Idaho is mountainous, forested, and pocked with lakes that have become prime recreation spots for Idahoans. The outside world, so eager to visit Yellowstone, seems barely to have discovered, so far, the wonders of Idaho just across the line.

Idaho's most stunning state park, Harriman, is located in the middle of a massive wildlife refuge where trumpeter swans and numerous other birds visit regularly. (There is no camping at Harriman, however.) Nearby Henry's Lake is widely considered one of the very best fishing spots in Idaho—high praise indeed.

There are scenic drives throughout this area, including the wonderful Mesa Falls drive, where the visitor can gaze as some of Idaho's best waterfalls and wander through a recently renovated visitor center.

This is also one of Idaho's best places to observe wildlife. Pronghorn antelope, mule deer, bald eagles, beavers, porcupines—and bears—are only a few of the animals wandering through the forests.

Much of this area is in the Caribou-Targhee National Forest, which, unlike most other national forests in Idaho, has a sixteen-day (rather than fourteen-day) limit on stays.

Note should be made here of a campground that falls outside of, but is accessed mainly through, Idaho (and is managed by the Ashton, Idaho, ranger station): Cave Falls. This campground, about 23 miles east of Ashton and along the Fall River, is on the southern border of Yellowstone National Park. (For that reason, special hiking permits are needed for anyone planning to hike north from the campground.)

For more information:

Island Park Area Chamber of Commerce
P.O. Box 83
Island Park, ID 83429
(208) 558-7755
www.islandpark.org

Targhee National Forest
420 North Bridge Street
St. Anthony, ID 83445
(208) 624-3151
www.fs.fed.us/tnf

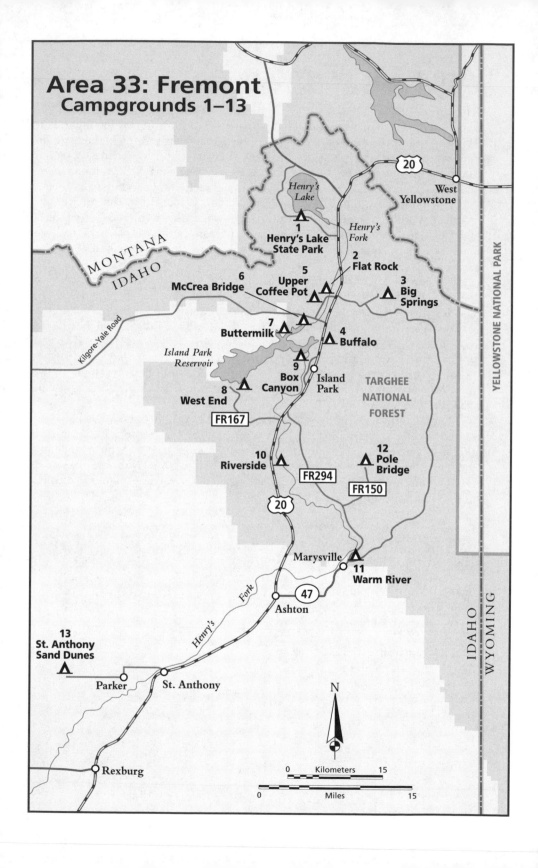

Area 33: Fremont
Campgrounds 1–13

MONTANA

IDAHO

Henry's Lake

20

West Yellowstone

△ 1
Henry's Lake
State Park

Henry's Fork

2
Flat Rock

6
McCrea Bridge

5
Upper
Coffee Pot

3
Big
Springs
△

△ △

Kilgore-Yale Road

7
Buttermilk
△ △

△ 4 Buffalo

Island Park Reservoir

9
Box
Canyon
△

Island
Park

TARGHEE

NATIONAL

FOREST

8
West End
△

FR167

YELLOWSTONE NATIONAL PARK

10
Riverside
△

12
Pole
Bridge
△

FR294

FR150

20

Marysville

11
Warm River
△

47

Ashton

Henry's
Fork

13
St. Anthony
Sand Dunes
△

Parker

St. Anthony

IDAHO

WYOMING

N

Rexburg

0   Kilometers   15

0   Miles   15

Area 33

	Town	Sites	Max. RV length	Electric	Picnic	Fire rings	Toilets	Showers	Water	Dump station	Disability access	Recreation	Can reserve	Fees ($)	Season	Stay limit (days)
1 Henry's Lake State Park	Island Park	45	40	•	•	•	F,V	•	•	•		BFH	•	$$–$$$	May–Sept.	14
2 Flat Rock	Island Park	40	32	•	•	•	F,V		•			BFH	•	$	May–Sept.	14
3 Big Springs	Island Park	15	32		•	•	V		•			H	•	$	May–Sept.	14
4 Buffalo	Island Park	127	34	•	•	•	F,V		•			F	•	$	May–Sept.	14
5 Upper Coffee Pot	Island Park	15	32	•			V		•			F		$$–$$$	May–Sept.	14
6 McCrea Bridge	Island Park	25	32				V		•			BF		$$–$$$	May–Sept.	14
7 Buttermilk	Island Park	54	32		•	•	V		•			BF	•	$	May–Sept.	14
8 West End	Island Park	19	22		•	•	V					BFS			June–Sept.	14
9 Box Canyon	Island Park	19	32		•	•	V		•			FH		$$	May–Sept.	14
10 Riverside	Ashton	56	34		•	•	V		•		•	BF	•	$$	June–Sept.	14
11 Warm River	Ashton	13	24		•	•	V		•		•	BFH	•	$$$	June–Sept.	14
12 Pole Bridge	Ashton	U	22		•	•	V		•			FH			June–Oct.	14
13 St. Anthony Sand Dunes	St. Anthony	U	32		•	•	V		•			H			May–Sept.	14

1 Henry's Lake State Park

Location: North of Island Park, south of West Yellowstone, Montana
Sites: 45
Facilities: Drinking water, flush and vault toilets, fire rings, showers, electric hookups, dump station, pets allowed
Fee per night: $$–$$$
Elevation: 6,500 feet
Road conditions: From U.S. Highway 20, a washboarded gravel road leads downhill toward the lakefront. An easy but sometimes bouncy ride for all vehicles.
Management: Idaho Department of Parks and Recreation, (208) 525-7121
Reservations: Available via Web site www.idahoparks.org
Activities: Boating, fishing, hiking, picnicking
Season: May 30–September 30
Finding the campground: From Island Park drive 12 miles north on US 20 to the park entrance on the west side of the road. From West Yellowstone, Montana, drive 15 miles south on US 20 to the park entrance.

The campground at Henry's Lake is a desert campground.

The campground: Amid all the forested federal campgrounds in the Island Park region, you'd expect Henry's Lake to be similar—but it isn't. Henry's Lake sits in a large, open bowl where the vegetation consists mainly of sagebrush. This is a desert campground, not a high mountain forest locale. That said, the lake is a highly popular boating and fishing spot and often fills with campers along its shoreline.

2 Flat Rock

Location: Northwest of Island Park
Sites: 40
Facilities: Drinking water, flush and vault toilets, fire rings, electric hookups, pets allowed
Fee per night: $
Elevation: 6,400 feet
Road conditions: Paved to the campground
Management: Forest Service, Ashton/Island Park Ranger District, (208) 652-7442
Reservations: About a dozen of the sites (including all of those with electric hookups) are reservable. Call (877) 444-6777 or visit Web site www.reserveamerica.com.

Activities: Boating, fishing, hiking, picnicking
Season: May 25–September 15
Finding the campground: From the Island Park Ranger Station, drive 5 miles north on US 20 to Macks Inn; the campground is located across the street from Macks Inn Resort.
The campground: This is another of the camping areas located on the Henry's Fork and one of the larger. It is an ordinary-looking wooded campground, more visible to the highway traffic than most other campgrounds in the area. Eight of the sites have electric hookups.

3 Big Springs

Location: Northeast of Island Park, south of West Yellowstone, Montana
Sites: 15
Facilities: Drinking water (faucet), vault toilets, fire rings, pull-through sites, grills, pets allowed, trash service (bearproof Dumpsters)
Fee per night: $
Elevation: 6,400 feet
Road conditions: Paved to and throughout the campground
Management: Forest Service, Ashton/Island Park Ranger District, (208) 652-7442
Reservations: Call (877) 444–6777 or visit Web site www.reserveamerica.com.
Activities: Hiking, picnicking
Season: May 25–September 15
Finding the campground: From Island Park on US 20, at the Big Springs exit, drive 4.5 miles east on Forest Road 059 (the Big Springs Loop Road).
The campground: Big Springs is a finely maintained campground back in the woods, with lush vegetation all around—but the lodgepole pines provide limited forest cover, so plenty of sun filters through. The campground is unusually thoroughly developed for a Forest Service site, even including trash service by way of Dumpsters located on-site. There's a campground host, and there are separate areas for groups and for day-use picnicking. Anyone interested in the river system of eastern Idaho will find plenty of interest here, because the springs that create the Henry's Fork of the Snake River are mostly in walking distance. Fishing is limited in some of these areas (check the local signage), but float trips along one of the streams (west toward Henry's Lake Outlet) are possible. Also within walking distance: the historic Johnny Sack Cabin, which is open from July 4 until Labor Day.

4 Buffalo

Location: South of Island Park
Sites: 127
Facilities: Drinking water (faucets), flush and vault toilets, fire rings, electric hookups (C Loop), pull-through sites, trash service (bearproof Dumpsters)
Fee per night: $
Elevation: 6,300 feet
Road conditions: Paved to the campground

Management: Forest Service, Ashton/Island Park Ranger District, (208) 652-7442

Reservations: Call (877) 444-6777 or visit Web site www.reserveamerica.com.

Activities: Fishing, picnicking

Season: May 25–September 15

Finding the campground: The campground is located within the (30-mile-long) city of Island Park, just off US 20, a quarter mile north of the Island Park Ranger Station, across the highway from Pond's Lodge. The Buffalo River, which runs nearby, is available for fishing (notably several varieties of trout).

The campground: Buffalo is by far the largest public campground in this region of Idaho, and it is well equipped to handle large numbers of people. Unlike the other sites in the area, sporting facilities (such as volleyball nets and fields) are available here, and one of the seven loops (E loop) is a single group site suitable for as many as 150 people. Another loop here (C loop) offers electric power hookups, unusual for a Forest Service campground. An amphitheater near the campground entrance is often used for night events during the summer. The campground also has a manager, located near the entrance at US 20.

5 | Upper Coffee Pot

Location: South of Island Park

Sites: 15

Facilities: Drinking water, vault toilets, electric hookups (6 sites)

Fee per night: $$–$$$

Elevation: 6,300 feet

Road conditions: From the highway, the last 2 miles of gravel road are sometimes washboarded but wide and flat—easy passage for any vehicle.

Management: Forest Service, Ashton/Island Park Ranger District, (208) 652-7442

Reservations: No

Activities: Fishing, hiking

Season: May 25–September 15

Finding the campground: From Island Park drive 2 miles south on US 20 and then 2 miles southwest on Forest Road 130.

The campground: Coffee Pot is so popular that the Forest Service doesn't even include it among some of its campground materials for the area—word of mouth alone keeps it filled. The location is one reason; an estuary of one of the Henry's Fork streams slowly meanders only feet from where campers set up. You needn't look for a Lower Coffee Pot campground, because there isn't one. However, there are upper and lower Coffee Pot Rapids on Henry's Fork. At the campground this river is placid. But a hike on the well-marked Coffee Pot Rapids Trail will take you to a canyon where the water runs fast and its sound may remind you of, yes, a coffeepot. Shade and sun are almost perfectly balanced at this campground. Six of the sites have electric power hookups, and veteran campers here often snap them up. A campground host monitors things at the entrance. Fishing, hiking, and other recreation options are available.

Except for the almost always full grounds, this campground exemplifies what people usually look for in Island Park–area camping.

6 McCrea Bridge

Location: South of Island Park
Sites: 25
Facilities: Drinking water, vault toilets, trash service (bearproof Dumpsters)
Fee per night: $$–$$$
Elevation: 6,200 feet
Road conditions: Paved nearly to the campground
Management: Forest Service, Ashton/Island Park Ranger District, (208) 652-7442
Reservations: No
Activities: Boating, fishing
Season: May 25–September 30
Finding the campground: From the Island Park Ranger Station on US 20, drive 3.5 miles south, then 2.2 miles northwest on the Fremont County Road 3 (Kilgore-Yale Road).
The campground: McCrea was closed for renovation in 2002, so that means fully upgraded services. Like nearby Buttermilk, this area provides good access to Island Park Reservoir, with a boat launch and four docks. The area is lightly wooded with lodgepole pines and other trees.

7 Buttermilk

Location: West of Island Park
Sites: 54, with group sites for up to 100
Facilities: Drinking water (faucet), vault toilets, fire rings, pull-through sites, trash service (bearproof Dumpsters)
Fee per night: $
Elevation: 6,200 feet
Road conditions: Paved nearly to the campground
Management: Forest Service, Ashton/Island Park Ranger District, (208) 652-7442
Reservations: Half of the camping sites are reservable; others are first come, first served. Call (877) 444-6777 or visit Web site www.reserveamerica.com.
Activities: Boating, fishing, picnicking
Season: May 25–September 30
Finding the campground: From the Island Park Ranger Station on US 20, drive 3.5 miles south, then 2.2 miles northwest on Fremont CR 3 (the Kilgore-Yale Road), and then 2 miles southwest on Forest Road 334.
The campground: This is probably the best place to access Island Park Reservoir; the campground sits on its northeast bank and features a concrete boat loading ramp and five docks. Various types of trout are available for the catching, and visitors engage in a wide range of boating activities (including Jet Skiing). Group sites are available.

8 West End

Location: West of Island Park
Sites: 19
Facilities: Drinking water (near but not in the campground), vault toilets, fire rings
Fee per night: None
Elevation: 6,200 feet
Road conditions: Mostly flat and smooth but intermittently rugged gravel road, with some climbing
Management: Forest Service, Ashton/Island Park Ranger District, (208) 652-7442
Reservations: No
Activities: Boating, fishing, picnicking, swimming
Season: June 1–September 15
Finding the campground: Drive 7 miles south of central Island Park on US 20, then turn west 15 miles on Forest Road 167.
The campground: The location is excellent, being right on the Island Park Reservoir and away from other development. The campground has few resources, however, and even the available water is located not on the grounds but within walking distance nearby. West End has decidedly informal camping; most campers here tend toward dispersal camping around the marked campgrounds. The lakeshore site makes it a favorite for boating and fishing.

9 Box Canyon

Location: South of Island Park
Sites: 19
Facilities: Drinking water (faucets), fire rings, garbage service (bearproof Dumpsters), vault toilets
Fee per night: $$ (more for groups)
Elevation: 6,320 feet
Road conditions: Paved nearly to the campground
Management: Forest Service, Ashton/Island Park Ranger District, (208) 652-7442
Reservations: No
Activities: Fishing, hiking, picnicking
Season: May 25–September 15
Finding the campground: From Island Park drive 7 miles south on US 20, then 0.3 mile southwest on County Road 34, and then 9 miles northwest on Forest Road 284.
The campground: Box Canyon is not exactly on the banks of the Henry's Fork but rather overlooks it from the rim of a canyon. But river access is available, and the campground is a favorite of anglers; note the fishing regulations, which for much of this area include a catch-and-release policy. There is also white water in this area, and float boaters often take the two-hour trip through Box Canyon to the Last Chance area. Several hiking trails are available, too.

This is a woodsy but only partially shaded campground, owing to the tall, thin stands of lodgepole pine. The campground has a resident host in the summer.

10 Riverside

Location: North of Ashton
Sites: 56
Facilities: Drinking water (faucets), vault toilets, fire rings, pull-through sites, barrier-free access (15 sites), trash service (Dumpster), pets allowed
Fee per night: $$
Elevation: 6,200 feet
Road conditions: Paved nearly to the campground
Management: Forest Service, Ashton/Island Park Ranger District, (208) 652–7442
Reservations: Available for 21 of the sites. Call (877) 444–6777 or visit Web site www.reserveamerica.com.
Activities: Boating, fishing, picnicking
Season: June 1–September 30
Finding the campground: From Ashton drive north on US 20 for 16.5 miles and then southeast 1 mile on Forest Road 304.
The campground: Ask a fly fisherman anywhere in the country about the "Henry's Fork," and you'll get a knowing look—but probably no tips about the best fishing spots, since those are usually closely held. Riverside is on the banks of the Henry's Fork (of the Snake River), though the main fishing area is catch-and-release only. Boating is good here, but you'll notice restrictions on that activity because the Upper and Lower Mesa Falls are only a few miles downstream.

11 Warm River

Location: Northeast of Marysville
Sites: 13
Facilities: Drinking water, vault toilets, fire rings, barrier-free access, pets allowed
Fee per night: $$$
Elevation: 5,200 feet
Road conditions: Paved to campground entrance; gravel within
Management: Forest Service, Ashton/Island Park Ranger District, (208) 652–7442
Reservations: Seven sites are reservable. Call (877) 444–6777 or visit Web site www.reserveamerica.com.
Activities: Boating, fishing, hiking, picnicking
Season: June 1–September 30
Finding the campground: From Ashton drive 10 miles northeast on Idaho Highway 47; exit at the campground.
The campground: The smallest incorporated city in Idaho is Warm River; censuses have placed its population at between two and eleven in recent

decades. The reason it became a city has to do with a private resort facility located here, within easy walking distance of the Forest Service campground (which came later). The campground sits in a sunny valley amid shade trees, next to the slow-running Warm River. It is slow here, and shallow, and warm enough that anglers often wade into the middle of it for their fly-fishing. Children can rent inner tubes nearby and slowly float the river as well. The campground has a ramp useful for anglers who have disabilities. The camp is also an entry point for a long trail, based on an abandoned railroad bed, which runs all the way to West Yellowstone, Montana.

12 Pole Bridge

Location: Northeast of Marysville
Sites: Undesignated number
Facilities: Drinking water, vault toilets, fire rings, pets allowed
Fee per night: None
Elevation: 6,300 feet
Road conditions: Paved up to Forest Road 150, which, although a wide and well-maintained dirt road and suitable for RVs, has some tricky turns and dips: Take it slowly.
Management: Forest Service, Ashton/Island Park Ranger District, (208) 652–7442 (managed in cooperation with the Idaho Department of Parks and Recreation)
Reservations: No
Activities: Fishing, hiking, picnicking
Season: June 1–October 31
Finding the campground: From Ashton drive 12 miles northeast on ID 47 and 5 miles north on Forest Road 294 (which is a continuation of ID 47), then go 7 miles northeast on FR 150.
The campground: This is a relatively primitive site set back in the mountains. The woods are thinned out here, but the Warm River (whose headwaters are nearby) does stream by, narrowly. Hikers and hunters will find it one of the best locations anywhere in Idaho. Hunters have long since discovered it, and the campground is sometimes full at the opening of hunting season in the fall. Small mountain streams are all around the campground, and several nearby beaver ponds are a great spot for children to practice their fishing. Hikers willing to trek about 7 miles will get one of the best views of Upper and Lower Mesa Falls, the last major undeveloped major waterfalls in the Columbia River system.

13 St. Anthony Sand Dunes

Location: North of Rexburg, west of St. Anthony
Sites: No designated spaces (room for about 30 RVs)
Facilities: Drinking water, vault toilets, fire rings
Fee per night: None
Elevation: 5,500 feet
Road conditions: Paved to the campground

Management: Bureau of Land Management, Idaho Falls, (208) 524–7500
Reservations: No
Activities: Hiking, picnicking
Season: May 25–September 15
Finding the campground: From Rexburg drive to the North Rexburg exit on US 20 and continue beyond it west on 1900 East for 6.3 miles, to the second flashing light; turn left and drive for just under a mile to the split in the road at railroad tracks; there, turn right (on 500 North) and drive for 2.9 miles to the campground area. Or, from downtown St. Anthony, follow the signs west to Parker and the sand dunes.
The campground: This is essentially a dispersal camping area but still heavily used, and likely to be developed into a full-scale campground in 2004. The Bureau of Land Management estimates room at the campground area for about sixty cars and about half as many RVs, but the use goes up beyond that—with some jammed-in crowds—on weekends and holidays. The sand dunes are certainly worth a look—as high as 600 feet, and stretching out over hundreds of acres. (They are similar to, but smaller than, the dunes at Bruneau, which has state park rather than BLM facilities). The heavy use notwithstanding, this campground just barely qualifies as such; there are no services (other than toilet facilities), and it is a considered an "informal" campground.

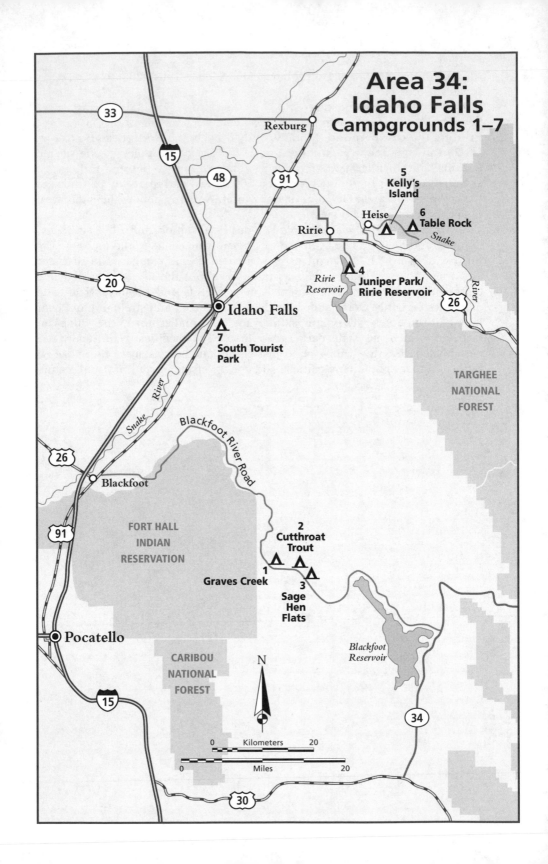

Area 34:
Idaho Falls
Campgrounds 1–7

33

15

Rexburg

48

91

5
Kelly's
Island

Heise

6
Table Rock

Ririe

Snake

20

Ririe
Reservoir

4
Juniper Park/
Ririe Reservoir

26

Idaho Falls

River

7
South Tourist
Park

Snake River

26

Blackfoot River Road

TARGHEE
NATIONAL
FOREST

91

Blackfoot

FORT HALL
INDIAN
RESERVATION

2
Cutthroat
Trout

1
Graves Creek

3
Sage
Hen
Flats

Blackfoot
Reservoir

Pocatello

CARIBOU
NATIONAL
FOREST

N

34

15

0   Kilometers   20

0   Miles   20

30

Area 34: Idaho Falls

The Snake River emerges into the Snake River plain at Ririe, and at that point several vacationer businesses have been established. There are not many others along the Snake, as the river winds through Idaho; in many places, the Snake is in a deep, inaccessible canyon or else is being drawn upon heavily for irrigation water. But at Ririe and Heise (home also of a hot springs), Idahoans do come to play in their big river.

The region from there to Blackfoot takes in much of the eastern Snake River plain, and a substantial number of Idaho's people live here—at Idaho Falls, Rexburg, Blackfoot, and other communities. This is farming country and food-processing country. But in the hills and along the riverfront, there are places to relax.

For more information:

Greater Idaho Falls Chamber of Commerce
505 Lindsay Boulevard
Idaho Falls, ID 83402
(208) 523–1010
www.idahofallschamber.com

Bureau of Land Management
1405 Hollipark Drive
Idaho Falls, ID 83401
(208) 524-7500

1 Graves Creek

Location: East of Blackfoot
Sites: 5
Facilities: Vault toilets, fire rings, river access
Fee per night: None
Elevation: 4,500 feet
Road conditions: Gravel roads maintained by Bingham County, good enough for a high-clearance sports vehicle in the summer but treacherous (muddy over a clay base) in the spring; RVs allowed but recommended only for experienced backcountry drivers
Management: Bureau of Land Management, (208) 524-7500
Reservations: No
Activities: Fishing, picnicking
Season: May 1–October 31
Finding the campground: From Blackfoot drive 9 miles north on U.S. Highway 91, then 10 miles east on Wolverine Road. Turn right onto Cedar Creek Road and continue for 13 miles, right onto Trail Creek Bridge Road for 6 miles, and then, after it becomes Lincoln Creek Road, go 1 more mile to the campground.

Area 34

	Town	Sites	Max. RV length	Electric	Picnic	Fire rings	Toilets	Showers	Water	Dump station	Disability access	Recreation	Can reserve	Fees ($)	Season	Stay limit (days)
1 Graves Creek	Blackfoot	5	15		•	•	V					F			May–Oct.	14
2 Cutthroat Trout	Blackfoot	U	15		•	•	V					F			May–Oct.	14
3 Sage Hen Flats	Blackfoot	5	15		•	•	V					F			May–Oct.	14
4 Juniper Park/ Ririe Reservoir	Ririe	49	42	•	•	•	FV	•	•	•		BFHS	•	$–$$	April–Oct.	14
5 Kelly's Island	Ririe	15	40		•	•	V		•			BFH		$	May–Sept.	14
6 Table Rock	Ririe	9	20		•	•	V		•			H	•	$	May–Sept.	14
7 South Tourist Park	Idaho Falls	U			•	•	F		•			H	•	$$	May–Sept.	1

The campground: Similar to Cutthroat Trout Campground, this one is well regarded as a prime fishing spot. The countryside is open sagebrush, desert in ambience. The campground has no drinking water, so be sure to pack your own.

2 Cutthroat Trout

Location: East of Blackfoot
Sites: Undetermined number
Facilities: Vault toilets, fire rings, river access
Fee per night: None
Elevation: 4,500 feet
Road conditions: Gravel roads maintained by Bingham County, good enough for a high-clearance sports vehicle in the summer but treacherous (muddy over a clay base) in the spring; RVs allowed but recommended only for experienced backcountry drivers
Management: Bureau of Land Management, (208) 524–7500
Reservations: No
Activities: Fishing, picnicking
Season: May 1–October 31
Finding the campground: From Blackfoot drive 9 miles north on US 91, then 10 miles east on Wolverine Road. Turn right onto Cedar Creek Road and continue for 13 miles, right onto Trail Creek Bridge Road for 6 miles, and then, after it becomes Lincoln Creek Road, go another 3 miles to the campground.
The campground: This is one of the more remote Blackfoot River campgrounds, semideveloped but well-enough equipped to appeal to hunters and anglers. It won't appeal to those looking for a shaded woodsy experience; the countryside along this stretch of the river runs to rolling sagebrush-covered hills, with some shade from juniper trees. It's a rugged stretch for an RV, though a practical drive in mid- to late summer, for the experienced and the patient.

Snake River canyon east of Ririe

3 Sage Hen Flats

Location: East of Blackfoot
Sites: 5
Facilities: Vault toilets, fire rings, river access
Fee per night: None
Elevation: 4,500 feet
Road conditions: Gravel roads maintained by Bingham County, good enough for a high-clearance sports vehicle in the summer but treacherous (muddy over a clay base) in the spring; RVs allowed but recommended only for experienced backcountry drivers
Management: Bureau of Land Management, (208) 524-7500
Reservations: No
Activities: Fishing, picnicking
Season: May 1–October 31
Finding the campground: From Blackfoot drive 9 miles north on US 91, then 10 miles east on Wolverine Road. Turn right onto Cedar Creek Road and continue for 13 miles, right onto Trail Creek Bridge Road for 6 miles, and then,

after it becomes Lincoln Creek Road, go another 6 miles to the campground.
The campground: Also in the mold of Cutthroat Trout, Sage Hen is a good
river site for anglers and hunters (and sometimes a destination for high school-
ers seeking a place away from adult supervision). This is an open-air campground area with spaces widely scattered around. Bring your own drinking
water; none is provided here.

4 Juniper Park/Ririe Reservoir

Location: South of Ririe
Sites: 49 (approximately)
Facilities: Drinking water, dump station, flush and vault toilets, fire rings,
electric hookups, barrier-free access, river access, showers, pull-through sites
Fee per night: $-$$
Elevation: 4,800 feet
Road conditions: Paved nearly to the campground
Management: Managed by Bonneville County Recreation Department, (208)
538-5126; property under control of the Bureau of Reclamation, (208)
678-0461
Reservations: Call Bonneville County at (208) 538-5126.
Activities: Boating, fishing, hiking, picnicking, swimming
Season: April 5–October 15
Finding the campgrounds: From Ririe drive east 2 miles on U.S. Highway
26.
The campgrounds: The Juniper Park area is one of the real gems among eastern Idaho public campgrounds, but it can get crowded given its location only
minutes away from Idaho Falls. Juniper's popularity is more than local,
though, since RV and other groups often use it for large group events, especially in the fall. For that reason you're well advised to call ahead to check for
availability if you plan to stay. The campgrounds are located on the Ririe
Reservoir, which meanders south from the Snake River; the reservoir is popular for boating and fishing. Bonneville County has put some work into this
one, adding utility hookups in the late 1990s and staffing a visitor center. (It
doesn't have the features of a museum, but the people there can answer your
questions and provide help.)

5 Kelly's Island

Location: East of Ririe
Sites: 15
Facilities: Drinking water, vault toilets, fire rings, river access
Fee per night: $
Elevation: 4,800 feet
Road conditions: Paved through Heise to the ski area, then gravel; it is main-
tained by Jefferson County but sometimes rough in spots. An adequate RV
road—for the patient.
Management: Bureau of Land Management, (208) 524-7500
Reservations: None ordinarily, but for information call (208) 524-7500.
Activities: Boating, fishing, hiking, picnicking

Season: May–September
Finding the campground: From Ririe drive 1 mile north on Archer Road, then 4 miles east on Heise Road. The campground is next to the Snake River.
The campground: Situated in a cottonwood grove, Kelly's Island is one of the most attractive BLM campgrounds in Idaho. At this stage of the Snake River, boating is easy and pleasant, and a nearby boat ramp is available.

6 Table Rock

Location: East of Ririe
Sites: 9
Facilities: Drinking water, vault toilets, fire rings
Fee per night: $
Elevation: 5,800 feet
Road conditions: Paved nearly to the campground
Management: Forest Service, Palisades Ranger Station, (208) 523–1412
Reservations: Call (877) 444-6777 or visit Web site www.reserveamerica.com.
Activities: Hiking, picnicking
Season: May 21–September 7
Finding the campground: From Ririe drive 12 miles east on US 26, then 1.5 miles east on Forest Road 218, and then 1.3 miles east on Forest Road 217.
The campground: This campground east of the Heise recreation area is close to the Kelly Canyon ski area (the national forest boundary in this area is at the ski area) and, like it, is nicely forested. A small springs shoots out above the campground, making for a pleasant setting. But the big draw here is for ATV and motorbike riders, who will find plenty of trails in the area.

7 South Tourist Park

Location: Idaho Falls
Sites: Variable
Facilities: Drinking water, flush toilets, fire rings
Fee per night: $$
Elevation: 4,750 feet
Road conditions: All paved
Management: City of Idaho Falls Parks and Recreation Division, (208) 529–1482
Reservations: Call (208) 529–1482.
Activities: Hiking, picnicking
Season: May 21–September 7
Finding the campground: In Idaho Falls, the park is located at 2800 South Yellowstone (or US 26).
The campground: This is a small urban campground for people passing through, not for long-term camping—there is a twenty-four-hour limit to stays. The park does have modern restrooms and an RV dump. South Tourist is next to North Tourist, which has golf and other facilities. From Yellowstone you can recognize the area by a tall totem pole perched out front.

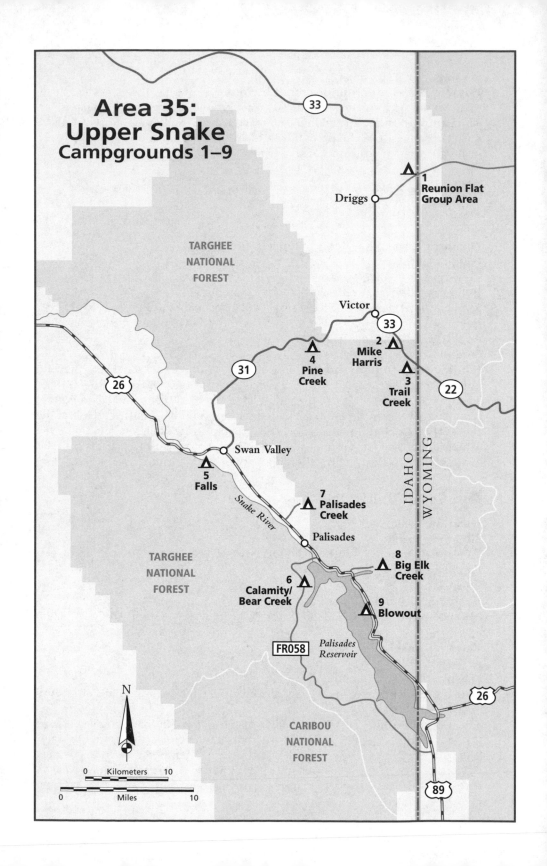

Area 35:
Upper Snake
Campgrounds 1–9

33

△ 1
**Reunion Flat
Group Area**

Driggs

TARGHEE

NATIONAL

FOREST

Victor

33

△ 2
**Mike
Harris**

△ 4
**Pine
Creek**

31

△ 3
**Trail
Creek**

22

26

IDAHO

WYOMING

Swan Valley

△ 5
Falls

Snake River

△ 7
**Palisades
Creek**

Palisades

TARGHEE

NATIONAL

FOREST

△ 8
**Big Elk
Creek**

△ 6
**Calamity/
Bear Creek**

△ 9
Blowout

FR058

*Palisades
Reservoir*

26

N

CARIBOU

NATIONAL

FOREST

0   Kilometers   10

0   Miles   10

89

Area 35: Upper Snake

The Idaho mountains adjoining Wyoming, just west of the Grand Teton Mountains (which are easily visible from Idaho and probably a better view than from the Wyoming side), have forged one of the state's prettiest areas. The reach of the Snake River just after it flows into Idaho—where it is halted by Palisades Dam—is one of the prettiest bodies of water in Idaho, and it is not yet heavily populated. (This area is becoming more popular with Idaho Falls residents.)

Just to the north of this area, over Pine Creek Pass, is the Teton Valley, one of the fastest-growing places in Idaho. There are good reasons: It is just over a mountain pass from world-famous Jackson, Wyoming, and just down the hill from the Grand Targhee Ski Area.

The whole area is full of wild critters of many types, from bald eagles and grebes among the birds to black bears, mule deer, moose, and elk among the mammals.

For more information:

Teton Valley Chamber of Commerce
74 North Main Street
Driggs, ID 83422
(208) 354–2500
www.tetonvalleychamber.com

Bureau of Land Management
1405 Hollipark Drive
Idaho Falls, ID 83401
(208) 524–7500

---

1 Reunion Flat Group Area

Location: East of Driggs
Sites: 3
Facilities: Drinking water, vault toilets, fire rings, pets allowed
Fee per night: $$$$
Elevation: 6,500 feet
Road conditions: Mostly paved; good gravel road approaching the campground
Management: Forest Service, Teton Basin Ranger District, (208) 354–2312
Reservations: Call (877) 444–6777 or visit Web site www.reserveamerica.com.
Activities: Fishing, hiking, picnicking
Season: June 1–September 15 (depending on weather)
Finding the campground: From Driggs turn east (at the Key Bank Building) on Ski Hill Road and follow it for 9 miles, and then continue 3 miles east on Forest Road 009.

Area 35

	Town	Sites	Max. RV length	Electric	Picnic	Fire rings	Toilets	Showers	Water	Dump station	Disability access	Recreation	Can reserve	Fees ($)	Season	Stay limit (days)
1 Reunion Flat	Driggs	3			•	•	V		•			FH	•	$$$$	June–Sept.	14
2 Mike Harris	Victor	12	20		•	•	V		•	•		FH		$	June–Sept.	14
3 Trail Creek	Victor	11	20		•	•	V		•	•		FH	•	$$	June–Sept.	14
4 Pine Creek	Victor	11	15		•	•	V		•	•		FH		$$	June–Sept.	14
5 Falls	Swan Valley	23	24		•	•	V		•			BFS	•	$$	May–Sept.	14
6 Calamity/ Bear Creek	Palisades	8	24		•	•	V		•			BFHS	•	$$	May–Sept.	14
7 Palisades Creek	Palisades	8	24		•	•	V		•			FH	•	$	May–Sept.	14
8 Big Elk Creek	Palisades	23	50		•	•	V		•			BFHS	•	$	May–Sept.	14
9 Blowout	Palisades	15			•	•	V		•			BFS	•	$$	May–Sept.	14

The campground: This campground, in the foothills below the Grand Targhee Ski Area, is right on the Idaho-Wyoming border. As the name indicates, it is strictly a group campground. The grounds are partly wooded and, despite the mountain location, flat; a wide range of recreational vehicles can be accommodated. Campers here often focus on hiking and mountain biking, and sometimes on fishing.

2 Mike Harris

Location: Southeast of Victor
Sites: 12
Facilities: Drinking water, vault toilets, fire rings, pull-through sites, garbage service (Dumpster), dump station
Fee per night: $
Elevation: 6,200 feet
Road conditions: Paved nearly to the campground
Management: Forest Service, Teton Basin Ranger District, (208) 354–2312
Reservations: No
Activities: Fishing, hiking, picnicking
Season: June 15–September 15
Finding the campground: From Victor drive 4 miles southeast on Idaho Highway 33 and then half a mile on Forest Road 239.
The campground: Mike Harris is located at the southeast edge of the Teton Valley, in the shadow of the Teton Mountains and just below the steep Teton Pass (which can be a formidable drive in winter, or even in summer if you're pulling a heavy trailer). This smallish, wooded campground is placed next to

Mike Harris Creek, about 5 miles from Victor. Mike Harris was a resident, decades ago, near the present campground location. But Forest Service records turned up nothing more about how he lived, when he lived there, or even why it named a campground after him.

3 Trail Creek

Location: Southeast of Victor
Sites: 11
Facilities: Drinking water (faucets), vault toilets, fire rings, pull-through sites, dump station
Fee per night: $$
Elevation: 6,600 feet
Road conditions: Paved to the campground
Management: Forest Service, Teton Basin Ranger District, (208) 354–2312
Reservations: Call (877) 444–6777 or visit Web site www.reserveamerica.com.
Activities: Fishing, hiking, picnicking
Season: June 15–September 15
Finding the campground: From Victor drive 6 miles southeast on ID 33; enter the campground from the highway.
The campground: Trail is located up the mountain en route to Teton Pass, above the Mike Harris campground, which it resembles. Though camping is allowed, it probably gets more use as a day-use site.

4 Pine Creek

Location: West of Victor
Sites: 11
Facilities: Drinking water (expected in 2004), vault toilets, fire rings, pull-through sites, garbage service (Dumpster), dump station
Fee per night: $$
Elevation: 6,600 feet
Road conditions: Paved to the campground entrance; but note that the campground is located nearly at the top of Pine Creek Summit, so some climbing is involved.
Management: Forest Service, Teton Basin Ranger District, (208) 354–2312
Reservations: No
Activities: Fishing, hiking, picnicking
Season: June 15–September 15
Finding the campground: From Victor drive 6.5 miles west on Idaho Highway 31; enter the campground from the highway.
The campground: Most campgrounds are in draws or valleys; this one is located close to a high mountain pass, just off ID 31. Though wooded, much of it is visible from the highway. Well drillers tried in 2002 and 2003 to tap into drinkable water underground but failed each time. They were planning to try again in the summer of 2004.

5 Falls

Location: West of Swan Valley
Sites: 23
Facilities: Drinking water, vault toilets, fire rings
Fee per night: $$
Elevation: 5,400 feet
Road conditions: Good gravel to the campground
Management: Forest Service, Palisades Ranger Station, (208) 523-1412
Reservations: Call (877) 444-6777 or visit Web site www.reserveamerica.com.
Activities: Boating, fishing, picnicking, swimming
Season: May 21-September 7
Finding the campground: From Swan Valley drive 4 miles west on U.S. Highway 26 and then 2.3 miles south on Forest Road 076.
The campground: Not on Palisades Reservoir, Falls is located next to the Snake River just downstream from Palisades Dam. The setting is at the bottom of a farm valley, a lightly forested location by the Snake River. It is a short hike from the community of Swan Valley.

Calamity/Bear Creek

Location: Southeast of Palisades
Sites: 8 (at Calamity; variable at Bear Creek)
Facilities: Drinking water, vault toilets, fire rings
Fee per night: $$
Elevation: 5,600 feet
Road conditions: Paved across the dam, good gravel (though steep in places) to Calamity Campground; the road gets much rougher from there to Bear Creek and should be left to high-clearance four-wheel-drive vehicles. There are several sharp turns (including a nasty one on the dam), so slow down and watch carefully.
Management: Forest Service, Palisades Ranger Station, (208) 523-1412
Reservations: Calamity only. Call (877) 444-6777 or visit Web site www. reserveamerica.com.
Activities: Boating, fishing, hiking, picnicking, swimming
Season: May 21-September 15
Finding the campgrounds: From Palisades drive US 26 southeast 2.6 miles, cross Palisades Dam, and then drive 1.1 miles southwest on Forest Road 058. Bear Creek is another 4 miles into the mountains on the same road.
The campgrounds: Calamity is a well-developed campground, one of the few on the south short of Palisades Reservoir. A wooded and forested campsite, it offers only limited views of the reservoir. This hosted campground offers RV-suitable spaces only in some locations; Loop C is considered too tight for turn-arounds. From here, however, ambitious boaters can access the reservoir. Bear Creek is a more remote and primitive area, good for fishing and hunting—but don't plan on bringing your RV back here, since the road is very narrow, steep, and rough.

7 Palisades Creek

Location: Northeast of Palisades
Sites: 8
Facilities: Drinking water, vault toilets, fire rings
Fee per night: $
Elevation: 5,600 feet
Road conditions: Good and relatively flat gravel leading into the campground
Management: Forest Service, Palisades Ranger Station, (208) 523-1412
Reservations: Call (877) 444-6777 or visit Web site www.reserveamerica.com.
Activities: Fishing, hiking, picnicking
Season: May 21-September 15
Finding the campground: From Palisades drive 1 mile northwest on US 26 and then 2 miles northeast on Forest Road 255 to the campground.
The campground: Know what you're getting here—focus on the word *creek* and not *Palisades*, which might lead you to think this campground is one of those beauty spots overlooking the reservoir. None of which is to argue against this campground, as long as boating isn't your aim. This area is still a pretty mountain campground, relatively isolated and close by a creek.

8 Big Elk Creek

Location: Southeast of Palisades
Sites: 23 (2 group sites)
Facilities: Drinking water, vault toilets, fire rings
Fee per night: $
Elevation: 5,800 feet
Road conditions: Paved to the campground
Management: Forest Service, Palisades Ranger Station, (208) 523-1412
Reservations: Reservations allowed for group sites only. Call (877) 444-6777 or visit Web site www.reserveamerica.com.
Activities: Boating, fishing, hiking, picnicking, swimming
Season: May 21-September 7
Finding the campground: From Palisades drive US 26 southeast 5.4 miles, and then go 1.4 miles northeast on Forest Road 262.
The campground: Partly perched on a bluff overlooking Palisades Reservoir and stretching out below to lakeside (where the group sites are located), this is not a place for seclusion. But it is a great place for views and for lake boat launches.

9 Blowout

Location: Southeast of Palisades
Sites: 15
Facilities: Drinking water, vault toilets, fire rings
Fee per night: $$

Palisades Reservoir near the Blowout Campground

Elevation: 5,800 feet
Road conditions: Paved to the campground
Management: Forest Service, Palisades Ranger Station, (208) 523-1412
Reservations: Allowed for some sites only; some sites in this campground were removed from the reservation system in 2002. Call (877) 444-6777 or visit Web site www.reserveamerica.com.
Activities: Boating, fishing, picnicking, swimming
Season: May 21–September 7
Finding the campground: From Palisades drive US 26 southeast 9 miles; campground is just off the highway.
The campground: Groups often use this site on the north side of the Palisades Reservoir; like other nearby sites, the view of the water is spectacular from here. A campground host lives here during the summer. It's also good for boating; Blowout has the second-biggest boating facilities along Palisades Reservoir.

Area 36: Blackfoot

Pocatello, on the Snake River plain, is Idaho's third-largest city, and through it flows the Portneuf River, which drains a large part of southeast Idaho. Follow the river from the "bottoms," where it pours into the Snake, back up toward its source and you find country changing from desert valley to lush mountains and high meadows. You find geologic anomalies that remind you of Yellowstone National Park—like the spectacular natural geyser at Soda Springs and the waters after which Lava Hot Springs is named—and some of the most unusual scenery in Idaho. As you do, reflect on what the early Oregon Trail pioneers thought as they considered this land, for they worked their way through much of this area.

The unusual geology has turned the Soda Springs area into Idaho's main mining district, but there is much more to see in the Portneuf country and in the highlands to the north and east of it.

Here, in this backcountry, lie most of the region's quality camping and recreational opportunities, not in the Portneuf River basin over a range of hills, but in the Blackfoot River basin (which merges with the Snake River near the city of Blackfoot). This remote backcountry, familiar mainly to locals—you won't often find crowds here—has some of Idaho's most pristine turf, and some of its fishing spots are prized.

Most of the public campgrounds in this area are managed by the Soda Springs Ranger District, which has only a limited recreation program; consequently, many of the campgrounds in this area have few facilities and are relatively primitive compared to the more-developed sites to the north along the Palisades Reservoir or to the south near Bear Lake. While none of these sites (except Big Springs) allow for reservations, none of them charge a camping fee, either, and they tend not to be as crowded as some of the sites elsewhere in the area. So this may be just the kind of camping you're looking for.

For more information:

Pocatello Chamber of Commerce
343 West Center Street
Pocatello, ID 83204
(208) 478–6340
www.pocatelloidaho.com

Soda Springs Chamber of Commerce
P.O. Box 697
Soda Springs, ID 83276
(208) 547–4964
www.sodaspringsid.com

Caribou National Forest
1405 Hollipark Drive
Idaho Falls, ID 83403
(208) 524–7500

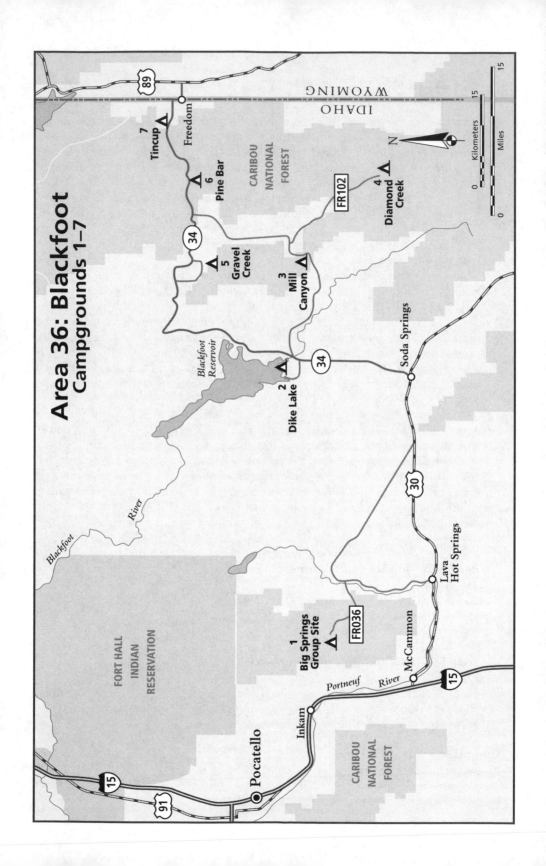

Area 36: Blackfoot
Campgrounds 1–7

Area 36

	Town	Sites	Max. RV length	Electric	Picnic	Fire rings	Toilets	Showers	Water	Dump station	Disability access	Recreation	Can reserve	Fees ($)	Season	Stay limit (days)
1 Big Springs	Lava Hot Springs	32	30		•	•	V		•			H	•	$	May–Oct.	14
2 Dike Lake	Soda Springs	35	25		•	•	V		•			BF			May–Oct.	14
3 Mill Canyon	Soda Springs	10	32		•	•	V					FH			June–Sept.	14
4 Diamond Creek	Soda Springs	12				•	V					FH			June–Sept.	14
5 Gravel Creek	Soda Springs	9	20			•	V					FH			June–Sept.	14
6 Pine Bar	Soda Springs	5	20		•	•	V					FH			June–Sept.	14
7 Tincup	Soda Springs	5	20		•	•	V					FH			June–Sept.	14

1 Big Springs Group Site

Location: North of Lava Hot Springs
Sites: 32
Facilities: Drinking water, vault toilets, fire rings, pets allowed
Fee per night: $
Elevation: 6,300 feet
Road conditions: Generally easy gravel roads; easy access for RVs and other larger vehicles
Management: Forest Service, Westside Ranger District, (208) 236-7500
Reservations: Reservations are needed to use this campground! Call (877) 444-6777 or visit Web site www.reserveamerica.com.
Activities: Hiking, picnicking
Season: May 15–October 1
Finding the campground: From Lava Hot Springs drive 10 miles north on the Bancroft Highway (old U.S. Highway 30), then 8 miles west on Forest Road 036.
The campground: Managed out of Pocatello, this group campground is the one relatively developed campground in this area, and it is the most popular, especially among eastern Idahoans and Utahans. (It's a favorite among church groups looking for a recreation outing or a retreat.) You'll find relatively little shade but plenty of recreation options, starting with the eponymous creek running through the grounds, and the forests all around. Horseback riding is accommodated in part of the campground. When it becomes especially busy, campers often overflow the campgrounds, dispersing to nearby woods for camping. Big Springs is just downhill from the Pebble Creek Ski Area (which is just east of Inkom)—but there's no road connection from Big Springs to the ski area, each of which must be accessed from different sides of the same mountain range.

2 Dike Lake

Location: North of Soda Springs
Sites: 35
Facilities: Drinking water, lake access, vault toilets, fire rings
Fee per night: None
Elevation: 5,900 feet
Road conditions: Good gravel road
Management: Bureau of Land Management, Pocatello office, (208) 478–6340
Reservations: None, but for information call (208) 236–6860.
Activities: Boating, fishing, picnicking
Season: May 31–October 31
Finding the campground: From Soda Springs drive 11 miles north on Idaho Highway 34; turn west at Chiua Cap Road, drive 2 miles, and then turn right at Dike Road; go 1 mile north to the campground.
The campground: Located at the southeast edge of Blackfoot Reservoir (about as close as the reservoir gets to paved road), Dike Lake is a good boat launch point—when the reservoir is high enough. BLM undertook some limited renovation of the campground in 2002 and 2003, and more is planned in coming years as funding becomes available.

3 Mill Canyon

Location: North of Soda Springs
Sites: 10
Facilities: Vault toilets, fire rings, pull-through sites
Fee per night: None
Elevation: 6,500 feet
Road conditions: Gravel road from the highway on out; conditions are widely variable. Watch for potholes and washboards.
Management: Forest Service, Soda Springs Ranger District, (208) 547–4356
Reservations: No
Activities: Fishing, hiking, picnicking
Season: June 1–September 30
Finding the campground: From Soda Springs drive 14 miles north on ID 34, then 13.5 miles east on the Blackfoot River Road, and then 6 miles west on Forest Road 099.
The campground: This may be the best site for fishing along the Blackfoot River (its popularity seems to have diminished over the years), though the Forest Service suggests checking fishing regulations carefully before dropping line. The fish may be plentiful, but the population is under close inspection. This is a thinly wooded but attractive remote area. Bring your own drinking water; none is provided on-site.

4 Diamond Creek

Location: North of Soda Springs
Sites: 12
Facilities: Vault toilets, fire rings
Fee per night: None
Elevation: 6,900 feet
Road conditions: Good, well-maintained, and mostly flat gravel road
Management: Forest Service, Soda Springs Ranger District, (208) 547–4356
Reservations: No
Activities: Fishing, hiking
Season: June 1–September 30 (depending on weather)
Finding the campground: From Soda Springs drive 14 miles north on ID 34, then 14 miles east on the Blackfoot River Road, then 4.9 miles northeast on FR 095, and then 12.5 miles southeast on Forest Road 102.
The campground: Though located on the like-named Diamond Creek, fishing isn't considered especially good at this remote mountain campground. Hunting of deer, elk, and moose, however, is—and this campground sometimes fills up during hunting season. Bring your own drinking water; the campground has none.

5 Gravel Creek

Location: North of Soda Springs
Sites: 9
Facilities: Vault toilets, fire rings, pull-through sites
Fee per night: None
Elevation: 6,500 feet
Road conditions: Good gravel road, regularly graded
Management: Forest Service, Soda Springs Ranger District, (208) 547–4356
Reservations: No
Activities: Fishing, hiking
Season: June 1–September 30
Finding the campground: From Soda Springs drive 34 miles north on ID 34, and then turn right at the sign for the campground and continue 5 miles south on the Wayan Loop Road. Watch for campground signs.
The campground: Like several of the other campgrounds in this area, this relatively remote site does not see a lot of family groups or big RVs or anglers (it's not well suited to any of those uses) but does see a lot of hunters in the fall. ATV enthusiasts also come by in the summer; there are no formally designated ATV trails, but a number of routes have become commonly used. The campground has no drinking water, so pack your own.

6 Pine Bar

Location: Northeast of Soda Springs
Sites: 5
Facilities: Vault toilets, fire rings
Fee per night: None
Elevation: 6,300 feet
Road conditions: Paved to the campground
Management: Forest Service, Soda Springs Ranger District, (208) 547-4356
Reservations: No
Activities: Fishing, hiking, picnicking
Season: June 1–September 30
Finding the campground: From Soda Springs drive ID 34 for 45 miles close to the Wyoming border (about 11 miles from Freedom, Wyoming). The campground is just off the highway.
The campground: Hunters (in season) and anglers do stop in here, and hikers can become enthralled with the nearby trails on the South Fork of Lau Creek to the Stump Peak Roadless Area. That said, Forest Service personnel report that much of Pine Bar's use is by travelers passing through, just spending the night by the roadside en route to Jackson, Wyoming. Bring your own drinking water; this campground has none.

7 Tincup

Location: Northeast of Soda Springs
Sites: 5
Facilities: Vault toilets, fire rings, pull-through sites
Fee per night: None
Elevation: 5,800 feet
Road conditions: Paved to the campground
Management: Forest Service, Soda Springs Ranger District, (208) 547-4356
Reservations: No
Activities: Fishing, hiking, picnicking
Season: June 1–September 30
Finding the campground: From Soda Springs drive ID 34 for 52 miles close to the Wyoming border (about 4 miles from Freedom, Wyoming). The campground is just off the highway.
The campground: Though located next to the highway, Tincup—which sits on the banks of Tincup Creek—is relatively secluded, which probably is why it gets less overnight traffic than nearby Pinebar. There are no major hiking trails nearby, but the fishing is said to be good at Tincup Creek. No drinking water is provided, so pack your own.

Area 37: American Falls

One of the largest dams in Idaho is the American Falls Dam, which decades ago actually forced the entire town of American Falls to relocate, since the dam would flood the old location. The American Falls Reservoir not only created a new city of American Falls but also led eventually to a number of recreation sites along its shores. Most of the land in this area is irrigated farm country, but there are wildlife refuges and park areas, and some attractive camping opportunities, both public and private.

Drive south down Interstate 15 toward Malad, and you'll see very different landscapes. One of the most spectacular areas is the Curlew National Grasslands west of Malad.

For more information:

American Falls Chamber of Commerce
239 Idaho Street
American Falls, ID 83211
(208) 226-7214

Curlew National Grasslands
1405 Hollipark Drive
Idaho Falls, ID 83403
(208) 524-7500

1 Sportsman Park

Location: East of Aberdeen
Sites: 29
Facilities: Drinking water, flush toilets, fire rings, electric hookups, pay phone
Fee per night: $$ (with electric hookups $$$)
Elevation: 4,350 feet
Road conditions: Good, flat and easy, paved up to and partly through the campground. The road leading into it, Boat Dock Road, originates in Aberdeen but can be tricky to find there: Look for the University of Idaho seed research complex.
Management: Bingham County, (208) 397-3000
Reservations: Call (208) 397-3000.
Activities: Boating, bird watching, fishing, picnicking, swimming
Season: Summer
Finding the campground: From Idaho Highway 39 in Aberdeen, drive to the north end of town to the University of Idaho agricultural research complex and the intersection with Boat Dock Road. Drive Boat Dock Road 3 miles east to the American Falls Reservoir; the campground is near the shoreline.
The campground: This is a rare local government campground, in this case operated by Bingham County. It is actually a multiple-use facility. It offers public swimming on a beach (within a roped-in area), boat launches, horse-

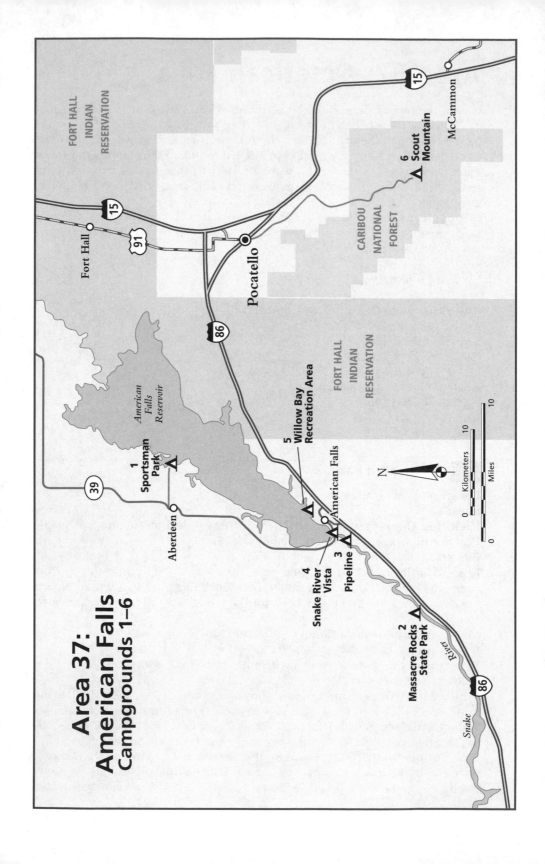

Area 37:
American Falls
Campgrounds 1–6

FORT HALL INDIAN RESERVATION

Fort Hall

15

91

Pocatello

86

CARIBOU NATIONAL FOREST

6 Scout Mountain △

McCammon

15

39

Aberdeen

American Falls Reservoir

1 Sportsman Park △

5 Willow Bay Recreation Area △

American Falls

3 Pipeline △

4 Snake River Vista △

FORT HALL INDIAN RESERVATION

N

0 Kilometers 10

0 Miles 10

2 Massacre Rocks State Park △

Snake River

86

Snake

Area 37

	Town	Sites	Max. RV length	Electric	Picnic	Fire rings	Toilets	Showers	Water	Dump station	Disability access	Recreation	Can reserve	Fees ($)	Season	Stay limit (days)
1 Sportsman Park	Aberdeen	29		•	•	•	F		•			BFS	•	$$–$$$	Summer	
2 Massacre Rocks State Park	American Falls	48	55	•	•	•	F	•	•	•	•	BFH	•	$	Year-round	
3 Pipeline	American Falls	5	17	•	•		V					BF		$	Year-round	14
4 Snake River Vista	American Falls	5	18	•	•		V					BF		$	Year-round	14
5 Willow Bay Recreation Area	American Falls	24		•	•	•	F		•	•		BS	•	$$	April–Oct.	
6 Scout Mountain	Pocatello	41	16	•	•		V		•			H		$$	May–Sept.	14

shoe and volleyball play areas, and a picnic area (including a large covered facility that can be rented) as well as camping spots. Some of the spots service RVs with electric power hookups, others do not; tents are allowed in some spaces. It looks more like a well-manicured private campground than a typical public campground. A couple restrictions of note (this being a local government facility): Pets must be kept on leash, and alcoholic beverages are prohibited.

2 Massacre Rocks State Park

Location: West of American Falls
Sites: 48
Facilities: Drinking water, flush toilets, showers, fire rings, electric and water hookups, dump station, pull-through sites, barrier-free access
Fee per night: $
Elevation: 4,300 feet
Road conditions: Excellent; paved to the campground, close to interstate
Management: Idaho Department of Parks and Recreation, Massacre Rocks State Park, (208) 548–2672
Reservations: Available via Web site www.idahoparks.org
Activities: Boating, fishing, hiking, picnicking
Season: All year, technically; as a practical matter, about May 1 through October 31 (depending on weather)
Finding the campground: Take Interstate 86 west of American Falls 10 miles to the Massacre Rocks State Park exit; the park is just off the interstate.
The campground: It's a desert campground but right next to the Snake River. There are two loops, the Upper Campground (closer to the visitor center and dump station) and the Lower Campground (closer to the Snake River and fishing access). The area is mostly unshaded, but the mountains around create picturesque scenery. Electric and water hookups are provided, and the restrooms

have hot showers. In the summer the park holds evening campfire programs, and 8 miles of hiking trails are designated. Wildlife and bird watching is popular in the area; park officials say that more than 200 species of birds have been seen there. About 3 miles downstream is the Register Rock group camping and picnic area. This is high desert, with all that implies, and close to the old Oregon Trail route; ruts from that trail still are visible.

3 Pipeline

Location: West of American Falls
Sites: 5
Facilities: Vault toilets, fire rings, lakeside access, pets allowed
Fee per night: $
Elevation: 4,300 feet
Road conditions: Paved until the last mile leading down to the campground; a well-packed gravel road down to the river
Management: Bureau of Land Management, Pocatello Office, (208) 548-2672
Reservations: None ordinarily, but for information call (208) 548-2672.
Activities: Boating, fishing, picnicking
Season: All year
Finding the campground: From the western American Falls exit to I-86 (the Rockland exit), take Eagle Rock Road west, toward the Neeley area; this is the frontage road for the interstate. On Pipeline Road turn north toward the Snake River and head downhill about a mile.
The campground: It's not one of the more evocative campground names (the namesake is a thin Intermountain Gas silver pipe crossing the Snake River from the campsite to the north side of the river), but it's one of the easier spots for anglers who want to launch their boats into the Snake River. Activity trails are available for ATV enthusiasts. The grounds are plainly developed in a desert-type environment but are located directly on the Snake River, and the location is beautifully scenic. (The boating area is several miles downstream of the American Falls Dam.) Bring your own drinking water; none is available here.

4 Snake River Vista

Location: West of American Falls
Sites: 5
Facilities: Vault toilets, fire rings, lakeside access, pets allowed
Fee per night: $
Elevation: 4,300 feet
Road conditions: Paved until the last mile leading down to the campground; a well-packed gravel road down to the river
Management: Bureau of Land Management, Pocatello office, (208) 548-2672
Reservations: None ordinarily, but for information call (208) 548-2672.
Activities: Boating, fishing, picnicking
Season: All year

Finding the campground: From American Falls cross the American Falls Dam, turn left on the first road on the northwest side of the dam, and follow the river road about 2 miles to the campground.

The campground: This campground is located almost directly across the Snake River from Pipeline Campground and is almost a mirror image of it. Like Pipeline, it's a good river input location. Also like Pipeline, it has no drinking water, so pack your own.

5 Willow Bay Recreation Area

Location: East of American Falls
Sites: 24
Facilities: Drinking water, flush toilets, showers, fire rings, electric hookups, LP gas, lake access, dump station, minimart, restaurant, pets allowed
Fee per night: $$
Elevation: 4,300 feet
Road conditions: Excellent; paved and well maintained into the campground
Management: A mixture of public agencies and a private contractor
Reservations: Call (208) 226-2688; credit cards accepted.
Activities: Boating, picnicking, swimming
Season: April–October generally (depending on weather)
Finding the campground: From American Falls drive east on ID 39 and then about 3 miles on Marina Road next to the American Falls Reservoir.

The campground: This is a borderline case for inclusion in this book: almost equal parts public and private and resembling in appearance a well-kept private campground more than a normal public facility. The land is owned mostly by the Bureau of Reclamation but in part by the city of American Falls (which got it in a trade with the state of Idaho). The agencies have contracted with a private operator, who runs the marina, cafe, campground, and related facilities. (In 2002 the operator signed a five-year contract for managing the property.) The lakeside location on the south shore of American Falls Reservoir, with convenient facilities, is the big draw, and the campground stays full much of the time.

6 Scout Mountain

Location: South of Pocatello
Sites: 41 (several group sites)
Facilities: Drinking water (faucet), vault toilets, fire rings
Fee per night: $$
Elevation: 6,900 feet
Road conditions: Paved to the campground but steep and winding in places
Management: Forest Service, Westside Ranger District, (208) 236-7500
Reservations: Reservations are needed for use of the group sites but not required for individual sites. Call (877) 444-6777 or visit Web site www.reserveamerica.com.
Activities: Hiking, picnicking

Season: May–September (depending on weather)

Finding the campground: From Pocatello drive 13 miles south on Mink Creek Road (Bannock County Road 38) and then 3.8 miles southeast on Forest Road 2000.

The campground: Located up in the mountains near the Scout Mountain Recreation Area, this is an attractive forested location seemingly a long way from the Pocatello desert valley country. Scout Mountain gets a good deal of traffic from the Pocatello area, so reservations are advised.

Area 38: Bear River

Almost all of Idaho lies within the Snake River Basin; the only areas that do not are the Panhandle in the far north and the southeast corner of the state, which is in within the Bear River system. (The Bear also runs through Wyoming and Utah.) This almost reflects society in this area, since the people who live in Preston and Franklin and the related communities in Idaho look more often to Utah as their social base. The small city of Franklin, Idaho's oldest continuously settled town, actually was settled under the impression it was located in Utah, not Idaho.

The Bear River twists and turns through this country, and much of it is not the desert of surrounding regions but a well-watered series of low hills and valleys. Wildlife is plentiful through much of this area.

For more information:

Preston Chamber of Commerce
32 West Oneida Street
Preston, ID 83263
(208) 852–2703

Caribou National Forest
1405 Hollipark Drive
Idaho Falls, ID 83403
(208) 524–7500

Bureau of Land Management
138 South Main
Malad City, ID 83252
(208) 766–4766

1 Hawkins Reservoir

Location: West of Virginia
Sites: 14
Facilities: Vault toilets, fire rings, laundry, river access
Fee per night: None
Elevation: 4,600 feet
Road conditions: Mostly paved, with some flat lane-and-a-half gravel road near the campground
Management: Bureau of Land Management, Pocatello office, (208) 236–6860
Reservations: No
Activities: Fishing, picnicking
Season: All year
Finding the campground: From the Virginia exit (south of McCammon) on Interstate 15, drive 10 miles west on Hawkins Reservoir Road.

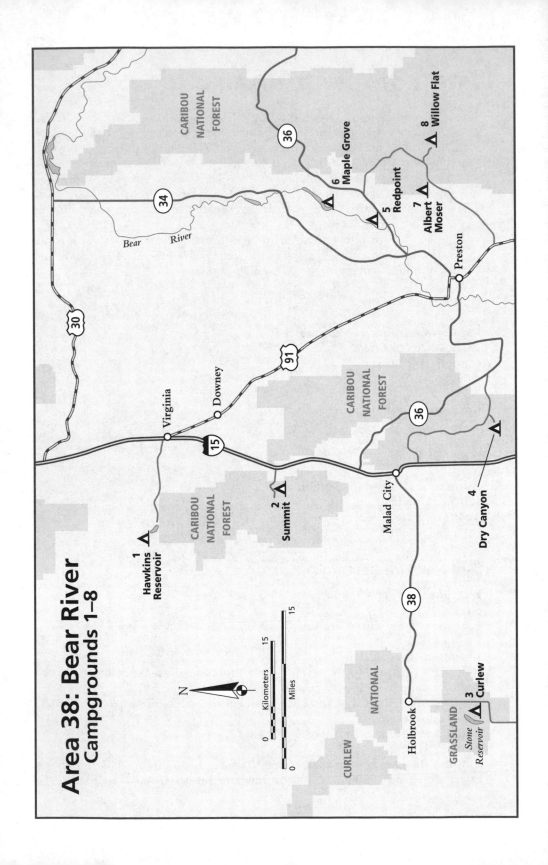

Area 38: Bear River
Campgrounds 1–8

N

Kilometers 15

0   15

0   15
Miles

CARIBOU NATIONAL FOREST

Bear River

34

30

91

Virginia

Downey

15

CARIBOU NATIONAL FOREST

1
Hawkins Reservoir

2
Summit

Malad City

36

4
Dry Canyon

38

Holbrook

CURLEW NATIONAL GRASSLAND

Stone Reservoir

3
Curlew

36

Maple Grove
6

5
Redpoint

7
Albert Moser

8
Willow Flat

Preston

Area 38

	Town	Sites	Max. RV length	Electric	Picnic	Fire rings	Toilets	Showers	Water	Dump station	Disability access	Recreation	Can reserve	Fees ($)	Season	Stay limit (days)
1 Hawkins Reservoir	Virginia	14	20		•	•	V					F			Year-round	
2 Summit	Malad	12	32		•	•	V		•		•	F		$	May–Sept.	14
3 Curlew	Malad	U			•	•	V		•			F	•		May–Sept.	14
4 Dry Canyon	Malad	U			•	•	V					F			May–Sept.	14
5 Redpoint	Preston	6	20		•	•	V					F		$		14
6 Maple Grove	Preston	20	17		•	•	V				•	F		$	June–Sept.	14
7 Albert Moser	Preston	9	16		•	•	V		•			F	•	$$–$$$	June–Sept.	14
8 Willow Flat	Preston	54	22		•	•	V		•			FH	•	$–$$	June–Sept.	14

The campground: This campground is a plain spot, unshaded, out in the desert and down in the Portneuf River valley. You'll find a few picnic tables and a small reservoir (some describe it as more like a pond). There's a broad vista across the valley to the mountains, but overall this is one of the less impressive campgrounds in the region. It has no drinking water, so pack your own.

2 Summit

Location: North of Malad City
Sites: 12 (11 individual, one for groups)
Facilities: Drinking water, vault toilets, fire rings, barrier-free access (1 site)
Fee per night: $
Elevation: 6,100 feet
Road conditions: Paved until you cross the interstate on House Road; gravel after that, but mostly high-quality road that can accommodate most vehicles
Management: Forest Service, Westside Ranger District, (208) 236–7500
Reservations: No
Activities: Fishing, picnicking
Season: May 20–September 30
Finding the campground: From Malad City drive 8 miles north on I-15, exit at the Devil's Lake exit (where the Devil's Lake private campground is located), continue north on Devil's Lake Road (which parallels the interstate) for 2 miles, then veer left and cross the interstate onto House Road (at the SUMMIT CAMPGROUND sign), and then follow it about 2 miles into the campground.
The campground: A secluded, forested campground just a few miles from the desert plains country of Malad City? Hard to imagine, but here it is, at the top of Malad Summit just north of town, a campground that looks as if it could be in the Idaho Panhandle. The burbling Mill Creek runs in front of it; there's plenty of shade; a national recreation hiking trail runs close by. The site spurs

The sign at Summit Campground, north of Malad City

are a little short, so very long RVs might not fit in well. The campground is hosted and is highly popular; locals often check in by Wednesday (staying there that night to meet campground rules, then heading back to town until Friday afternoon) to beat the weekend crowds.

3 Curlew

Location: West of Malad City
Sites: Unspecified number
Facilities: Drinking water (faucets), vault toilets, fire rings
Fee per night: None
Elevation: 5,000 feet
Road conditions: Paved nearly to the campground
Management: Forest Service, Westside Ranger District, (208) 236-7500
Reservations: Reservations are required for the group sites. Call the Forest Service office at Malad City at (208) 766-4743.

Activities: Fishing, picnicking
Season: May–September (generally)
Finding the campground: From Malad City drive west 17 miles (on marked county roads) to Holbrook and then south on Stone Road about 5 miles to the Curlew Grasslands and the campground entrance. The campground is just north of the Utah border.
The campground: This group campground (with some individual camping also allowed) is located in the Curlew National Grasslands and is one of the newer campgrounds in Idaho, built in 1999. This is an open-air, unforested, flat location, but it's great for wildlife viewing. Picnic tables here are built with covers and wind barriers, and the amenities are modern; groups can use a large pavilion building for events, and the campground lawn is watered and mowed. Stone Reservoir is close by for water recreation. A host is on-site.

4 Dry Canyon

Location: East of Malad City
Sites: Unspecified number
Facilities: Vault toilets, fire rings
Fee per night: None
Elevation: 5,800 feet
Road conditions: Gravel on Dry Canyon Road but an easy drive
Management: Forest Service, Montpelier Ranger District, (208) 847–0375
Reservations: No
Activities: Fishing, picnicking
Season: May–September (generally)
Finding the campground: From Malad City drive 2 miles north on I–15, exit east on to ID 36, drive 18 miles southeast to Dry Canyon Road, and then continue about 4 miles west.
The campground: This is an unusual no-fee group campground, one heavily used (maybe in part for that reason) by groups regionally. There is space here for two or three individual campers as well. The grounds are out in a nearly treeless meadow, and parking is open-air, but forests are close by, and hiking trails branch out from the grounds in all directions. Bring your own drinking water; none is provided at the campground.

5 Redpoint

Location: Northeast of Preston
Sites: 6
Facilities: Vault toilets, fire rings, river access
Fee per night: $
Elevation: 5,000 feet
Road conditions: Narrow (just barely one lane in places), twisting, steep, and rugged—the last few miles of this road are not good for the faint of heart or for large trailers.
Management: Bureau of Land Management, Pocatello office, (208) 236–6860

Reservations: No
Activities: Fishing, picnicking
Season: Not noted; check with BLM, (208) 236–6860.
Finding the campground: From Preston drive 5.5 miles northeast on Idaho Highway 34, then 3 miles northeast on Idaho Highway 36, and then 4 miles north on Oneida Narrows Road.
The campground: Similar to Maple Grove, this is a nicely forested site with some views of the mountain area, and it is a little easier (comparatively) to get into. Also like Maple Grove, there's no drinking water provided here, so you'll have to bring your own.

6 Maple Grove

Location: Northeast of Preston
Sites: 20
Facilities: Vault toilets, fire rings, barrier-free access, river access
Fee per night: $
Elevation: 4,900 feet
Road conditions: Narrow (just barely one lane in places), twisting, steep, and rugged—the last few miles of this road are not good for the faint of heart or for large trailers.
Management: Bureau of Land Management, Pocatello office, (208) 236–6860
Reservations: No
Activities: Fishing, picnicking
Season: June 15–September 5
Finding the campground: From Preston drive 5.5 miles northeast on ID 34, then 3 miles northeast on ID 36, and then 8 miles north on Oneida Narrows Road.
The campground: Maple Grove is a very pretty site that draws carloads of Utahans in season, despite the difficulties of getting there. The fishing is average, the scenery above average. This campground has no drinking water, so pack your own.

7 Albert Moser

Location: East of Preston
Sites: 9
Facilities: Drinking water, vault toilets, fire rings
Fee per night: $$–$$$
Elevation: 5,500 feet
Road conditions: Paved until the last 2 miles; good road easily passable by most vehicles
Management: Forest Service, Montpelier Ranger District, (208) 847–0375
Reservations: Call (877) 444–6777 or visit Web site www.reserveamerica.com.
Activities: Fishing, picnicking
Season: June 15–September 5
Finding the campground: From Preston take U.S. Highway 91 southeast for 4 miles, then Cub River Road northeast for 12 miles to the campground.

The campground: This mountain location on the Cub River is popular with Utahans but usually not very crowded. It is a good site for hiking and fishing. It is named for Albert Moser, a prominent resident of Preston and a Franklin County commissioner in the 1960s.

8 Willow Flat

Location: East of Preston
Sites: 54
Facilities: Drinking water, vault toilets, fire rings
Fee per night: $-$$
Elevation: 6,500 feet
Road conditions: Narrow and winding dirt road for the last 6 miles but passable by most vehicles
Management: Forest Service, Westside Ranger District, (208) 236-7500
Reservations: Call (877) 444-6777 or visit Web site www.reserveamerica.com.
Activities: Fishing, hiking, picnicking
Season: June 15-September 5
Finding the campground: From Preston take US 91 southeast for 4 miles, then Cub River Road northeast for 16 miles to the campground.
The campground: This is the most popular site in the region with ATV and motorbike enthusiasts, and they use a number of trails near the campground that have been etched into the landscape. This campground is less forested than some of the others in the area.

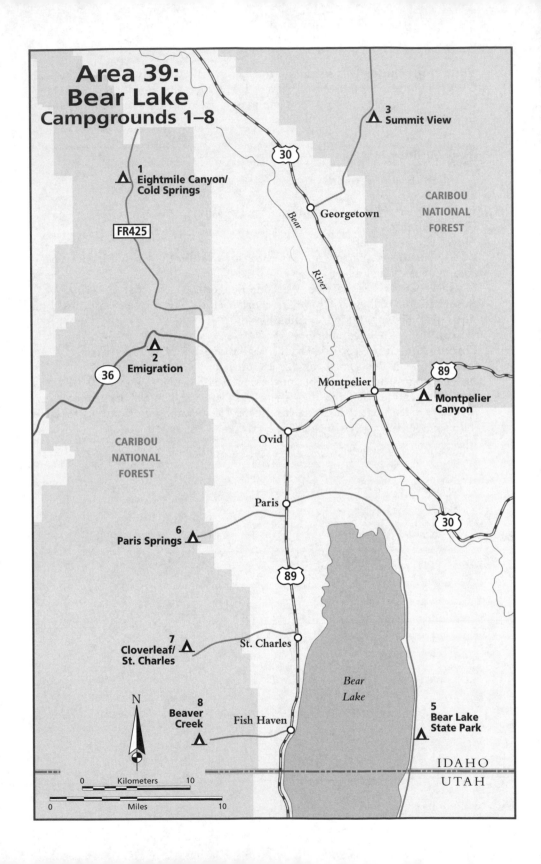

Area 39:
Bear Lake
Campgrounds 1–8

3 Summit View

30

1
Eightmile Canyon/
Cold Springs

CARIBOU
NATIONAL
FOREST

FR425

Bear

Georgetown

River

2
Emigration

36

89

Montpelier

4
Montpelier
Canyon

CARIBOU
NATIONAL
FOREST

Ovid

Paris

30

6
Paris Springs

89

Cloverleaf/
St. Charles **7**

St. Charles

Bear
Lake

N

8
Beaver
Creek

Fish Haven

5
Bear Lake
State Park

IDAHO

UTAH

0   Kilometers   10

0   Miles   10

Area 39: Bear Lake

The largest lake in southern Idaho is only half in Idaho; Bear Lake is split with Utah. No matter; plenty of Idahoans love to go sailing and fishing on it.

But the lake is only the beginning of attractions here. The biggest Oregon Trail Center in Idaho—one of the biggest along the trail—is located just north of Montpelier. The Minnetonka Cave just south of Montpelier is probably the most stunning underground trip you can take in the state. And the Paris Tabernacle, built by early Mormon settlers in the area, is one of the foremost examples of pioneer architecture anywhere in the state.

For more information:

Bear Lake Convention and Visitors Bureau
P.O. Box 26
Fish Haven, ID 83287
(208) 945-2072
www.oregontrailcenter.org

Caribou National Forest
1405 Hollipark Drive
Idaho Falls, ID 83403
(208) 524-7500

Area 39

	Town	Sites	Max. RV length	Electric	Picnic	Fire rings	Toilets	Showers	Water	Dump station	Disability access	Recreation	Can reserve	Fees ($)	Season	Stay limit (days)
1 Eightmile Canyon/ Cold Springs	Soda Springs	10	16		•	•	V					FH		$	May–Oct.	14
2 Emigration	Ovid	26	22		•	•	F,V	•	•		•	H	•	$	June–Sept.	14
3 Summit View	Georgetown	22			•	•	V		•				•	$	June–Sept.	14
4 Montpelier Canyon	Montpelier	13	32		•	•	V		•			F	•	$	May–Sept.	14
5 Bear Lake State Park	St. Charles	48	60	•	•	•	•	F		•	•	BFS	•	$–$$$	May–Oct.	
6 Paris Springs	Paris	12	22		•	•	V		•			H	•	$	June–Sept.	14
7 Cloverleaf/ St. Charles	St. Charles	19	22		•	•	F		•			FH	•	$$	June–Sept.	14
8 Beaver Creek	Fish Haven	5	22		•	•	V					FH		$	June–Sept.	14

1 Eightmile Canyon/Cold Springs

Location: South of Soda Springs
Sites: 10 (7 at Eightmile, 3 at Cold Springs)
Facilities: Vault toilets, fire rings, picnic tables
Fee per night: $
Elevation: 6,500 feet
Road conditions: Paved except the last 3 miles to the campground, which are gravel and periodically prone to severe wear (especially after particularly cold winters)
Management: Forest Service, Montpelier Ranger District, (208) 847-0375
Reservations: No
Activities: Fishing, hiking, picnicking
Season: May 31-October 31 (depending on weather)
Finding the campgrounds: From Soda Springs drive south 14 miles on the Bailey Creek/Eightmile Road (Forest Road 425).
The campgrounds: Both of these campgrounds are in Eightmile Canyon, in wooded areas. Both are relatively primitive, with picnic tables and fire rings and toilets, and not much more (no water). Garbage is strictly pack it in, pack it out. A Forest Service guard station is located nearby. The most remarkable feature of these campgrounds (and Emigration as well) is the location within a short walk of part of the proposed Great Western Trail, a corridor and collection of trails that would run from Canada to Mexico. In Idaho part of the trail would run west of Bear Lake in national forest land along the higher mountain reaches. More information about the trail is available at the Web site www.gwt.org/gwt.

2 Emigration

Location: West of Ovid
Sites: 26 (3 disabled-accessible)
Facilities: Drinking water, flush and vault toilets, shower, fire rings
Fee per night: $
Elevation: 7,500 feet
Road conditions: Paved to the campground
Management: Forest Service, Montpelier Ranger District, (208) 847-0375
Reservations: Call (877) 444-6777 or visit Web site www.reserveamerica.com.
Activities: Hiking, picnicking
Season: June 15-September 5
Finding the campground: From Ovid (which is 6 miles west of Montpelier), drive 10.5 miles west on Idaho Highway 36.
The campground: Located next to the small but fast Emigration Creek, this campground is high up in the mountains that separate the Bear from the Cache valleys and just off the highway that provides road connection between the two. One of the most picturesque campgrounds in the area, Emigration features an unusual collection of trees (mixed conifers and others). This is a good hiking area.

3 Summit View

Location: Northeast of Georgetown
Sites: 22
Facilities: Drinking water, vault toilets, fire rings
Fee per night: $
Elevation: 7,500 feet
Road conditions: Mostly paved (through the county road), with well-maintained forest road beyond
Management: Forest Service, Montpelier Ranger District, (208) 847-0375
Reservations: Call (877) 444-6777 or visit Web site www.reserveamerica.com.
Activities: Picnicking
Season: June 15-September 5 (depending on weather)
Finding the campground: From Georgetown drive 2.4 miles east on Bear Lake County Road 20102 and then 6 miles north on Forest Road 449.
The campground: The name is a misnomer, since there are no real views from this campground, which is well shaded (with lodgepole pines) and thoroughly forested. The undergrowth inside the campground is full of huckleberries, so you don't even have to leave the grounds to go berry picking. Don't (as some campers have) confuse this Summit with the similar-named campground north of Malad City.

4 Montpelier Canyon

Location: East of Montpelier
Sites: 13
Facilities: Drinking water, vault toilets, fire rings
Fee per night: $
Elevation: 6,100 feet
Road conditions: Paved to the campground
Management: Forest Service, Montpelier Ranger District, (208) 847-0375
Reservations: May return to reservation system in 2004. Call (877) 444-6777 or visit Web site www.reserveamerica.com.
Activities: Fishing, picnicking
Season: May 25-September 5
Finding the campground: From Montpelier drive east on U.S. Highway 89 for 3.3 miles; enter the campground from the highway.
The campground: This is a side-of-the-highway campground in a relatively open-air atmosphere along Montpelier Creek. (Why, one might ask, is there no campground on Montpelier Reservoir, which is another 3 miles or so east of town?)

5 Bear Lake State Park

Location: East of St. Charles
Sites: 48
Facilities: Drinking water, electric hookups, dump station, fire rings, lake access, group shelter, pull-through sites, pets allowed

Fee per night: $-$$$
Elevation: 6,000 feet
Road conditions: Paved to the campground
Management: Idaho Department of Parks and Recreation, Bear Lake State Park, (208) 847-1045
Reservations: Available via Web site www.idahoparks.org
Activities: Boating, fishing, picnicking, swimming
Season: May 1-October 1 (depending on weather)
Finding the campground: From St. Charles drive 11 miles east on East Beach Road.
The campground: Bear Lake is an unusual body of water in many ways. For one thing, it looks more turquoise than blue. For another, it is home to the Bonneville Cisco fish, which can be found nowhere else on earth. The lake is popular in the region for fishing, boating, and swimming—but before you plan your trip, be sure to check the water levels, because they vary greatly from season to season and year to year. The lake is to the south of the park; to the north is the Bear Lake National Wildlife Refuge, a marshy area that is home to many kinds of birds, some of them rare. The campground itself is located on the northeast side of the lake, away from the population centers. A wide variety of campsites are available here; some have electric hookups. There is some shade, but mainly this is a marsh and beach area. The area is popular for snowmobiling in the winter (the Bear Lake Valley gets lots of snow). One other note: The park's office is not located even close to the park; it can be found on the north end of Montpelier on U.S. Highway 30 in the Oregon Trail Center building.

6 Paris Springs

Location: Southwest of Paris
Sites: 12
Facilities: Drinking water, vault toilets, fire rings
Fee per night: $
Elevation: 6,100 feet
Road conditions: The county road is dirt but well maintained.
Management: Forest Service, Montpelier Ranger District, (208) 847-0375
Reservations: Call (877) 444-6777 or visit Web site www.reserveamerica.com.
Activities: Hiking, picnicking
Season: June 1-September 5
Finding the campground: From Paris drive 2 miles south on US 89 and then 3.8 miles west on Bear Lake County Road 30027.
The campground: The grounds are located just inside the national forest boundary and in a relatively flat basin area, not in the mountains (where most of the forest lands are). Some of this sprawling campground is in a forest area, however, and several hiking options are available.

7 Cloverleaf/St. Charles

Location: West of St. Charles
Sites: 19
Facilities: Drinking water, flush toilets, fire rings
Fee per night: $$
Elevation: 7,000 feet
Road conditions: Paved to the campgrounds. (The reddish soil in the mountains here is often blown onto the road and may make it look like a dirt road, but it isn't.)
Management: Forest Service, Montpelier Ranger District, (208) 847-0375
Reservations: Call (877) 444-6777 or visit Web site www.reserveamerica.com.
Activities: Fishing, hiking, picnicking
Season: June 15–September 5 (depending on weather)
Finding the campgrounds: From St. Charles on US 89, drive west on the St. Charles Road (toward Minnetonka Caves) about 6 miles.
The campgrounds: These campgrounds, located on the St. Charles Road west of that town, are up in the mountains and tucked into small forested draws. Some space is set aside (notably at Cloverleaf) for group activities. These sites are on the road to Minnetonka Cave, which gets tens of thousands of visitors every year and is one of the two or three best caves for visiting in Idaho.

8 Beaver Creek

Location: West of Fish Haven
Sites: 5
Facilities: Vault toilets, fire rings
Fee per night: $
Elevation: 6,000 feet
Road conditions: The county road is dirt but well maintained.
Management: Forest Service, Montpelier Ranger District, (208) 847-0375
Reservations: No
Activities: Fishing, hiking, picnicking
Season: June–September
Finding the campground: From Fish Haven drive 5 miles north on US 89 to St. Charles. From St. Charles drive the Green Canyon Road west 7 miles toward the mountains. Watch for the campground sign.
The campground: Often full on the weekends in the summer, Beaver Creek is a true backwoods site—more than most in this area—and quite primitive, without drinking water or other services.